W9-AAO-649

COLOSSIANS & PHILEMON

THE IVP NEW TESTAMENT COMMENTARY SERIES

ROBERT W. WALL

GRANT R. OSBORNE, SERIES EDITOR

D. STUART BRISCOE AND HADDON ROBINSON,
CONSULTING EDITORS

An imprint of InterVarsity Press
Downers Grove, Illinois

For our children

InterVarsity Press
P.O. Box 1400, Downers Grove, IL 60515-1426
World Wide Web: www.ivpress.com
E-mail: email@ivpress.com

InterVarsity Press® is the book-publishing division of InterVarsity Christian Fellowship/USA®, a movement of students and faculty active on campus at hundreds of universities, colleges and schools of nursing in the United States of America, and a member movement of the International Fellowship of Evangelical Students. For information about local and regional activities, write Public Relations Dept., InterVarsity Christian Fellowship/USA, 6400 Schroeder Rd., P.O. Box 7895, Madison, WI 53707-7895, or visit the IVCF website at <www.intervarsity.org>.

Design: Cindy Kiple
Images: Einzug in Jerusalem - Entry into Jerusalem by Wilhelm Morgner at Museum am Ostwall, Dortmund, Germany. Erich Lessing/Art Resource, NY.

ISBN 978-0-8308-4012-0

Printed in the United States of America ∞

InterVarsity Press is committed to protecting the environment and to the responsible use of natural resources. As a member of Green Press Initiative we use recycled paper whenever possible. To learn more about the Green Press Initiative, visit <www.greenpressinitiative.org>.

Library of Congress Cataloging-in-Publication Data

Wall, Robert W.
Colossians & Philemon/Robert W. Wall.
p. cm.—(The IVP New Testament commentary series)
Includes bibliographical references.
ISBN 0-8308-1812-X
1. Bible. N.T. Colossians—Commentaries. 2. Bible. N.T. Philemon—Commentaries. I. Title. II. Title: Colossians and Philemon. III. Series.
BS2715.3.W365 1993
227'.707—dc20 *93-21557*
CIP

P *18 17 16 15 14 13 12 11 10 9 8 7 6 5 4 3 2 1*
Y *25 24 23 22 21 20 19 18 17 16 15 14 13 12 11 10*

General Preface — *9*
Author's Preface — *11*
Introduction to Colossians — *13*
Outline of Colossians — *30*
Commentary on Colossians — *33*
Introduction to Philemon — *179*
Outline of Philemon — *192*
Commentary on Philemon — *193*
Bibliography — *219*

General Preface

In an age of proliferating commentary series, one might easily ask why add yet another to the seeming glut. The simplest answer is that no other series has yet achieved what we had in mind—a series to and from the church, that seeks to move from the text to its contemporary relevance and application.

No other series offers the unique combination of solid, biblical exposition and helpful explanatory notes in the same user-friendly format. No other series has tapped the unique blend of scholars and pastors who share both a passion for faithful exegesis and a deep concern for the church. Based on the New International Version of the Bible, one of the most widely used modern translations, the IVP New Testament Commentary Series builds on the NIV's reputation for clarity and accuracy. Individual commentators indicate clearly whenever they depart from the standard translation as required by their understanding of the original Greek text.

The series contributors represent a wide range of theological traditions, united by a common commitment to the authority of Scripture for

Christian faith and practice. Their efforts here are directed toward applying the unchanging message of the New Testament to the ever-changing world in which we live.

Readers will find in each volume not only traditional discussions of authorship and backgrounds, but useful summaries of principal themes and approaches to contemporary application. To bridge the gap between commentaries that stress the flow of an author's argument but skip over exegetical nettles and those that simply jump from one difficulty to another, we have developed our unique format that expounds the text in uninterrupted form on the upper portion of each page while dealing with other issues underneath in verse-keyed notes. To avoid clutter we have also adopted a social studies note system that keys references to the bibliography.

We offer the series in hope that pastors, students, Bible teachers and small group leaders of all sorts will find it a valuable aid—one that stretches the mind and moves the heart to ever-growing faithfulness and obedience to our Lord Jesus Christ.

Author's Preface

I wish to thank the *koinōnia* of graduate students who studied Colossians and Philemon with me during the spring of 1991. Along with their weekly preparation, they were given the task of reading a draft of this commentary and offering their comments and suggestions for improvement. I am grateful for the contribution they made to me and to this book. I am also indebted to Mark Abbott, pastor of the First Free Methodist Church in Seattle, who read a draft of the commentary with a critical eye to how well it "preached." His encouragement and wisdom helped to make this labor more enjoyable for me and, I hope, more profitable for the teachers and pastors who will use this commentary. I am grateful to Grant Osborne, the series editor, for his many suggestions, which enriched my understanding of these letters. And to many colleagues, whose conversations and insights have continued to sustain me both intellectually and spiritually. In this regard I note especially my New Testament colleagues at Seattle Pacific University, William Lane and Eugene Lemcio, along with Scott Bartchy, whose letters to me are the lens through which I now read and understand Paul's letter to Philemon.

My work as a scholar and my vocation as Christ's disciple are profoundly influenced by my wife, Carla. Those who know her well will easily find the traces of her theological vision and practical spirituality in this book; she influences me as none other. This commentary is lovingly dedicated to our children, Zachary, Cara, Andrew and Benjamin. Our experiences of trying to parent them—my most demanding and humbling devotion—spark innumerable questions and testimonies that bring to light the meaning of Scripture for life. We pray that God will help our family live together in *koinōnia* so that in holy partnership with the risen Lord Christ we might be empowered to do the good work of a reconciling God in a troubled and fragmented world.

Rob Wall

Introduction to Colossians

Interpreting Scripture is an act of worship. One of the most surprising gains of recent biblical scholarship is the recognition that a historical and literary analysis of biblical texts, however informed and judicious, cannot be the primary aim of the church's interpretation of its Scripture. We do not study Scripture simply by applying some technique to it. We believe God intends that every text of Scripture be used to form the faith and guide the witness of every Christian, and so Bible study should properly concern itself with people who desire to worship God in spirit and truth and bear witness to the Lord in their daily lives. Walt Brueggemann has nicely said that Scripture "is God's house and God wants his children to play there" (1991:121).

To say this does not dismiss or even demote the modern concern to understand biblical texts in their first-century context; authors always shape their compositions in the light of historical circumstance and current literary convention. Yet faithful interpretation must wait upon the Bible for divinely inspired words that make sense of today's faith and life. Studying a biblical book at the point of its origin—the preoccupation of most modern scholars—is meaningful only when its yield can address the contemporary questions and struggles of the ordinary believer.

This orientation toward the study of the Bible is consistent with the decisions made by our earliest forebears in the faith. It was they who first recognized God's inspiration of certain writings, preserved these writings, canonized them as useful and trustworthy and finally shaped them over time into our biblical "rule of faith." When interpretation is guided by the church's own intentions for the biblical canon, its primary objective will be to nurture faithfulness to the Word of God made flesh in Jesus Christ. A good interpreter's exposition of the Bible makes "plain sense" of its meaning, not only in ways consistent with the core theological convictions of Christian faith but also in ways that provide concrete and practical guidance for daily living.

In the introductions to my commentary on Colossians and Philemon I will take up several historical questions and survey the scholarly opinion about each: Who was the author? What ancient literary conventions did he use in composing his letters? Who were his first readers, and what spiritual crises occasioned the writing of these letters? These historical questions are important only as they help clarify the meaning of the biblical text. Any "occasional" composition, a category that includes all of Paul's letters, embodies the immediate concerns of both author and audience at the point of the composition's origin. Even so, the interpreter's desire to reconstruct the environment that produced a particular biblical writing should not displace a more primary, pastoral concern. As an interpreter of Colossians and Philemon, I am ultimately concerned with what relevant connections can be drawn between Paul's first readers and today's Christians. Such is the dynamic nature of the Bible's authority. Thus, rather than locating the so-called "conflict at Colosse" in the first century and freezing its significance there, my inclination is to search out the conflict's contemporary counterparts in today's congregations so

Notes: Introduction [1]The perceived scholarly value of the modern debate over the authorship of Colossians resides in the equation of its canonical authority with its Pauline (i.e., apostolic) authorship. In my view, this way of stating the problem is incorrect if a historical interest (the author's identity) then justifies a theological interest (the book's authority). In fact, the Bible is largely an anonymous book, perhaps so to distract attention from the authors' identity and to underscore the fundamental importance of the subject matter. Although the New Testament letters are not anonymous, except for Hebrews, this

that Paul's letter will continue to instruct believers about what it means to be the church and to do as the church should.

□ The Author of Colossians

The author of the letter identifies himself as Paul (1:1; 4:18), and the ancient church accepted the book's own attribution at face value. Since the beginning of the modern period of biblical scholarship and the rise of a "hermeneutics of suspicion," however, Paul's authorship of Colossians has been challenged on literary and theological grounds. Some scholars argue that Colossians shows a more mature theological perspective than Paul's "genuine" letters and uses different vocabulary. Because historical questions of authorship are typically linked to theological questions of authority, those who reject Paul's authorship of Colossians tend to undervalue its religious significance for today's church. Even those who champion Paul's authorship of Colossians tend to do so for theological rather than historical reasons: they contend that the inspiration (and therefore the canonicity) of Colossians depends upon the apostle's having written it.

I believe both sides make a fundamental mistake in equating the question of a book's *authority* with the question of its *authorship.* At the very least, if the interpreter is interested in the historical aspect of a book's authorship, he or she must provide evidence that is apropos to the historical issues at hand.[1]

In all probability Paul wrote Colossians with Timothy's help (see commentary on 1:1). Of course, this verdict is judged by history, not ideology. Two criteria are typically employed by scholars to determine the validity of such a historical judgment: (1) whether the language and writing style of Colossians conform to Paul's other letters, and (2) whether its content and practical application agree with the theology and hermeneutics found in Paul's other letters. In the case of Colossians,

---

general rule still applies: Scholarly quests after the identity of the author and his audience should not distract the interpreter from the content of the canonical text.

This is especially true for Colossians. Most modern scholars, with some variation, have concluded that Colossians was not written by Paul but by a pseudepigrapher—that is, by someone after Paul who belonged to the Pauline school of thought and who then credited his writing to Paul, following ancient literary custom. When interpreters equate apostolic authorship with authority and then reject Paul as the author of Colossians, the practical result

Timothy's employment as Paul's scribe and his part in composing this letter may qualify how we understand these two criteria. Additionally, a third criterion is sometimes added by scholars: whether Colossians derives from Ephesians or from some other preformed collection of Pauline ideas that was in circulation among his converts. The application of this third criterion, however, is so fraught with difficulty, requiring speculation after speculation, that few scholars use it today. At the very least, it seems highly presumptuous for a scholar to suppose that a single author could not write two similar compositions for two different audiences and modify one or the other in light of different concerns or relationships. I rather suspect this is a common practice among letter writers of every generation. How many of us, for example, have used a computerized form letter when writing to family and friends at Christmas or Easter, adding to or subtracting from it as we move down our mailing list?

The scholar's first challenge to Paul's authorship of Colossians is based on *literary* grounds. Such a scholar will note that Colossians contains some different vocabulary from that in other Pauline writings (Lohse 1971:84-91; Schweizer 1982:18-19). At last count, some thirty-four words can be found in Colossians that appear nowhere else in the New Testament—a high number for a brief composition. In addition, there are peculiarities in the author's style as he alternates between more formal theological and ethical formulations and more pastoral and pointed polemic.

George E. Cannon (1983) has argued, however, that most of the literary evidence judged to be "unauthentic" by those who oppose Pauline authorship comes from sections of the letter (1:12-20; 2:9-15; 3:5—4:6)

---

is that they reject its authority and its usefulness for Christian nurture.

My response to this scholarly tendency is *not* to mount a countervailing and more convincing historical argument, which then would only fall victim to the same misguided equation of authorship with authority. Nor do I appeal to a different definition of biblical authority or of the pseudepigrapher's task (cf. David Meade's *Pseudonymity and Canon*). Rather, I seek to clarify and distinguish between two methodological interests regarding a book's authorship. In the case of Colossians, the debate over authorship assumes the historian's interest, requiring the interpreter to gather appropriate historical evidence and to subject it to critical inquiry: is Colossians written by Paul or by a pseudepigrapher? Yet the debate also assumes the theologian's interest: is the content of Colossians apostolic and therefore authoritative?

In pointing out the theological aspect of this discussion, I make a distinction between an *apostle,* which refers to a particular person, and a book's *apostolicity,* which has to do

where Paul has purposely departed from his normal style to quote theological formulations already in use by Christians as either confessions of faith (e.g., 1:15-20) or codes of moral conduct (e.g., 3:18—4:1). Cannon contends that these formulations were composed by the Colossians themselves and subsequently edited by the apostle for use in this letter.

This strategy of accommodation allows Paul, who has never met his audience, to speak his mind in a theological idiom that would be familiar to them. Crosscultural communication enhances the prospect of understanding. Think of the missionary who makes use of both the language and the customs of an unevangelized people in order to make the gospel message more meaningful to them. Paul the missionary uses the same strategy to communicate more persuasively to an unknown congregation. According to Cannon, Paul uses Colossian theology in order to remind the Colossians that what they confess to be theologically true and ethically correct conforms to his own message of the Gentile mission (cf. 1:24—2:3). Indeed, when we examine carefully the vocabulary and stylistic features of the more personal portions in Colossians (e.g., 2:4-8 and 2:16—3:4), where the apostle's voice is more clearly heard, we find considerable correspondence to the vocabulary and style of Paul's "genuine" letters. Thus, when Paul moves from Colossian Christian tradition (1:12-23) to personal polemic (1:24—3:4) to comment on the specifics of false teaching at Colosse (see below), he is better able to clarify how what the Colossian Christians affirm, which coheres with the themes of his own message, is incongruent with the aberrant teaching.

This literary strategy of restating his readers' central beliefs in order to comment on their legitimacy for a particular situation is characteristic

with the theological tradition belonging to a particular apostle. The purpose of this distinction is to shift the interpreter's chief concern from the authority of the one who writes (apostle versus pseudepigrapher) to the authority of what is written (apostolic versus nonapostolic). So even if one concluded on historical grounds that the apostle Paul did not write Colossians, one could still maintain its authority on the theological grounds that its content belongs to the Pauline tradition, is apostolic and is therefore authoritative for those who belong to the "one holy catholic and apostolic church."

Beyond all the historical data that may settle the debate over who wrote Colossians, I accept the authority of Colossians because the church has already determined the theological integrity of its content. Both the church that formed the Christian Bible and the church that continues to read it recognize that when Colossians is picked up as a witness to the person and work of Jesus Christ and read by generation after generation of believers, it is inspired by God and therefore profitable for "teaching, rebuking, correcting and training" (2 Tim 3:16).

of Paul's preaching and writing. In fact, in his portrait of Paul's missionary work in Acts, Luke shows how Paul always presents his message in the idiom of his audience, whether Jewish (e.g., Acts 17:1-15) or Greek (e.g., Acts 17:16-33). On the basis of these reflections, then, I side with Kümmel, who concludes his own discussion of Paul's authorship of Colossians by saying that "on the basis of language and style, there is no reason to doubt the Pauline authorship of the letter" (1975:342).

In preaching or teaching from Paul's letters, we must keep in mind that he did not write letters as academic briefs, devoid of passion and composed of unchanging ideas and universal truths for a fixed, permanent biblical canon. His letters always comprise a practical theology, for the apostle adapts the unchanging convictions of his gospel to the actual problems facing a particular congregation in practical and concrete ways. Paul is an itinerant missionary, not a professor of biblical studies! He writes his letters from a martyr's prison, a missionary's tent or a pastor's office to address the spiritual needs of the rank-and-file. Our exposition should seek to embody Paul's spirit—even when we are dealing with Colossians, whose philosophical tone makes practical exposition more difficult.

The second criterion measures the content of a book's teaching, whether its *theological themes* are developed in continuity with themes found elsewhere in the Pauline writings. Again, the historian can give weight to this criterion only by assuming that a writer's stated ideas remain rather static and do not change over time. If we accept this assumption, we would judge any theological shift from Paul's "genuine" letters as "non-Pauline." Scholars who use this criterion on Colossians find its view of Christ more cosmic than crucified (cf. 1:15-20; 2:9-10), its eschatology more realized than futuristic (cf. 2:11-12; 3:1-2) and its ecclesiology more universal than congregational (cf. 1:18). Therefore they conclude that Colossians diverges from the "authentic" Pauline writings (cf. O'Brien 1982:xliv-xlix). This is especially true for those who explain the differing theological emphases in light of the sociohistorical forces at work within Gentile Christianity after Paul's death (Käsemann 1964:149-68).

Again, Cannon's important work challenges this line of argument. Even if we conclude that the theological shifts found in Colossians are too dramatic to be reconciled with the historical Paul, we must acknowledge that the theological adjustment takes place within the letter's "traditional" sections, where the Colossian voice (rather than Paul's) is heard. The distinctive Christology of Colossians, for example, is introduced in 1:15-20, a hymn composed, according to Cannon, by the Colossian church. Where Paul departs from the tradition of his readers and addresses them as their apostle, both his content and his intent conform to his other letters.

Moreover, the attempt to determine the boundaries of Paul's theological formation is a highly dubious enterprise. When does a new emphasis in his teaching about Christ or a different dimension to his understanding of salvation actually contradict a fundamental of his previously held faith? As with anyone who is nurtured by God's grace within a community of believers, Paul's thinking developed and deepened over time. His personal experiences of God and also of his various opponents on the mission field challenged him to think in new ways. His theological formation did not happen in a vacuum but in the context of real life.

Nor did Paul write his letters in a vacuum; the infant church was itself developing in the midst of conflict and confusion. Paul's writing reflects this; his letters are full of life, each prompted by the problems of a specific people and by Paul's desire to send practical advice to them in difficult times. We make a mistake in supposing Paul intended to write his letters as "books of the New Testament," addressing an amorphous congregation of future believers rather than real people in his own day. Often Paul reminds his readers that he has their problems clearly in mind as he writes to them; what he writes, then, is shaped not only by his personal history but also by the history of his readers. To the extent that his readers changed, Paul adapted his message to better communicate the gospel of God to the people of God.

Perhaps it is best to understand any shift in Paul's thinking as reflecting the dynamic of a single person who is intent on communicating theological convictions in practical ways to different audiences at different moments in the course of a long career. Shouldn't we expect a similar dynamic to be reflected over time in our own letters? In summary, then, any difference in theological formulation that the interpreter might find in Colossians is best explained either by Paul's literary strategy or by the ferment of his historical and personal situation.[2]

□ The Congregation in Colosse

The ancient city of Colosse was located in the fertile valley forged by the river Lycus in the Asian province of Phrygia. Centuries earlier, Colosse had served as a center for the valley's prosperous wool and textile industries; its place on a major trade route only enhanced its economic advantage. But by the time of Paul its influence had waned. Neighboring Laodicea (2:1; 4:13, 15) had replaced Colosse in economic and political importance, while Hierapolis (4:13), some fifteen miles away, had grown in prominence as a tourist town, famed for its mineral baths and as a sanctuary for members of the prominent Phrygian mystery cult. (Hence the name *Hiera polis* means "holy city" in Greek.) In all likelihood, then, this letter first addressed a small congregation in a rather unimpressive town.

In fact, there is no indication from Paul's writings or from Acts (cf. Acts 19:10) that Paul ever reached Colosse during his evangelistic campaign in the Lycus valley. Paul's strategy was to visit only the most prominent urban centers of a particular region, to recruit mature colleagues, such as Epaphras (1:7-8; 4:12-3; cf. Philem 23) and Tychicus (4:7-8), and to advance his Gentile mission to additional places and people. Significantly, the pivotal references to Epaphras, himself a Colossian (cf. 4:12), indicate that this congregation was founded through his preaching ministry (1:7-8) rather than through Paul's. Obviously the apostle was pleased with its results. Not only does he express confidence that the gospel Epaphras proclaimed conformed to his own (1:23, 28; cf. 2:6), but he also com-

---

[2]J. C. Beker's discussion of Paul's interpretive strategy provides another interesting perspective for modern students of Paul on the problem of the apostle's developing theology. According to Beker, Paul's core theological convictions are never expressed in his letters as unchanging, static truths. Paul's letters are by nature "hermeneutical writings" in which his stable convictions about God are refocused on a moving target—the changing contingencies of a particular congregation's situation—in order to show practically how God deals with a specific congregation of people. While Paul has a "core" theology (which according to Beker is rooted in Jewish apocalypticism), when writing he "does" theology. He gives new expression to his beliefs depending upon the changing historical circumstances and spiritual crises that face his first readers. Thus his timeless ideas about God's transforming grace, Christ's atoning death, the faith community's covenant with God for salvation, or the present status and future realization of that salvation are theological abstractions commu-

mends the Colossians for their faithfulness to it (1:2-6; 2:5-8) and often alludes to the radical change brought about by their growing confidence in God's transforming grace (1:13-14; 2:7, 13). Specifically, Paul notes that because of their vital faith they now have a share in Christ's destiny as heavenly Lord (1:15-20; 3:1-2) and will participate fully in God's final triumph over evil when Christ returns to earth (3:3-4).

☐ The Crisis at Colosse

Although the Lycus valley was a well-known haven for Diaspora Jews, apparently Epaphras's ministry was exclusively to Gentiles (cf. 4:11-12) and was viewed by Paul as an extension of his own Gentile mission (cf. 1:24-2:3). So the specific spiritual crisis addressed in this letter must be understood against the general background of Paul's controversial Gentile mission. Both from Paul's writings and from Luke's Acts, we know that Paul's evangelistic ministry provoked the wrath of "official" Judaism and made untenable the already fragile relationship between Judaism and the first followers of Christ. Even within the earliest church, some Jewish Christians were offended that Paul's evangelistic mission did not require Gentile converts to jump through the same hoops that Judaism required of its Gentile converts (cf. Acts 15:1, 5; Col. 2:9-12). Other Jewish believers objected to the egalitarianism of Pauline Christianity by which Jews and non-Jews alike participated with Christ and through his Spirit in the salvation of God (cf. Acts 10:44—11:18; Col 3:11-12).

While Paul maintained his Jewish identity (cf. Rom 11:1; Acts 21-26), his Jewish brothers and sisters were alarmed, thinking that he had abandoned his religious heritage. The issue for them, however, was more

---

nicated to no one in particular! The apostle is not interested in disembodied ideas; he is interested in how ideas are fleshed out in the ordinary practice of faith and the daily witness of a faithful people.

But precisely because of his pastoral interest in his readers, Paul's letters reflect how everyday life influences how Christ is understood and trusted for salvation. For example, Paul's own traumatic experience of imprisonment (cf. Phil 1:12-26), when Colossians was apparently written (4:18; cf. 1:24; 2:1), and the presence of the "hollow and deceptive philosophy" that threatened the Colossian congregation (2:8) challenge him to find new dimensions of Christ's redemptive work in order to communicate his gospel to his readers in useful ways. The practical point for us is this: only when the current readers of Paul's compositions learn to identify with his first readers can we better understand how the truths of Paul's message continue to interpret our faith and life.

than religious. Because the apostle did not make the same demands of Gentile converts that Judaism did, some Jewish believers felt that Gentile believers were not being properly assimilated into the faith community and that there could be serious sociopolitical consequences at the hands of the Roman government (Dunn 1983:95-122). Without Torah (Law) and tradition (i.e., interpretations of Torah) to provide social and spiritual boundaries, Jewish believers were worried that Christianity as a whole would fail to remain a distinctive community, covenanted with God for salvation, and would be absorbed into the pagan world.

According to Paul, membership in the "Israel of God" is gained *and* maintained by trusting in the salvation that God has already accomplished through Christ's atoning death. Social and political distinctives between the church and the synagogue are redrawn in terms of the requisite "obedience of faith." According to Paul, all believers, whether Jew or not, are now reunited with God in Christ Jesus (3:11). Moreover, Paul considers obedience to the dietary and religious traditions of Judaism unnecessary for converted Gentiles (2:20-23): God calls Gentiles out of the world for salvation by the preaching of Christ (cf. Acts 15:13-21; Rom 10:5-13; Gal 2:1-10). To depend on Jewish tradition rather than Christ's dependable work is to deny the singular significance of his cross and invalidate the empty tomb. In effect, Paul's Gentile mission transformed (or ended!) the first Jewish-Christian dialogue by altering how the "true" Israel conceived of its relationship with God, which the exalted Lord Jesus Christ now mediates and maintains, and with non-Jews, whom God calls out of the world for salvation by the preaching of the Christian gospel (Rom 10:1-15).

The more specific crisis facing the first readers of Colossians is the relationship between Judaism and Pauline Christianity in the town of Colosse, if not also throughout the Lycus valley. According to Acts, Paul's evangelistic crusade in this area had been conducted in the shadow of the synagogue (Acts 19:8); both Jews and Gentiles heard the gospel (Acts 19:10), the truth of which was validated by the extraordinary things God did through Paul (Acts 19:11-12). Significantly, Luke refers to Christianity in Acts 19:9 as "the Way" (cf. Acts 19:23), the name given it as a sectarian movement within Judaism. According to Luke, then, the relationship between Jews and Gentiles was apparently a critical feature of

Paul's message in the Phrygian province. This background information may help identify Paul's opponents at Colosse and the theological crisis he was writing to correct.

Several scholars have recently concluded that the clipped references in Colossians (cf. 2:9, 18, 21, 23) to a "hollow and deceptive philosophy" that "depends on human tradition and the basic principles of this world" (2:8) to fashion "fine-sounding arguments" (2:4) suggest that the Colossian congregation was being influenced by a Hellenized form of piety (Francis 1975), probably of Jewish origin (Bornkamm 1975). If to be a Christian meant in some important sense to be Jewish, as opponents to the Gentile mission would have argued, then believers would quite naturally look to their Jewish-Christian teachers (perhaps even to the rabbinate of the local synagogue) for instruction. While this sectarian form of Judaism cannot be described with any certainty, many now believe it emphasized learning the *ideas* of a truly Jewish religion at the expense of practicing and proclaiming it. In fact, many such theological ideas were borrowed from the margins of Jewish teaching and were "otherworldly" (cf. 2:16-19); it was practically impossible to apply them to real life (cf. 1:9-10). Devotion to God was expected to be expressed through ascetic rules and by moral codes that prevented believers from living life (cf. 2:20-23). When such instruction led the Colossians away from the gospel of the Gentile mission, Paul contended that the result was spiritual poverty rather than theological maturity.

Another feature of the Colossian crisis has to do with the tenuous relationship between this congregation and its founding father, Epaphras (1:7; 4:12-13; see below, 1:3-12). Paul is very careful in this letter to express support for Epaphras and his ministry, perhaps because it is Epaphras and not Paul who is under attack at Colosse. After all, this congregation had never met the apostle, and his visit to this region had been brief. Paul's quotes from Colossian tradition may well serve more than a rhetorical purpose (see above): they may also reflect the theological idiom of Epaphras's message. Thus the apparent agreement between Paul's message and the Colossian confessions of faith may be mustered in support of the reputation of the imprisoned Epaphras, who, as author of their theological tradition, has direct charge of this congregation's spiritual welfare.

□ Paul's Response to the Colossians

Paul's letters all contain a practical theology. And his practical theology is rooted in a practical wisdom: he considers theology's results, or "fruit" (1:5-6, 9-10), important. In the letter to the Colossians, the apostle is primarily concerned to correct a Christianity whose "hollow and deceptive" sophistry has reproduced an untenable discipleship among the believers in Colosse. The influence of Phrygian Judaism upon certain Christian teachers, however peripheral, threatens to produce a faith that denies the inherent goodness of God's creation and the potential power of God's new creation, the church.

In a sense, Paul is concerned with how believers define and understand the working of divine grace. According to Paul, the theological center of "true" religion must never be shifted from our ongoing participation in the life of the Risen Lord, because it is "in Christ" that God's grace transforms people from death to life. To shift the center of faith from Christ to the intellectual domain of philosophical speculation and ascetic piety is to understand divine grace in terms of "human tradition" (2:8) and "rules" (2:20-21); a Christless version of Christianity is self-deception. Its foolishness is evident in its inability to mediate God's saving grace, which comes only through our participation with Christ (cf. 1 Cor 1:18-25).

Paul's worry in this regard is also that the Colossians have lost interest in the work of evangelism, replacing it with the legalistic observance of religious traditions (2:16) and moral codes that restrict what is handled, tasted and touched (cf. 2:21). Paul's polemic repeatedly draws attention to the arrogance of such asceticism (2:18, 23), supposing that people can put off the "sinful nature" (cf. 2:11) by human activity rather than by trusting in divine grace (cf. 2:12-15). In fact, Paul worries that this preoccupation with the flesh, although seeking to deny it, actually indulges its power over their lives (cf. 2:23). When believers locate evil in "things," they tend to imagine that they are not personally responsible for sin. Sin exists outside the self; holiness is objectified and codified as rules that demand abstinence from a particular food or a certain kind of music or a "worldly" appearance, and is set up as a closed system of theological dogma.

While I prefer that my children listen to classical music and wear conservative dress, I must never make my personal taste the measure of their relationship with God. A Christian spirituality focused on the rejection of "things" and the acceptance of certain ideas rather than on relationships rejects the essentially *covenantal* and *concrete* character of true religion. For Paul, the species of spirituality that results from God's triumph over sin and evil by the cross (2:13-15) is demonstrated by transformed human relationships (3:5—4:6) which are held together by the exalted Christ (2:19) and not by "written codes" or "the basic principles of this world" or invisible "powers and authorities."

☐ Paul's Message for Today

As a religious Jew, Paul thinks of his faith as an ongoing story of God's covenant-saving acts. His core convictions retain the essential shape of the Old Testament story of God's salvation of Israel. God's story begins with the creation of all things and the call of a chosen people to come out of the evil world for the promised salvation. God's story will conclude with a final triumph over the evil powers that were responsible for creation's fall, and with God's full blessing of the covenant community that has remained faithful to the Lord. For Paul, the church must always find its present compass in the foundational truths of the biblical story, which has been retold and confirmed in the death and resurrection of the Lord Christ.

The purpose of Paul's letters is to chart the present orientation of the faith community: what are the present results of being a congregation of believers called out of Colosse (or Seattle!) by God for salvation? As a Christian, Paul is convinced that the promise contained in the biblical story was fulfilled by the death and resurrection of Jesus Christ (2:9-15). Given the emerging threats of facile intellectualism and legalistic asceticism in Colossian Christianity, Paul draws upon traditions that stress Christ's lordship over everything material and spiritual, external and internal (1:15-20). God's Risen Son is custodian of the created world as well as the world of ideas. As disciples of Christ, we must never see our life of faith in private or sectarian terms, nor should we be so arrogant as to suppose that God's salvation is based on the elegance of our theological formulations. If Christ Jesus is Lord over both the natural and the spiritual orders of human life, we his followers must engage ourselves in the world as agents of reconciliation.

Paul's understanding of Christ's ultimate importance in the present dispensation of God's salvation has two integral parts. First, Christ is Lord over God's old and new creations; he is Lord over the entire history of God's salvation. His "cosmic" lordship is an expression of God's triumph over evil and death; through Christ's lordship, God's good intentions for the now fallen creation are currently being worked out in the history of the new creation, the church. And the transforming grace of God, which believers are already experiencing, will bear its full fruit at Christ's return. Paul's message promises the experience of conversion, of human transformation. Every change from bad news to good news that takes place in human relationships—from the forgiveness of sin (1:13-14) that reconciles us with God (1:21-22) to the empowering of a "new self" (3:10) that reconciles us with each other (3:11)—marks a fulfillment of God's promise to restore all things and return them to the Garden.

Second, Paul justifies his claim that Christ is Lord over all things by appealing to the actual experience of God's transforming and empowering grace, which has practical effect in our daily relationships with God and each other. Paul repeats two phrases, "in Christ" and "with Christ," to underscore the vital importance of the church's ongoing relationship with Christ as the location of God's gracious action within human history. Given their tendency toward intellectualizing their Christian faith, this more practical emphasis is central to Paul's letter for the Colossians. It seems ironic to me that many commentators on this book fail to emphasize Paul's participatory Christology, preferring to discuss his cosmic Christology. While Paul is certainly concerned to establish the spatial boundaries of Christ's lordship (that is, over the entire cosmos), he is more concerned to press the status of the believer, who in partnership with Christ already experiences (that is, participates in) the various fruits of God's salvation. Thus the faith community is the "body" of Christ, who is its "Head" (1:18; 2:19); the church has been raised with Christ by God from sin and death (2:11-15) and made to live "with Christ in God" (3:3). That is, believers share in the totality of God's triumph in Christ!

There is nothing mystical or abstract in Paul's Christology; he does not overemphasize Christ's transcendent lordship. Rather, Paul draws on the traditions of Christ's status as Lord over all things to express and impress the larger truth that the community of faith participates with its triumphant Lord in God's continuing triumph over sin and death.

Paul's stress on the present fulfillment of God's promised salvation ("realized eschatology") and his softening of the importance of Christ's return ("futuristic eschatology") only add to this emphasis. Because God has already fulfilled the promise of salvation through Christ's death, the transforming power of divine grace is relocated *within* the history of God's people (salvation is already realized) rather than at its end when Christ returns (salvation is not yet realized). Paul is quite careful when appropriating the "already/not-yet" and "hidden/revealed" motifs of Jewish apocalypticism (3:1-4) to focus on what God has already revealed and fulfilled. Christianity is not an esoteric religion of private morality, nor do its members sit passively and wait for the end to come. The grace of God has already been disclosed in the death and resurrection of the historical Jesus and is now transforming the believing community in the public square for all to see.

Surely Paul's extended comments in Colossians about his own missionary work (1:24-2:5), Epaphras's gospel ministry in Colosse (1:5-8) and others engaged in the work of the Gentile mission (4:7-17) seek in part to encourage the Colossians to measure devotion to Christ in terms of evangelistic zeal and public life rather than by a life hidden away in the inner self. God's grace transforms more than the mind and heart of the individual believer; it has its positive effect in various public arenas—social (3:5-14; 4:2-6), familial (3:18—4:1) and worshiping (3:15-17). According to Paul, then, God's grace is currently mediated through Christ (2:9-10), who is Lord over everything (1:15-20); this confession is the eschatological reality that envisions the church's active and public response to every part of God's creation. Christianity is practiced not "on the side" but in the public square for all to see.

Contemporary Christianity is like Colossian Christianity in many ways. Especially in America, cultural myths of the self-sufficient individual lead to a private discipleship, interested in personal experience more than responsible action, in personal rights more than public morality, in personal benefits more than worship and witness to God. As a result, our preaching is typically centered on the personal blessings derived from a privatized relationship with God. And in turn, the consequence is that many congregations have an immature ecclesiology, gathering together to meet personal needs rather than to worship God as an inclusive community.

One of the fastest-growing religious movements in both America and Europe proclaims a "prosperity gospel," promising material wealth and physical healing to those whose spiritual life is also rich and healthy.[3] The theological foundation of this heretical movement, which continues to flourish in some parts of the charismatic renewal (such as the "Word of Faith"), is dualistic, dividing human existence into spiritual and material realms. The two are in eternal conflict with each other at every level. Thus, according to this "gospel" we are liberated from material evil (physical sickness and economic poverty) as we participate in the "spiritual" realm through revelatory experiences. Such experiences are thought to provide a special knowledge of God that not only anchors faith but also provides the basis for God's gifts of healing and wealth. Recipients of this revelation see themselves as members of a spiritual elite within the church—an ecclesiology that leads to the very arrogance Paul warns against in Colossians 3:16-19.

In many ways, the Colossian heresy is analogous to this modern religious movement; thus Paul's response to the ancient falsehoods provides us with an important resource for today. According to Paul, a theology that makes the spiritual mutually exclusive of the material distorts the truth of the gospel and will contaminate its fruit (1:3-12). Foundational to both theological (2:4-15) and ethical (2:16—4:1) formation is the confession that Christ is Lord over both realms (1:15-20). Moreover, central to Paul's Christology is that the "spiritual" has been revealed to us within history and in the *physical* Jesus (1:18-20; 2:9).

Within other quarters of evangelical Christianity, legalistic asceticism is mistaken for devotion. Outsiders have noted our spiritual arrogance and theological triumphalism and called us self-righteous. We are often similar to the Colossian legalists, more interested in following a codified form of holiness than in nurturing a holy heart. In some quarters evangelicals champion their closed system of theological ideas, often specializing in minor issues and differences with other believers. New litmus

[3]Hummel (1991) provides an excellent introduction to this heresy.

tests other than the great fundamentals of the faith have been fashioned to measure the "orthodoxy" of the faithful. Rather than promoting a practical and practiced Christianity, intolerant believers view worship as a search-and-destroy mission, sermonizing against those who do not believe exactly as they do.

Paul's letter is for us too. We have become Colossian sophists, more interested in knowing theology than doing it, more interested in disqualifying others from the prize than in pressing on toward it ourselves. May God use Paul's letter to bring about our repentance and spiritual renewal.

Outline of Colossians

1:1-2 __________Paul's Greeting

1:3-12 _________Paul's Prayer of Thanksgiving

1:13-23 ________The Foundation of Faith: God's Grace in Christ

1:13-14 ______The New Exodus

1:15-20 ______The New Creation

1:21-23 ______The New Age

1:23—2:3 _____Paul's Defense of His Ministry

2:4-15 _________PAUL'S ARGUMENT AGAINST CHRISTLESS THEOLOGY

2:4-8 __________The Error of Sophistry

2:9-15 _________Paul's Response to the "Philosopher"

2:9-10 _______Christ Is God Within History

2:10-15 ______Christ Is Lord over History

2:16—4:1 _____PAUL'S POLEMIC AGAINST CHRISTLESS ETHICS

2:16-23 ________The Error of Ascetic Piety

2:16-17 ______Accusation Without Foundation

2:18-19 ______Righteousness Without Relationship

2:20-23 ______Religion Without Results

3:1—4:1 ______Paul's Response to the "Spiritual Umpire"

3:1-4 ________The Foundation of Pauline Ethics

3:5-11 ______The Community's Conversion from Vice
3:12-17 ______The Community's Conversion to Virtue
3:18—4:1 ____Virtue Illustrated by the Christian Family

4:2-18 ________Benediction
4:2-6 ________Paul's Evangelistic Concern for Outsiders
4:7-17 _______Paul's Apostalic Concern for Insiders
4:18 ________Final Farewell

COMMENTARY

Colossians

□ Paul's Greeting (1:1-2)

Following the literary conventions of the ancient world, Paul begins his letter to the congregation at Colosse by introducing himself and greeting his readers. Such introductions had a function similar to that of business cards in today's professional world. Business cards make introductions and help to establish relationships with potential clients. Likewise, Paul greets his readers in order to establish a relationship with them, creating a positive setting for their reading (or listening—see 4:16) and responding to what he has written.

In Paul's letters, however, variations on the opening formula convey important theological content that helps to introduce his message. The various phrases Paul uses to introduce himself or to greet his audience frame his relationship with them: his apostolic message is authoritative for them and is useful for their spiritual nurture.

The Author (1:1) At the head of Paul's letter is his Roman name, Paul, perhaps used here as an expression of solidarity with his unknown Gentile readers. More important, Paul describes himself as *an apostle of Christ Jesus.* Houlden calls this title a "badge of office" (1970:145); the writing of the letter to the Colossians is an exercise of his office and carries the weight of its authority. Literally, the word *apostle* derives from a verb that means "to send on a mission"; it refers to a public official with the authority to represent and act on behalf of the one who has sent him. Schweizer suggests a more Jewish background to the word (1982:29): like the Old Testament prophets, Paul has been sent on God's mission to proclaim the "word of the Lord" (cf. Is 61:1; Luke 4:16-19; Acts 9:14-15; Gal 1:11-16; 1 Cor 1:17).

In other letters where Paul calls immediate attention to his apostolic office (cf. Gal 1:1; 1 Cor 1:1; 2 Cor 1:1), his authority is being challenged from within the congregation. Firm reference to his apostolic authority at the outset seems warranted. While Lohse suggests that at Colosse the "unique position of the apostle is undisputed, so that Paul is presented as an apostle only in the opening verse" (1971:6), Paul returns to speak of the responsibilities of his Gentile mission in 1:24—2:5 to clarify his "official" relationship with his readers. The interpreter does well to compare Paul's use of autobiographical material in Colossians with the apologetical role that autobiography plays in his other letters (such as Galatians and 2 Corinthians) where he recounts his missionary work in response to opponents. While he has not yet met with his Colossian readers, no doubt there is opposition to his ministry and teaching among them.

Recall that Paul's Gentile mission was quite controversial in earliest Christianity, when many believers understood themselves as belonging to a messianic movement *within* Judaism. Boundaries between the church and synagogue were still quite fuzzy; Paul's preaching of a "law-free" gospel (as in Galatians) and his conversion of Gentiles without compliance to the most basic proselyte requirements of Greek-speaking Judaism (as in Romans) were increasingly difficult for religious Jews, and even for many Jewish Christians, to accept (see Acts 11:1-18; 15:1-5; 21:15-26). Moreover, although Paul had witnessed the resurrection of Christ on the Damascus Road, some early Christian leaders still doubted his apostolic credentials. After all, he had persecuted Christ's disciples and had not been with Christ from the beginning (see Acts 1:21-22; 1 Cor 15:8-11).

Notes: **1:1-2** The compositions by Paul found in the NT are distinguished by their literary form and function. Each writing consists of four parts: a greeting, a thanksgiving (except for Galatians), often including a prayer, a main body and a benediction. Together, they form a personal letter written to respond to a particular congregation's spiritual crisis (see Aune 1987:158-225). Notice that the form of Paul's letters corresponds to the form of a Christian service of worship. Rather than coincidental, this correspondence may well be the product of the public reading of letters as a typical and central feature of early Christian worship (compare Eph 3:4 and Rev 1:3; see Lohse 1976:13-14).

1:1 For a review of recent scholarship on the New Testament idea of *apostle* see Agnew 1986:75-96. Munck contends that Paul's Damascus Road experience of the Risen Christ is properly understood as a "call" rather than a "conversion" (1967:80-83). Certainly Paul's

This ambivalence toward Paul's apostolic credentials within the early church is reflected in Acts, where Paul's ministry is commissioned by the Lord (Acts 9:15-6) but his apostleship results from a congregation's ordination (Acts 13:3; cf. 1 Thess 2:6-7). Even the church's mission to the Gentiles was initiated by Peter, the leader of the Twelve who immediately succeeded Jesus; he, not Paul, was appointed by God to bring salvation to the Gentile soldier Cornelius. Paul himself adds other reasons, including the itinerant nature of his evangelistic ministry, which was widely scorned in the ancient world (cf. 1 Thess 2:1-16).

Against this background of controversy, then, the pointed manner of Paul's introduction is made necessary by readers who know him only by "muddy" reputation. Paul reminds them that his personal authority (and by implication the trustworthiness of his advice) is not granted by another person nor by some more prominent congregation but by *Christ Jesus,* the Lord of the church. Moreover, Christ's decision to do so was *by the will of God.* Since *the will of God* is the redemption of all creation, Paul does not use this idiom to "strong-arm" his readers into an undesirable submission. Rather, he understands that his ministry to the Colossians—given by Christ, who gave himself for their redemption (1:14)—conforms with the will of the One who wills their rescue from the reign of darkness (1:13). Some have even linked this reference to *the will of God* with Paul's commission on the Damascus Road (cf. Acts 22:14), an event that harks back to God's calling of the biblical prophets as carriers of God's word. In this sense Paul's apostleship is prophetic, since he is called by God to bring the word of salvation to a people who have need of it.

Besides Paul, there is Timothy, his coworker and Christian *brother.* The

---

view of Jesus changes: Paul can no longer contend that Jesus is but a pretender to the messianic throne; instead, in his resurrection Jesus has been confirmed by God as Messiah. However, the real purpose of the christophany is to commission Paul to an evangelistic ministry among both Jews and Gentiles (cf. Acts 9:14-15). Further, the language both Luke and Paul use to describe Paul's vision of Christ parallels the recountings of God's calling of the Old Testament prophets to their tasks. No doubt Paul understood his experience as something similar to what happened to the prophets of old; and no doubt he understood his apostleship accordingly.

Ellis argues that by adding the pronoun *our* to *Timothy,* the NIV suggests more intimacy than is required by Paul (1971:437-52).

appearance of Timothy's name in the greeting may serve a couple of purposes. Unlike Paul, Timothy may be known to the readers, so Paul may have mentioned his name to persuade them of Timothy's support for the content and purpose of this letter (cf. Martin 1981:44; Lohse 1971:7). While Paul does not indicate that the Colossians actually know Timothy personally (but see Schweizer 1982:29-30), he is apparently well-known as an important leader of the church's Gentile mission in this part of Asia (cf. Acts 16:1-5). Thus, Paul's reference to the Colossian congregation as *faithful brothers* in verse 2 expresses a desire that the close relationship he enjoys with Timothy is also shared with his readers.

Because of the constraints of prison life, Paul may have used Timothy as the letter's scribe and messenger (see Phil 2:19). Evidence for this suggestion comes from the letter itself. In the closing benediction, Paul writes the letter's final blessing "in my own hand" (4:18). The implication is that the rest of his letter is written by Timothy's "hand," following a common practice in the ancient world. In fact, the role of a servant-scribe in the early church was based on the scribal role in the synagogue. The Jewish scribe was not so much a stenographer who merely wrote down what was dictated as he was an editor who composed writings based on what the teacher said. Paul's Jewishness, coupled with his perception that he was engaged in a collaborative ministry, would have allowed Timothy to serve him as a scribe in this sense. Timothy's part in composing Colossians may partially explain the extant differences in writing style and vocabulary between this and Paul's other letters (see introduction, under "Author").

The Audience (1:2) Having introduced himself, Paul next greets the Colossians as a *holy and faithful* congregation. Christians are not holy by their own efforts to please God; they are transformed into a holy people for a holy God by the Lord's gracious initiative. The added phrase

---

1:2 Lohse objects to the NIV translation, which takes the noun *saints* to be an adjective, *holy.* He contends that *saints* for Paul is a synonym for the church (cf. 1 Cor 1:2) and refers specifically to "the holy people whom God has chosen for himself in the end-time" (1976:7). For support of the NIV rendering see C. F. D. Moule, who contends that because the phrase *faithful brothers* lacks an article, *holy* can be connected with *faithful* as adjectives of *brothers* (1962:45). Schweizer agrees with Moule's analysis of Paul's grammar but concludes that here Paul is guilty of "careless usage," since elsewhere he uses *saints* in a substantival sense (1982:30). Also of interest is Wright's comment that the conjunction, *and,*

in Christ deepens the significance of this core conviction (cf. Phil 1:1) in that it expresses Paul's "participatory" Christology: God's grace positions the *holy and faithful* community *in Christ* to participate in the glorious results of his messianic work. The readers of this letter are not outsiders who are unable to understand Paul or unable to act upon his advice. They are insiders whose proximity to God's transforming grace promises new life for those who obey the apostle's admonitions. They should read the letter accordingly.

Paul's glad greeting of his readers as those who possess the prospect of being transformed *in Christ* also intends to draw them together into a community for Christian witness. Wright stresses the importance of the parallelism between *in Christ* and "in Colosse" (unfortunately obscured in the NIV translation, *at Colosse*): those who are faithful believers in Christ are also responsible citizens in Colosse, and the two worlds must never be separated. Their public witness to Christ in the town of Colosse must always reflect their participation with him in the power of God's salvation (1986:47). In drawing this parallelism, Paul has the Colossian conflict in mind, for this congregation of saints is struggling to connect their life in Christ with their life in Colosse. In fact, their religious observance tends toward moral asceticism and spiritual mysticism, which actually disconnect them from the world around them. Added to these tendencies, their interest in philosophical speculation has given rise to a variety of Christian devotion that is much too private and esoteric, and largely irrelevant to unbelievers in Colosse.

Because Paul is writing to a congregation that specializes in theological abstraction, his advice often takes on a similar cast. Colossians is difficult to preach and teach because it is the ideas of faith that are at stake, not the actions of faith. Yet we will find that Paul always holds the two together. All that he writes envisages the parallelism "in Christ" and

---

between *holy* and *faithful* is explanatory (1986:47). For Wright, then, the phrase *faithful believers* expands and clarifies the meaning of Paul's address to the saints: "To the saints—that is, to the faithful believers—at Colosse."

While Bratcher and Nida contend that Paul's *in Christ* formula is one of the most difficult expressions in the NT to translate, in part because it is so theologically laden (1988:5), Colossians is a primary source of its exposition. See my note to 1:16 for a summary of the modern debate over what *in Christ* means for Paul.

"in Colosse," which is the focal point of Christian life: those *in Christ* who are made *holy and faithful* by divine grace must live "in Colosse" as public agents of divine grace.

In stressing *faithful brothers,* Paul may very well have the audience's religious confusion in mind. In fact, Houlden suggests that Paul differentiates those who resist false teaching (the *faithful brothers*) from those who are susceptible to it (1970:148). Paul uses "faithful" three other times in Colossians (1:7; 4:7, 9) to characterize the work of trusted colleagues whose ministry of evangelism is exemplary. In every sphere of public life, whether at home or at work, whether in the marketplace or in the town square, believers embody the grace by which God in *Christ* has saved them from the terrible consequences of sin.

The Greeting (1:2) The apostle's conventional salutation wonderfully expresses the theology of his Gentile mission. *Grace to you* was a common greeting between people living in the Roman world. In Paul's vocabulary of God's salvation, however, it underscores the stark contrast between God's saving grace and the secular forms of salvation offered by the ruling elites of the Roman world. Every event Paul recites in the story of God's salvation—beginning with God's election of a people for salvation (3:11-12), climaxing with God's sending of Jesus as Son (1:15-20) in order to lead that people on a new exodus from sin (1:13-14), and concluding with God's call of Paul as apostle (1:24—2:5) in order to lead Gentiles into God's final triumph over evil in Christ (1:21-23)—is understood as the work of God's grace. That is, grace empowers a holy and faithful life from which death and sin are absent (see Rom 6:4). Unlike the Roman offer of secular salvation, often repressive and always conditional, God's salvation is offered as a free gift, even to those without social merit or political power.

The second critical word of Paul's salutation, *peace,* has a biblical background, reflecting the prophetic catchword *shalom.* The prophets of the Old Testament speak of *shalom* when describing the fulfillment of God's promise to restore all things to their created order: *peace* is the word that summarizes a "new world," transformed from its fallen state into the form of life intended by the Creator God. More than a reference to internal and spiritual contentment, then, the biblical idea of peace embraces every dimension of human existence—past, present and future. Certainly in Colossian Christianity, God's victory in Christ is celebrated and confessed as a cosmic event: the exalted Christ now mediates God's rule over the natural order as well as over the spiritual order (1:15-20). As a result, peace is more than a good feeling or mystical experience; it presumes a universal condition, in which all of human life is brought into conformity with the Creator's intentions for all things (3:5—4:6). The glib distinction that pundits and preachers often allow between a "public morality," typically secular, and a "private morality," typically religious, is frankly unbiblical. The lordship of the Risen Christ demands complete consistency in the norms and values that characterize those gathered *in Christ,* and the same when scattered "in Colosse."

☐ Paul's Prayer of Thanksgiving (1:3-12)

Typically, the second section of Paul's letters expresses his thanksgiving for the spiritual formation of his readers. In this way Paul continues the practice of other letter writers in the ancient world, who offered thanks to their gods for blessings received, often the deliverance from some physical calamity or economic ruin (O'Brien 1982:7-9). The thanksgivings that typically introduce Paul's letters are quite different; they suggest dependence on the biblical psalms more than the secular literary conventions of his day. The tone of Paul's thanksgivings is worshipful, often fashioned as a prayer. It is offered to his readers much like a pastor's invocation at the beginning of a worship service, which calls a congregation to worship God.

Paul's long sentences (1:3-8 and 1:9-11 are each a single sentence) evoke the sense of sustained conversation with God as the proper setting for reading or hearing Paul's letter. Further, Paul's thanksgivings are full of important theological themes that will be taken up again in what follows. My point is this: Paul's purpose in thanking God with profound prayer and praise is to locate his instruction in a setting of worship. Here, in perhaps the most worshipful portion of his letter, Paul remains very much a pastor seeking to nurture his flock. He does not compose his letters from a scholar's study in some ivory tower; his prison cell is a pastor's study, and as he writes, the concerns of his flock weigh on his heart and mind.

Paul's expression of thanksgiving serves not only a pastoral role within the congregation but also an introductory role within the composition. At an emotional level, Paul's prayer for the well-being of his readers helps to establish a constructive environment for reading his often critical letter. Especially by offering intercession for the Colossians' spiritual growth (1:9-11), Paul projects the image of a caring pastor rather than a judgmental patron. His warm and worshipful tone is especially important since his readers do not know Paul on a first-name basis and, even though he is their apostle, they may well require his acceptance of them before they are ready to accept his advice.

More important, the letter's thanksgiving includes a hint of the spiritual crisis at hand. Wright comments that Paul's references to his prayer are not "devotional musings" detached from the more important "main body" of the letter (1986:49). Quite deliberately, the prayer forms the logical basis for Paul's subsequent admonitions. In the case of Colossians, the second half of Paul's thanksgiving (vv. 9-11) petitions God for the congregation's understanding of the gospel, so that it will *live a life worthy of the Lord.* By equating the "worthy life" with *every good work* (1:10), this theologian of grace introduces his message to the Colossians in a provocative way: a more thorough knowledge of the gospel they have heard and accepted (vv. 7-8) is required to produce a practical Christianity of good works and transformed lives (vv. 9-11).

Upon closer reading, even the chiastic structure of the thanksgiving portion of Paul's letter illumines his message. A *chiasmus* (from a Greek word that means "marked with an X") is a literary pattern used by a skilled writer to help readers remember the important points. In a passage formed in a chiastic pattern, the author presents a sequence of key ideas and then repeats the same ideas in inverted order. What distinguishes a chiasmus from an inverted parallelism, found frequently in the Old Testament psalms, is the presence of a new idea located between the two inverted sequences. Scholars call this new idea found at the *X* the chiastic "vertex"; this pivotal idea expresses the chief concern around which the other ideas find their meaning. The vertex of a chiasmus works rather like the point guard of a basketball team or the quarterback of an American football team: he is the team's playmaker who controls the surrounding action and enhances the play of his teammates.

Viewed as a literary chiasmus, Paul's thanksgiving contains two parallel although inverted series of three theological ideas (vv. 3-6 and vv. 9-12), with the vertex in between (vv. 7-8), as follows:

A We always thank God, the Father of our Lord Jesus Christ, when we pray for you (v. 3),

B because we have heard of your faith in Christ Jesus and of the love you have for all the saints—the faith and love that spring from the hope that is stored up for you in heaven (vv. 4-5)

C and that you have already heard about in the word of truth, the gospel that has come to you. All over the world this gospel is bearing fruit and growing, just as it has been doing among you since the day you heard it and understood God's grace in all its truth (vv. 5-6).

D You learned [the gospel] from Epaphras, our dear fellow servant, who is a faithful minister of Christ on our behalf, and who also told us of your love in the Spirit (vv. 7-8).

C′ For this reason, since the day we heard about you, we have not stopped praying for you and asking God to fill you with the knowledge of his will through all spiritual wisdom and understanding. And we pray this in order that you may live a life worthy of the Lord and may please him in every way: bearing fruit in every good work, growing in the knowledge of God, being strengthened with all power according to his glorious might (vv. 9-11)

B′ so that you may have great endurance and patience, and joyfully (v. 11)

A′ giving thanks to the Father, who has qualified you to share in the inheritance of the saints in the kingdom of light (v. 12).

Paul first (A/A′) gives thanks to God, because he has heard reports of the readers' piety, described by two related triads of good works (B, faith, love and hope, and B′, endurance, patience and joy). He concludes by interpreting their piety to be the natural fruit and logical growth of accepting the gospel's truth (C/C′).

Paul actually interrupts his prayerful thanksgiving to mention the ministry of faithful Epaphras, through whom the gospel first came to the Colossians. This interruption works to draw the readers into the vertex, or pivotal point, of Paul's opening comments. Epaphras is a well-known exemplar of practical piety. Like Timothy (1:1), he is a "fellow servant" and "faithful minister" in the hard work of the Gentile mission. That is, Epaphras embodies the "right stuff" that Paul desires for all his readers, whose spiritual crisis is their failure to incarnate their faith in practical, life-transforming forms. Their tendency is rather to exchange *the word of truth* (v. 5), which Epaphras proclaims and embodies, for "fine-sounding arguments" (2:4) that are rooted in a "hollow and deceptive philosophy" (2:8).

Perhaps Paul is concerned about Epaphras's current status among the Colossian believers and places this comment at the thanksgiving's vertex to help secure his reputation as an exemplary believer. While it remains impossible for us to know just why Paul makes this strategic reference to Epaphras, two biblical clues fashion an outline of Epaphras's story that help confirm my speculation. First, church tradition asserts that the Epaphras who shared Paul's prison cell according to Philemon 23 is the same Epaphras Paul mentions in Colossians. While the references to Epaphras in Colossians do not suggest that he is in prison, Philemon, which was written before Colossians, could refer to an earlier imprisonment. Epaphras's past imprisonment could well have resulted in a prolonged absence from Colosse, during which time others (including theological opponents) could have taken charge of the congregation's spiritual nurture. Now that he is able to return to his former ministry, Paul's prayer recalls the importance of Epaphras's earlier ministry to reestablish him in this congregation.

A second and more important clue comes from Colossians 4:12-13, where Paul vouches for Epaphras's commitment to the Colossian congregation. Why would Paul sense a need to vouch for Epaphras and to stress the close tie the two men share in the Gentile mission? Masson has suggested that Paul wants to overturn Epaphras's reputation for incompetence, and even laziness, which has helped the false teachers succeed (1950:156). While this speculation seems strained to me, it is true that Paul is concerned with Epaphras's reputation. I suspect Paul is concerned because the truth of Epaphras's teaching, which had converted the readers to Christ, is now jeopardized. In this sense, Paul's letter defines and defends the content of Epaphras's teaching and witness.

In any case, I am convinced that Epaphras's relationship with the Colossian church is a key to unlocking the reason Paul wrote Colossians. Certainly the reputation of any congregation's spiritual mentors, past and present, is an important issue to consider. I recall as a young boy seeing the portraits of former pastors displayed prominently in our church's narthex. They were a loving reminder of our congregation's spiritual heritage and encouraged all of us not to depart from it. In a similar way, Paul's desire to promote Epaphras's work in Colosse has the effect of an exhortation to follow his faithful example and to maintain *the word of truth* he had proclaimed to them.

Thanks Be to God (1:3) Paul always gives thanks for God's work in the lives of others. Here he uses the plural pronoun—*we always thank God . . . when we pray for you*—in order to emphasize the corporate nature of his ministry. The prayers he regularly shares with others, such as Timothy (1:1) and Epaphras (1:7-8; see also 4:12), seek to benefit others spiritually without assuming any special status for himself. Further, Paul's prayer is centered on *God, the Father of our Lord Jesus Christ.* Worship never congratulates people or focuses on their material needs; rather, Christian worship is rooted in our singular devotion to God, from whom and to whom our salvation is directed.

Paul's frequent use of *Father* alludes to an important Old Testament metaphor for God's covenantal relationship with Israel. Thanksgiving is given to God, then, within the framework of a covenant of mutual fidelity. Thus, to express thanks to God as our Father not only acknowledges God's faithfulness to us but also assumes our covenantal obligation to obey God in return, even as the child is responsible to bring honor to his or her father. So thanksgiving anticipates our own faithfulness to a faithful God, which is made possible by God's grace through faith in Christ (see Eph 2:8-10).

The Fruit of Colossian Faith (1:4-5) Paul next characterizes the congregation's life by the familiar triad of faith, love and hope (1 Thess 1:3; 1 Cor 13:13).

I work best under the pressure of a deadline. Having a particular goal in mind for a task helps me to accomplish it more quickly and effectively.

And Paul here lays a goal before his readers. While he uses the triad of faith, love and hope to commend the Colossians, it also serves to set out the objectives of Christian life. Every task that we perform, every calling we hear, every burden we respond to, every act of worship and every opportunity to witness should aim to strengthen our faith, love and hope.

Paul mentions *faith* first; faith for him occupies the place of prominence in the Christian life. (More than one-half of all the New Testament references to "faith" are found in Pauline writings!) Unlike John, who emphasizes the act of believing, Paul's phrase *your faith in Christ Jesus* probably does not refer to personal decisions for Christ as the object of faith (but see Schweizer 1982:33). Rather, Paul's idea of faith emphasizes a relationship with Christ which nurtures a distinctive religious identity. Typically, Paul distinguishes the church's relationship with Christ from other religious traditions (especially Judaism) whose identity in the world is fashioned by different practices (such as observance of the law). Further, in continuity with the Old Testament writers, the content of faith for Paul is a narrative of God's salvation. The believer trusts in the God whose promised salvation is fulfilled in the life of God's people through a sequence of historic events, climaxing with the dying and rising of the Messiah. Often, as in the confessions of Colossians 1:13-23, Paul provides his readers with a recital of the redemptive events which are to be trusted as true and effective for salvation (see also Rom 10:9).

Also note that Paul often uses various prepositions with *faith* to express different aspects of the church's vital relationship with Christ. For example, *through (dia)* is combined with *faith* to express the means by which reconciliation with God is achieved during the new dispensation (as in Col 2:12 and Rom 3:25). Or when Paul wishes to specify the precise object of human trust, he will use *on (epi):* a relationship with Christ requires trusting *on* God's gracious action in Christ (Rom 4:5). In the triadic formula of Colossians 1:4-5, Paul uses the preposition *in (en)*

Notes: **1:4-5** The apocalypticism of earliest Christianity interpreted the effect of Christ's death in spatial and temporal terms. Spatially, God's salvation is already realized in heaven but not yet realized on earth. According to Revelation, for instance, God's triumph over evil, the essential result of Christ's death, has already had its full effect in heaven (Rev 5:9-10; 11:19; 12:1-12). God's triumph over evil *on earth,* however, has not yet been realized, for Christ must return before evil and death are purged from the created order (Rev 14:6—

to indicate a place or even a community where people live. A community of faith has been cleansed of sin; it is a place, created by divine grace through human faith, where the Spirit reigns and where believers are liberated from the power and consequences of sin. In this sense, faith in God is the way into Christ, where spiritual resources are found that empower faithful living.

Paul sees salvation as something Christians experience together. To enter the living Christ by faith is to experience intimate fellowship with him and also with other believers (1 Cor 12; Gal 5:6-11). Christianity is not the private religion of a particular believer. Rather, every believer is baptized with other believers into Christ, where they worship God together and where God's grace forms them into a community to love one another.

Appropriately, *love (agapē)* comes next in Paul's triad. He uses an article with love (literally, "*the* love") to make more definitive and concrete his idea of love. Paul resists abstractions; for him love is a transforming act, not a moral principle or an empathetic feeling. Love is faith in motion (Gal 5:6), so that even divine love is understood by specific acts, such as Christ's death. Further, the phrase *for all the saints* suggests love's unconditional and inclusive character: it embraces the entire congregation. Here too the preposition *for (eis)* is crucial, because it points love in the direction of another person; love is always for someone else.

Finally, the community's shared faith and mutual love result in their common *hope* for God's coming salvation. The NIV's loose translation of the difficult phrase *dia tēn elpida,* "for the sake of hope," correctly indicates that faith and love are the effective yield of hope: *faith and love . . . spring from hope.* This should not seem remarkable to us (cf. Moule 1968:49), even though we might expect Paul to view faith or love as the ground of hope. He does speak elsewhere about the impossibility of a hopeless faith (1 Cor 15:12-19) or a hopeless love (1 Thess 3:12-13), and

20:15). Temporally, what has already taken place because of a past event (the death of Jesus) awaits a future event (the Second Coming of Jesus) to complete God's salvation as a "new creation." According to Revelation, then, Christ's death and exaltation have triggered a new age of God's salvation that will ultimately fulfill in human experience what has taken place in heavenly existence. See my *Revelation* (Wall 1991:12-25) for a discussion of the spatial and temporal ingredients of Christian apocalypticism.

in 1 Thessalonians he combines faith and love to make hope their common foundation (1 Thess 1:3; cf. 5:8). The curious phrase which speaks of hope as *stored up in heaven* (see also 1:23, 27) may point to the tension between a salvation already realized in heaven but not yet fully realized on earth (3:1-4). Paul recognizes that our experience of God's salvation is partial, our love still imperfect and our faith yet incomplete (1 Cor 13:10-12). Hope projects the completion of love and perfection of faith into a certain future, when the Risen Christ returns to earth and God triumphs over sin and death "on earth as it is in heaven."

Hope may also point to a crisis of faith and love. Biblical writers, especially Paul, are quite clear about the logical relationship between eschatology and present life. For example, if we believe that a restored creation awaits the end of history when Christ returns, then we are likely to view the present order in pessimistic, world-denying ways. We are less likely to work for changes within the cultural order if our hope for change rests only in Christ's future return. We are likely to view salvation as personal rather than public and as spiritual rather than social. Paul's concern is for a balanced perspective. On the one hand, he agrees that Christ's work will have its perfect result in the restoration of all things at his future return. On the other hand, Christ's work already is transforming believers into the community of faith and love, and the presence of that transformed community does make a positive difference in the surrounding social order.

Illustrations of this abound. Even now, evil cannot triumph over grace! Paul never promotes a world-denying discipleship; he underscores how life within the world is transformed by God's grace. Believers who trust Christ for their salvation belong to him and not to the world; they are "in him" and under his lordship (1:15-20), where all things spiritual and material are made new by grace (3:9-10).

In the case of the Thessalonians, both faith in Christ and love for one another were threatened by a faulty hope. Apparently, new Christians had become confused about the status of those who had died before Christ's return. They supposed that the "dead in Christ" could not now partic-

---

1:5-6 Luke's version of the sower parable in Luke 8:1-15 is about the preaching of the "word of God" as the essential messianic act and also then for his apostolic successors. This emphasis agrees with Paul's sentiment expressed in 1:5-6. The fruit proper to the gospel

ipate fully in God's final triumph over sin, discouraging those still "alive in Christ." Paul wrote 1 Thessalonians to correct a faulty futuristic eschatology (see 1 Thess 4:13—5:11), in order to comfort believers (1 Thess 4:18; 5:11) and encourage a more mature faith (1 Thess 3:2-10; 4:14; 5:8) and active love (1 Thess 3:11-13; 4:9-10; 5:8).

Perhaps Paul introduces his letter to the Colossians with the faith-love-hope triad to correct another faulty hope that threatened the faith and love of early Christians. Paul's emphasis in Colossians, however, is on a "realized" rather than "futuristic" eschatology (see introduction; also see R. Martin 1991:48 for a different view). Indeed, there is some evidence that Paul's Colossian opponents promote a futuristic view of salvation, resulting in a retreat from society (2:16-23; O'Brien 1982:12). While I do not think eschatology is a primary feature of the false teaching at Colosse, Paul clearly writes this letter to find a proper balance between what portion of God's salvation is already possessed and what portion will be possessed at Christ's return (3:1-4). Moreover, Paul opposes any retreat from society that neglects the church's responsibility to confront and convert the lost. I suspect Paul's stress on hope may even carry evangelistic freight: only when the lost are made to see the hope of their salvation will faith and love spring forth from them.

The Fruit of the Gospel (1:5-6) Paul shifts from thanking God for what *we have heard* about the Colossians to what *you have already heard about . . . the gospel.* The common verb *hear* logically relates Paul's favorable report of the Colossians' life with the Colossians' reception of the gospel, so that the one results from the other: because the Colossians have *already heard* the Christian gospel (and presumably believed it to be true), their lives have been transformed. This connection of proclamation and transformation makes perfect sense to Paul, whose missionary experience is of the *gospel . . . bearing fruit and growing* (see Luke 8:1-15). Moreover his personal experience is validated by Scripture, whose stories of Old Testament prophets heralded the good news of God's salvation as the final solution to Israel's spiritual and sociological woes. We should not be surprised, then, that Luke's narratives of Paul's

---

is itself! Thus if the gospel proclaims the *word of truth,* then the embodiment of God's truth is its effective yield.

calling on the Damascus Road (cf. Acts 9:1-19; 22:6-21; 26:9-23) and Paul's own allusions to the same event reverberate with echoes of the prophets called by God to their evangelistic tasks (compare Gal 1:11-17 and Jer 1:4-19). Like the prophets of old, Paul is called to preach the gospel; and as with the Israel of old, the church's believing response results in restoration by God's powerful grace.

The content of Paul's gospel is *the word of truth.* Even as the prophets of God proclaimed "the word of the Lord," so does Paul. The subject matter of Paul's gospel is theological because its source is God; its claims can be trusted as true because God is Truth. Significantly, the phrase *word of truth* translates a Hebraism more naturally rendered "God's true word" (as in Ps 119:43). In the Old Testament the phrase refers to the content of God's revelation given in Torah (literally, Law), which is a reliable guide to God's promised blessing. This intimate union of revealed truth and experienced life is noted elsewhere in Paul's writings, where the reconciling "word" (2 Cor 5:19) comes from God (1 Cor 14:36), the Lord (1 Thess 1:8) or Christ (Col 3:16) in order to shape the life of the faith community (Phil 2:16). This equation of divine revelation and human experience anticipates Paul's argument against the Colossian "philosopher," whose teaching is a "word of falsehood" and results in spiritual and eschatological death rather than in life (see O'Brien 1982:12). The "deceptive philosophy" of Colosse, which fashioned a private and mystical religion, would also diminish interest in the work of evangelism and thereby undermine the prospect of changed lives.

In order to highlight the importance of evangelism, Paul cites two results of his Gentile mission. First, the proclaimed gospel is being heard *all over the world.* Paul's phrase does not refer to the universal scope of his Gentile mission (as Houlden and Lohse suggest) but rather to its "triumphal progress" (as O'Brien says) that now *has come* to Colosse. Perhaps Paul's phrase echoes Jesus' "parables of growth," in which growth (of a tree, a tiny mustard seed, a loaf of bread) signals the ultimate triumph of God's covenant people. In this sense, the progress of the Gentile mission to Colosse fulfills in part the promise contained in Jesus' parables.

1:7-8 The interpreter may wish to connect Paul's reference to Epaphras with G. E. Cannon's argument that Colossians is composed of one part Colossian "tradition" and another part Pauline polemic (see introduction, under "The Author of Colossians"). Paul claims that

Second, the gospel message is the medium by which the whole world comes to understand the *truth* about *God's grace.* Nowhere in Paul's writings is there a more succinct expression of the importance of evangelism than here: the proclamation of the gospel clarifies the intentions and results of grace. God's grace is a difficult notion for most people to grasp, partly because it contradicts so much of what we learn and experience from the non-Christian society that surrounds and conditions us. Secular humanism teaches that only the self-sufficient individual survives; secular materialism teaches that only the self-interested individual prospers. Everyday experience teaches us that receiving gifts from others is conditioned on first giving gifts. In Western society, as in ancient Colosse, the myths and idols of secular humanism provide no resources for understanding the gospel's truth that one's humanity survives and prospers only because of the loving interest of God and the sufficiency of God's grace. And the medium of the message is the proclamation of the gospel for conversion.

The Central Point: Let Epaphras Be Your Example (1:7-8) A third "just as" clause (omitted by the NIV) issues in the prayer's vertex, where Paul's pivotal point is made (see the discussion of chiasmus, above): the *fruit* proper to the hearing and understanding of the gospel is exemplified by the evangelist Epaphras (see "The Crisis at Colosse" in the introduction). In another sense, Paul's pastoral concern provides his readers with a personal illustration of his earlier triad: Epaphras is faith, love and hope in action. Thus, his *faith in Christ Jesus* (1:4) is embodied in his work as a *faithful minister of Christ;* his love for all the saints (1:4) is embodied in his support of Paul and ministry to the Colossians (Lohse 1976:23; compare Rom 5:5; 15:30; Gal 5:22); finally, his ministry, through which the Colossians *learned* the good news of God's grace, has grounded them in their *hope that is stored up . . . in heaven* (1:5). Epaphras, then, is the exemplary mediator of the message. He illustrates what Paul insists upon: that the good news about God's salvation in Christ must be proclaimed.

---

the Colossian believers first learned the *word of truth* from Epaphras. If so, then perhaps Epaphras is the primary source of the three confessions of faith (1:13-14, 15-20, 21-23) that Paul uses, edits and incorporates into his letter. The critical theological sections of this

I am not at all convinced of the value of "church growth" strategies that encourage church planting without evangelism; nor am I convinced of the value of expository preaching that fails to call the congregation to conversion and spiritual renewal by the simple preaching of the gospel. Even mature believers must be reminded with some regularity of the truth that calls people to Christ. Central to Paul's definition of the church is its missionary activity: we must be a people of the gospel. Paul contends that the preaching of the gospel yields a healthy harvest in the congregation's spiritual life. The ministry of evangelism is prudent not only because it illumines the truth about Christ and leads people into Christ, but also because there, in Christ, lives and relationships are transformed. The example of Epaphras reminds believers that the ministry of evangelism can revitalize the whole church, making it stronger and even more productive for the Lord.

The Fruit of the Gospel (1:9-11) The second part of Paul's prayer repeats in reverse order the words and ideas found in 1:3-6, but this time in intercession for the Colossian believers. The content of Paul's petitions reflects the nature of his pastoral concern. This concern is clearly marked out in the text as a purpose clause: Paul intercedes for the Colossians in order that God may *fill you with knowledge* so that *you may live a life worthy of the Lord.* The essence of this "worthy life," exemplified by Epaphras, is defined by two participles, each modified by a prepositional phrase, which together recall the yield of the gospel ministry (1:6): *bearing fruit in every good work, growing in the knowledge of God.*

While the apostle Paul is impressed by the report of the congregation's spiritual development, his petition seems to detect a certain immaturity in them that fails to discern what is spiritually important. Hence, he asks

---

composition, then, express the central claims of the gospel ministry of Epaphras, with whom Paul collaborates in the Gentile mission. Paul mentions Epaphras favorably not only as an exemplar of practical Christianity but also to show their theological unity. The theology Epaphras has taught among the Colossians agrees with Paul; it is apostolic and therefore authoritative. This would be an important implication if the decline of Epaphras's influence at Colosse had resulted in the denial of his theological claims.

1:8 The phrase *in the Spirit* is striking because Paul refers to the Spirit only here (and probably not in 2:5) in Colossians, and even then without an article. It may well be that the cosmic Christology of Colossian Christianity has so overwhelmed the Holy Spirit's role

God for increased *knowledge* and *spiritual wisdom and understanding* for them. This accumulation of similar terms for true knowledge underscores its importance to Paul. The progress of Christian formation follows up rebirth with retraining. While the Colossians have *learned* the *word of truth* from Epaphras, they are apparently too easily confused by false teaching; their faith in Christ Jesus is not "as hard as nails," and their Christian witness has suffered as a result. At its root, the Colossian crisis is a crisis of knowing God. And so it is with every challenge to a congregation's spiritual formation.

Paul's concern for a more comprehensive knowledge of God's will as the basis of living for God in the world is profoundly Jewish in nature (see Schweizer 1982:41). Knowledge for its own sake—as "fine-sounding arguments" (2:4) or as philosophy "which depends on human tradition and the basic principles of this world" (2:8)—is simply not valued by Paul. Knowing God, the yield of an active spiritual life, sparks obedience to God, and obedience finds its eschatological reward (3:1-5; compare Rom 2:5-11). In a similar sense, the writer to the Hebrews warns against being satisfied with a rudimentary understanding of "the elementary truths of God's word" and calls for a more mature wisdom that can "distinguish good from evil" (Heb 5:12, 14). That is, a mature knowledge of God's Word always yields a practical and public result: behavior that conforms to the will of God, which is "doing good" (compare 1 Pet 3:17).

The biblical illiteracy that characterizes so many clergy and congregations today is largely responsible for a church that seems powerless to stem the tide of secular materialism. In fact, often there is really nothing except words glibly confessed that distinguishes the believer from the nonbeliever (see 1 Cor 4:20). It might seem to those outside of faith that

---

in the church's theological formation that they do not have any developed or substantive idea of the Holy Spirit. Schweizer speculates that Paul may intend to draw a contrast between "spiritual love" and the "worldly love" that is encouraged by the false teaching (1982:38-39).

1:9 The Greek word for *knowledge* gained from personal experience *(epignōsis)* is often used by Paul in his prison letters. Perhaps later in his ministry he encountered a more academic form of the gospel that emphasized theory and theological abstraction, which is expressed by another Greek word for knowledge, *gnōsis*, and which is the mode of Greek speculative philosophy.

Christ makes no difference in the way we live or think. Even when we place ourselves under Scripture's claim, we do so for individual reasons, with individual questions, for individual direction. In such cases the result of submitting to Scripture's witness to God is rarely repentance that leads to transformed relationships with others. Paul's concern and his prayer for the Colossians, therefore, have their counterpart today.

The expression *every good work* is not typical of Paul, especially since he links it to a life that *pleases [God] in every way;* but it is not unlike Paul to stress the practical outcome of knowing God (compare Phil 1:10), as some commentators have reminded us (see Lohse 1976:29-30). This reminder seems especially appropriate in light of the (I think false) distinction some conservative expositors make between our confessions that "Jesus is Savior" and "Jesus is Lord." Paul's theology is centered by the Old Testament idea of covenant that binds together a gracious God and a people of faith (see Rom 9—11). A covenant between two partners is the product of concrete actions by each one for the other. In the case of the biblical covenant, God's gracious initiatives toward God's people and their obedient responses secure a relationship that results in a lasting salvation. Without one or the other there would be no relationship, no covenant, no blessing.

Paul's gospel, as reflected in his letters, emphasizes God's gracious initiative in Christ. In fact, so keen is Paul's emphasis on God's covenanting grace that it is quite possible to mistake his idea of salvation as consisting only of God's unilateral and unconditional act in Christ. More precisely, however, Paul retains a biblical understanding of God's covenantal relationship with Israel: Israel's actual participation in God's promised salvation depends on its response to God. While salvation is unconditionally offered, it is entered into only when certain conditions are met. "Obedience of faith" (see Rom 1:5; 16:26) and "good works"

1:11 The participle *being strengthened* is conveyed by Paul in the passive voice, indicating that the source of strength is not the congregation itself but God.

The syntax of Paul's second triad is uncertain and difficult to translate. The final member of my proposed triad, "joy," stands syntactically orphaned, with the preposition "with," and may well belong to what precedes it in the last part of verse 11 or with what follows it in the first part of verse 12 (Harris 1991:33). My decision to place the clause with *great endurance and patience* to form a second Pauline triad is based primarily on literary rather than on grammatical grounds. My proposal fits the chiastic pattern of Paul's thanksgiving

(Rom 2:5-11) are required before God's positive verdict is given. Of course, for Paul good works are the public indications of a believer's "obedience of faith" in Christ; they are the results of participating with him in God's salvation. For Paul, then, a firm dependence upon what God has already accomplished through Christ is the single requirement for getting into—and staying in—the community covenanted with God for salvation. The emphasis of his prayer of intercession, then, must be understood in terms of the deeper "theo-logic" of his gospel: to understand *God's grace in all its truth* by the preaching of the gospel (1:6) will produce good works, not independent from but the result of divine grace (compare Phil 2:12-13).

A third circumstantial participle, *being strengthened,* along with its adjoining prepositional phrase *with all power,* introduces a second triad of virtues—endurance, patience and joy. The second triad interacts with the first (1:4-5) to describe the congregation's new life in Christ. In this case Paul links the knowledge of God with the power of God, additionally alluding to the Old Testament idiom *[God's] glorious might.* God's grace is not a theological abstraction; it is God's power that empowers a community to walk in a way that pleases the Lord (compare 1 Cor 2:5; 4:19-20; 12:10; Eph 1:18-19). Grace makes the promises of God real in people's lives. The additional reference to God's glory is rooted in the Old Testament concern for God's reputation. God's *might* enabled Israel to wage war against God's enemies so that the nations might come to know "the power of his might" (Lohse 1976:30). In this context, Paul prays that God's gracious power may transform the Colossians to live in the marketplace and town square in a manner that upholds God's reputation.

The life that demonstrates God's *glorious might* is characterized by endurance, patience and joy. Like the first triad, this one has an eschatological basis: it characterizes a people in whose life the new age has

(see above); further, the structure of this triad is similar to the first (1:4-5). The first combined faith and love before introducing its third member, hope, with a preposition; likewise, this formulation combines its first two members, endurance and patience, before adding a third, joy, also with a preposition. Also for good reasons the NIV places "joy" with the final participle of verse 12, *giving thanks,* since "prayers are said with joy" (Lohse 1971:33); it preserves the balance of the preceding participial phrases (O'Brien 1982:25) and parallels the Paulinism found in Philippians 1:4 (Harris 1991:33).

already dawned (compare Gal 5:22-23), with the capacity to maintain hope in God's future triumph (Col 1:5; 1 Thess 5:14) even in the midst of present adversity (2 Cor 6:4-5; Jas 1:2-4; 5:10-11). Yet the second triad also extends the significance of the first. While the first establishes the ideal characteristics of true religion (faith, love, hope), the second triad envisions the characteristics that are necessary to overcome spiritual conflict in maturing toward the ideal Christian life.

Difficult circumstances that place the believer under spiritual siege may well be obvious to a congregation: a recent tragedy in a member's family, a current controversy in the surrounding community, perhaps some transition taking place within the church. Yet often the signs of spiritual warfare are less obvious. The secular values of society shape habits of mind and heart that are utterly antagonistic toward God. For example, today's Christians too easily detach the virtue of love from its spiritual and biblical moorings, replacing it with an anti-Christian humanism that specializes in self-love.

In this light, *endurance* refers to the act of hanging on to one's most essential commitments, whereas *patience* refers to one's capacity to do so. Each reflects the sort of person who has been formed by difficult circumstances in order to respond favorably toward God in adversity. Both dispositions are rooted in joy, which like hope is disposed toward the future, where the costs of Christian existence bear their promised reward (see Jas 1:2-4). Paul's praise of this sort of believer presumes the active participation of the Spirit, whose good work yields this favorable fruit (compare Gal 5:21-22; 1 Thess 1:6). His concluding reference to joy may also presume his own apostolic influence (cf. Phil 1:25; 2:2; 4:1); his missionary ministry provides the context for the Spirit's work and fruit (compare 1 Cor 3—4). Thus the final phrase, *joyfully* (or "with joy"), may well embed a call that is critical to Paul's larger purposes: Reject the falsehoods of Paul's opponents and embrace the truth of his gospel in order to be formed by God's Spirit into a redeemed people (compare 2 Tim 2:8-10).

Thanks Be to God (1:12) The final participle, *giving thanks,* found in verse 12, returns Paul to the point where his prayer began (1:3), thereby fashioning a literary *inclusio,* which "includes" everything mentioned in between as reason to be thankful. Especially since Paul repeats his confession that God is *Father,* the reader senses his confidence that his concerns for the Colossian congregation will be addressed by a concerned God. If the first thanksgiving remembers God's faithful work on their behalf, this final thanksgiving invokes God's continuing work, which promises to bring to fullness the work of grace the gospel has begun.

Paul's prayers are rich in theological treasure, and this one is no exception. Those who teach Colossians will surely want to mine the themes Paul so simply and elegantly introduces here. Before Paul talks about God, he first talks *to* God as a personal, covenant-keeping Savior. Thanksgiving for and confidence in God's grace provide the theological foundation for prayer. Given society's tendency toward self-interest and modernity's emphasis on self-sufficiency, we believers need constant reminders that prayer allows us to express our core conviction that God is faithful. And it is in the context of worship, within our various expressions of thanksgiving, that the congregation of believers is empowered to be for and with others in prayer.

The second half of verse 12 is transitional. The words *share* and *inheritance* link Paul's thanksgiving (1:3-12) to his confession of Christian faith (1:13-23). These two words are often found together in the Old Testament to describe the distribution of the Promised Land among the tribes of Israel (e.g., Deut 32:9). In this context, land is a metaphor or type of God's salvation. Like salvation, land is a good gift given by God to the faith community. In fact, to occupy the land of God's promise was to experience God's salvation and to know with certainty that the Lord is a promise-keeper. Now Paul locates the *saints* (compare 1:2) in a new promised land, the *kingdom of light.* As before, the people of God are led there by divine grace; for it is the Father *who has qualified* the saints for entrance into the kingdom (v. 13). The aorist tense of this verb suggests that God has already made a positive verdict about the believing community. The *saints* have, in effect, already been granted entrance into the kingdom, since they are "in Christ" and God's Son already rules there.

☐ The Foundation of Faith: God's Grace in Christ (1:13-23)

By beginning his letter with thanksgiving to God, Paul has encouraged his readers to consider more carefully why they should be thankful as Christians. Most especially, they should be thankful because Epaphras's preaching ministry has introduced them to the truth about God's grace (1:6) and the nature of the fruit that springs from it. What follows in 1:13-23 expands Paul's understanding of God's grace; it is his "confession of faith" adapted from and for his Colossian readers.

Believers have always given various public expressions to their common experience of God's love and confidence in God's redemption. From the beginning, Christian congregations have followed the custom of Jewish synagogues in composing hymns to sing and confessions to recite together for guiding their celebration of a shared faith. From childhood, we learn to recite the Apostles' Creed or sing "O for a Thousand Tongues" to supplement our memorization of Bible verses, all to aid us in remembering and applying the story of God's salvation to our daily lives. And we often bear witness to that faith by including lines from hymns or verses in letters we write to friends.

We should not be surprised, then, to find remnants of similar spiritual resources in Paul's writings. Paul often cites or alludes to Scripture and frequently draws upon traditional hymns and creeds in his written correspondence in order to remind his readers that the gospel they confess together is true. Paul realizes, of course, that it is often more persuasive to use familiar expressions of his audience's faith in making a particular point or dispensing difficult advice. We sometimes refer to this strategy as "seeking the common ground," so important when entering into a conversation with someone we do not know well. Indeed, the phrases found in this portion of Paul's letter represent compressed, even shorthand versions of a confessed and sung faith.

Paul's dependence on hymns and confessions about Christ used by Colossian Christians is especially important since he did not plant this congregation—Epaphras did—and his apostolic authority may well be somewhat tenuous there as a result. By basing his advice on what they

---

Notes: **1:13-23** According to form critics such as R. P. Martin, Paul often adds "preformed" materials to his letter in order to expand and delimit his understanding of God, as in 1:12 ("the Father, who has qualified you to share in the inheritance of the saints"), or following a relative pronoun, as in 1:14 *(in whom we have redemption).* In addition, Paul will sometimes indicate his use of another source by a change in pronouns, as in 1:11-12,

themselves confess to be true and celebrate in song, Paul finds a way to align himself with them. His readers would come to recognize that their understanding of Christian faith agrees with Paul's, thereby allowing them to stand more firmly under his apostolic authority. Moreover, if the Colossians learned the truth about God's grace from Epaphras (1:7), it seems likely that Paul constructs this confession of faith to defend the gospel proclaimed first by Epaphras for and to the Colossians.

Paul's confession of faith consists of three parts, each echoing an important biblical typology or type of God's saving grace. Richard Hays has recently argued that Paul's allusions to and citations of Scripture provide his readers with specific clues that clarify his understanding of God and his audience's struggle to trust God in the face of some crisis of faith (Hays 1989). The biblical typologies of God's saving grace form the very bedrock of Paul's own understanding of his faith in Christ. For example, the first part of his confession (1:13-14) echoes the Bible's story of Israel's exodus. In Paul's handling of this saving event, the salvation of Christians is a type of exodus: Christians have experienced an exodus from sin; God's grace has once again delivered them from evil and death, this time by forgiving their sins, and has transformed them into a reconstituted and restored Israel.

The second part of Paul's confession of faith (1:15-20) alludes to God's creation, natural and spiritual, as yet another type of God's saving grace. In this case, believers populate God's new creation, and their celebration of and participation in Christ's lordship over the entire created order show that God's original intentions for humanity, corrupted by the Fall, are now being carried out by God's grace in their congregational life.

The final part of Paul's confession (1:21-23) alludes to the new age of prophetic promise, when God's salvation will be worked out in the life of God's people. Those who live in Christ live already in this promised dispensation, when the Redeemer's intentions for the created order are realized. Together, these three Old Testament types of God's grace—

---

where Paul shifts from *you* ("that you may have great endurance") to *us* ("who has qualified us to share"). Typically, these materials, shaped by and for worship, will be poetic, consisting of a different and often exalted vocabulary, and stated in a more rhythmic meter. The symmetrical pattern of the text, often indicated by the translators, is yet another clue, as is the repetition of key words.

resulting in a new exodus, a new creation, a new age—provide the biblical basis of truth to which Paul will consistently appeal in the rest of the letter, in order to encourage a more mature faith at Colosse and to correct a dangerous false teaching.

Finally, Paul organizes his confession of faith by prophetic typologies found in each of the three sections of his Bible: the "new exodus" derives from Torah, the "new creation" from the Writings, and the "new age" from the Prophets. Thus Paul uses all of his Scripture to reflect upon the eschatological significance of what God has already accomplished for believers who participate with Christ Jesus in the salvation of God.

The New Exodus (1:13-14) The outworking of divine grace within the history of the faith community is first of all understood by Paul as God's rescue of sinners from the dominion of the evil one. The special vocabulary of this passage—"inheritance of the saints" (1:12), *rescued us, brought us into the kingdom, redemption, the forgiveness of sins*—employs the "terminology of conversion . . . which makes fit for service those who are unfit" (Schweizer 1976:50). Also, Paul is able to frame the experience of conversion by a familiar historical event (the exodus) and a particular people (the Israelites; compare Lohse 1971:33-35). Jewish religion seems a prominent source for the teaching of Paul's opponents in Colosse, and Jewish holy days and dietary rules continue to be observed by some believers there, so the apostle draws on biblical traditions that remind his readers that the authentic celebration of exodus belongs to those who are *brought into the kingdom of the Son* through the proclamation of the Christian gospel.

Paul's conviction that believers already realize the promises of God's future salvation—a "realized eschatology"—is actually informed by his "realized Christology": the true Israel (see Rom 2:28-9) enters the place where God's salvation is found because of what the crucified Christ has already accomplished for them. Characterizing the congregation as belonging to the realm of *light,* Paul sets up a contrast with *the dominion*

1:13-14 G. S. Shogren has rightly argued that the Old Testament background of this passage seeks to correct a "radical individualism" of the kind that the visionary mysticism of the Colossian false teaching might encourage (1988:173-80). Although our sources are cultural and secular, North American Christianity engenders the same error. Paul's emphasis

of darkness (1:13), a metaphor for evil. That is, the church's rite of passage from *darkness* into *light,* out of sin and death into holiness and life, is through Christ's completed work. In Christ the new exodus of the true Israel has already occurred, and God's people have already entered their promised land to receive the good gifts of their Lord and Savior.

God's Rescue Operation (1:13) Paul's confession of God's gracious decision to usher the church into the promised land continues by specifying its result: God *rescued us . . . and brought us into the kingdom of the Son.* God's action is described in the aorist tense *(has rescued),* which suggests that the defeat of demonic enemies and the church's entrance into God's kingdom have already taken place. The verb translated *rescue (rhyomai)* echoes the Old Testament stories of God's intervention to deliver an embattled Israel from its enemies, especially the master story of the exodus, when God delivered Israel from the pharaoh's tyranny and the avenging angel. For Paul, the climactic act of God's intervening grace, which constitutes the church's Passover, occurred when Christ trusted God even to death. In a sense, the saving result of Christ's death reoccurs whenever a person trusts in Christ for salvation (compare Rom 3:22; 7:24—8:1).

The perverseness of sin is such that those who live within the *dominion of darkness* will consistently choose against God's good intentions for them. Sin is not simply rebellion against God; rather, it is the refusal of God's grace, which aims to bring the sinner from death into life, from bad news into good news. It would be absurd to think that God desires the ugliness of death or the self-destructiveness of sin (see Jas 1:13-18); God wants to rescue us from the terrible results of sin.

God's salvation, then, is a rescue operation, because sin imperils the redemption of the sinner. Sinful humanity is seduced by the fictions and falsehoods of the secular order, which promise that good things result from individual effort aided by technological advancement and that military superiority assures our national sovereignty and economic prosperity. According to Paul's teaching, the spiritual struggle we routinely ex-

---

on a people entering Christ's kingdom *with* him is a crucial reminder for us that our salvation is not to be privatized or personalized; rather, our salvation is corporate and public.

For a recent and rigorous treatment of the cosmic dualism in Pauline thought and how it relates to the crisis at Colosse, see Lincoln 1981, esp. 110-34.

perience is prompted by invisible forces that belong to two competing kingdoms. The evil one works to separate us from God (and thus from the transforming power of God's grace), while the other works to reconcile us with God (and so to participate with Christ in the wondrous results of God's grace). For those who belong to Christ's kingdom, God has triumphed over the powers of the evil realm; the sense of personal well-being we now experience results from our liberation from the evil powers.

Paul's worldview prevents the separation of spiritual from historical. Whatever happens in the spiritual and invisible realm will have its historical consequence in human life. Thus, God's triumph over the evil powers at Christ's death and exaltation has its current effect in transformed human lives and will have its full historical effect at Christ's return, when all of creation will be restored. While Paul imagines the church's salvation to be an exodus from one spiritual kingdom into another, the results of conversion are experienced and very real. This emphasis by Paul throughout Colossians is a very important corrective to the false teachers, who insist on the importance of heavenly visions (2:18) and earthly asceticism (2:20-23) as the means of divine grace. In fact, God has already done everything necessary in heaven (through the work of Christ on earth) to transform human existence, both spiritually and materially, personally and publicly.

One final comment about the *kingdom of the Son [God] loves,* which is the church's destination as it is liberated from the evil kingdom. Several expositors have suggested that this phrase alludes to God's promise made to David about his eternal kingdom (2 Sam 7:8-17, esp. v. 16) and to his subsequent coronation as Israel's king (see Ps 2:4-9). Paul recognizes that Jesus, not David, has established God's eternal kingdom and is the *Son he loves* (see Mt 3:17; 17:5). This implied meaning may be important to Paul's readers, if they have heard from messianic Jews in Colosse that the biblical David is the ordained pattern the coming Messiah would follow as David's son (compare Mt 1:1). Like David, Messiah would enjoy an intimate relationship with God and mediate God's rule over Israel. But messianic Jews believed that unlike David, whose disobedience prevented God from fulfilling the promise of an eternal kingdom, the coming "son of David" Messiah would mediate God's reign forever. Some Jews even believed that the Messiah's reign would be inaugurated by Israel's return from its spiritual exile in an "old age" of disobedience into a "golden age" of holiness. I think Paul understands the result of Christ's work in exactly this way (compare 1 Cor 15:24-28): those believers who are now in Christ have returned from their spiritual exile and participate daily in the "golden age" of grace, enjoying the pleasure of God.

God's Forgiveness as Exodus (1:14) Under the pressures of the crisis in Colosse (see the introduction), Paul's description of God's rescue operation modifies his earlier teaching. For example, Paul's futurism is softened by his emphasis on the new life believers already attain by the working of God's redeeming grace in Christ Jesus. Thus, believers now experience the reality of God's *redemption* as *the forgiveness of sins.* Earlier in his ministry, Paul spoke of human "sin" (singular) as a world force, "a power which found entrance into the world through Adam's deed and since then has exercised its tyranny over men" (Lohse 1971:39; see Rom 5:12—8:2; 2 Cor 5:16-21). When Paul uses the plural *sins,* as he does here, he means specific acts of disobedience and their real and terrible consequences. Thus the idea of redemption, which pictures slaves set free from the Roman slave market, takes on a personal and practical meaning as well: God rescues us from the results of our sinful acts which we experience in our daily lives and read about in our daily newspapers.

As a feature of Paul's retelling of the exodus story, God's gracious work in Christ liberates a true Israel from the consequences of their former rebellion against God, which had prevented God from transforming them in accord with his original intentions at their creation. Grace not only rights our relationship with God; it also redeems us from those actions that deny God access into our lives, so that God can heal us and help us along the narrow way that leads into the promised land.

The New Creation (1:15-20) This is one of the most debated passages in the history of New Testament interpretation and requires more care than any in Colossians. In part the modern debate is over the meaning of its poetic language, which is understood against the backdrop of ancient literature and religion. Another aspect of the debate, however, is over its theological significance and especially the role this passage plays within the whole of Colossians. Let me offer a few introductory comments regarding Paul's pivotal confession of Christ before I comment more specifically on its meaning.

In this passage Paul employs various images of creation to clarify "the word of truth, the gospel" (1:5-6). By linking the lordship of Christ to God's creation of the entire cosmos, Paul's tacit claim is that Christians have been remade into a new humanity, characterized by their holistic spirituality. Against his ascetic opponents at Colosse, who have rejected the material for the spiritual, Paul confesses Christ as Lord over *both* worlds; he is the "cosmic Christ." Therefore, believers are to resist any teaching that divides their life into separate spheres, material and spiritual, which would also divide their loyalty to Christ. If Christ is Lord over all of God's creation, then those in Christ have been re-formed into a new creation and embody God's reconciliation of all things (v. 20).

By using the creation typology to underscore the holistic result of God's saving grace, Paul can also introduce the importance of Jesus' death (v. 20). The Creator's ultimate goal for the fallen creation is the reconciliation or restoration of all things; and this goal has already been achieved on the cross. Though the material effects of sin and fallenness remain all too evident, Paul can claim that the Creator's goal has already been realized through Christ and is already being demonstrated in the life of a new creation, the church.

Paul's point challenges today's church to change. More and more believers divide more and more things up. What we value in the privacy of our homes is often at odds with what we value in our public lives. At work, we often reflect the commercial values of survival and self-interest rather than the biblical values of self-sacrifice and fidelity. Modernity's dream of economic affluence and political influence often determines even the believer's behavior outside of home and congregation.

I recently spoke on "Human Sexuality and the Christian" at a singles'

1:15-20 N. T. Wright has recently demonstrated the christological importance of reading this passage as a poem about Christ (1990:444-68). According to Wright, the poetic quality of the passage is best captured as an inverted parallelism, where Christ is praised as the "firstborn of God's creation" (A, vv. 15-16), the "supreme being over all things" (B, vv. 17), the "head of the church" (B′, v. 18), and the "beginning of the new order" (A′, vv. 18-20).

convention. My discussion of the Bible's teaching about homosexuality provoked many in the audience to make the modern distinction between sexual orientation and sexual practice, as though God's grace affected one's sexual practices (external) but not one's sexual orientation (internal). Paul's point is that such dichotomies between the visible and invisible, public and private, external and internal are false. His confession of Christ's lordship over all things shows his confidence that Christ's death establishes God's grace in every nook and cranny of God's creation.

This point is further clarified by a literary analysis of the passage. Commentators continue to debate its literary history, trying to identify its form and trace its function in the earliest church to its final form in this composition. Suffice it to say that no clear consensus has emerged on any of these issues. Most argue, however, that the poetic quality of this passage and its non-Pauline vocabulary suggest that Paul did not compose it from scratch; rather, he edited a hymn or confession that was already in use, probably by the Colossian readers (see introduction, under "The Author of Colossians"). Scholars arrive at this conclusion by carefully distinguishing the poetic images used to guide a congregation in prayer, to confess its faith in Christ or to sing its devotion to Christ from the more didactic descriptions of Christ used to instruct a congregation. The phrases used in this passage to express Christ's lordship are actually poetic metaphors and do not intend a literal description. These metaphors seek to point us to the truth about Christ's significance for human and salvation history.

Clearly, the poetic quality of this passage makes it more difficult for the modern interpreter to discern Paul's intended meaning for his first readers, although many scholars have attempted to so do. In its canonical form, its rhythmic pattern remains uneven and its stanza markers unclear (unlike what we expect in today's hymnals). Many agree with me, however, that two roughly parallel stanzas about Christ are introduced by a

---

Wright concludes that these four claims make up a "christological monotheism" that is characteristically Pauline.

For the importance of the Jewish Wisdom tradition as the theological background for this passage, see Dunn's excellent summary (1980:163-212).

common grammatical construction. Thus, in verses 15 and 18 Christ is introduced by a relative pronoun (*hos,* "he") combined with the linking verb (*estin,* "is"), resulting in a crucial parallelism that sets forth Paul's essential convictions about the lordship of Jesus Christ: (1) *he is the image of the invisible God, the firstborn over all creation* (v. 15) and (2) *he is the beginning and the firstborn from among the dead* (v. 18).

This grammatical clue is crucial for interpretation, not only because it provides a nice balance to the passage but, more important, because it divides the passage into two integral christological themes that Paul will develop in the main body of his letter. The first theme, introduced in verses 15-17, considers the role of Christ within the created order, while the second, introduced in verses 18-20, considers his role within the new order of his kingdom now populated by God's people (compare v. 13). Paul's parallel claims about the Lord Christ nicely frame the Bible's conviction that God's creation and redemption are two parts of an integral whole. This theological conviction implies a practical point as well: the redeemed community is a new creation, and the current demonstration that God's grace has reconciled and reintegrated all things spiritual with all things material in accord with God's will.

The similarity of terminology with Jewish interpretation of Wisdom's work in both creation (Prov 8) and salvation (Is 40) provides yet another important clue to the teacher of this passage. Many religious Jews of the first century, such as Paul, ordered their lives by biblical Wisdom, not only because it provided practical advice for a wide assortment of daily affairs but indeed because this advice was viewed as the very "word of God" (Prov 30:5-9), necessary for salvation (Wisdom 6:24). Various New Testament writers make this same point. James, for example, views Wisdom as the heavenly "word" from God, necessary for salvation (Jas 1:17-21; compare 2 Tim 3:15). Matthew's gospel shows how Jesus taught his disciples the Wisdom of God for their salvation (Mt 7:24; 10:24; 11:25; 24:45; 25:1-9). Paul makes it clear that he follows in the way of the earliest church, then, by drawing upon Jewish Wisdom to explain his faith in Christ (compare 1 Cor 1:30).

Two core convictions of biblical Wisdom are important as background to Paul's understanding of Christ's cosmic lordship. First, Wisdom teaches that every aspect of human life (including its religious, social, political, family and economic dimensions) is to make visible the Creator's invisible intentions (see Heb 11:1-2). If God is true and good, so are the intentions for all that the Creator has made. So Israel's sages distilled their observations of human life into the Old Testament Proverbs to express the Creator's good intentions as guides toward the good life and away from misfortune.

Second, the messianic Jews (Jews waiting for Messiah to come) who lived around the time of Jesus and Paul linked Israel's practice of biblical Wisdom to the coming of the Messiah. What had first been composed as a social ethic to order Israel's national life now took on eschatological importance: the practice of Wisdom became a condition for Israel's entrance into God's promised salvation.

Taken together, then, these two convictions derived from the Wisdom tradition of Judaism inform Paul's convictions about Christ, who is the personification of Wisdom, and the church, which belongs to him: God's good intentions for all of creation are embodied in the Lord and are realized in the community of his kingdom.

Let me make one final comment in introducing this passage. Paul's confession of the lordship of Christ provides one of the New Testament's most important models for understanding the deity of Christ. In a day when many believers hold firmly to the incarnation of God in Christ but do not understand why, this passage takes on an even greater practical importance. For the apostle's confession that Jesus is cosmic Lord makes the even more profound claim that in the Lord Jesus Christ, God has been made one of us, for us. Certainly Paul's primary point in this compositional context is to claim something decisive for the Lord's *messiahship:* that is, Jesus' messianic work, especially his death (v. 20), embodies or incarnates the work of God. In fact, the truth about God's grace (vv. 4-5) is disclosed personally and within history by Jesus from Nazareth.

On this basis Paul revises the fundamentals of Jewish monotheism as well as his interpretation of Jewish Scripture; for him, true religion is no longer expressed by Judaism's daily recitation of the biblical *Shema* (Dt 6:4, an affirmation of faith in Israel's God) or compliance with biblical Wisdom's instruction through observance of Torah legislation or temple practice. Rather, all of God's truth contained in Jewish tradition has been made flesh in Jesus; further, the Creator's good intentions for all things, incarnated in Jesus, are embodied in the new creation, which is by and for and in him (1:16-17).

Christian orthodoxy does not conclude with incarnational Christology but with incarnational ecclesiology. The God whose grace and truth is made flesh in Christ's life is now incarnated in the church's life. Thus Paul's claim for the Lord Christ issues in a practical claim upon the Christian's life and constitutes yet another typology of God's grace: sinful humanity is transformed into new humanity with the capacity to live in accord with God's pleasures and to delight in the blessings God intended for the first man and woman. For this reason, Paul's defense of Christian faith in chapter 2 will give way to his description of Christian life in chapter 3.

God's Son Is Lord of Creation (1:15-18) The first stanza of this confession relates Christ to creation, beginning with the claim that Jesus is *the image of the invisible God.* Most scholars locate the important idiom *image* within the Hellenistic world, where it referred to various media of divine revelation. For example, according to Platonic thought, the entire cosmos is the visible "image" of the invisible God (see Lohse 1971:47) and the natural order properly guides our imagination about God's identity. In fact, under the influence of Plato, Hellenistic Judaism interpreted God's act of creation as informed by preexistent and eternal images or expressions of God's Wisdom. In this mythic sense, then, creation is the visible, historical counterpart of invisible, heavenly reality. The precepts and principles of God's Wisdom form the very substance of all things. These "images" of the Creator do not merely "represent" or help us "visualize" God; rather, they actually make what is hidden in God concrete and knowable, so that we may know and enter into fellowship with God.

Paul's understanding of Christ's significance takes shape in a Greek philosophical environment that defined *image* in this way. In referring to Jesus as *the image of the invisible God,* Paul means that Jesus is the very substance of God's purposes and intentions for creation. He is God's pattern for all of life, and through him God will restore a broken and fallen creation in his likeness. In this regard, Paul's claim for Jesus may be intended as more than an apologia for his cosmic importance as Lord Christ. I think Paul uses *image* to echo the biblical story of creation, when God created male and female in God's own image (Gen 1:27). Paul's ultimate point is that the Christ event brings to historical expression the ultimate purpose of God's creation of all human life. On the one hand, Jesus exemplifies humanity's faithful response to God; but on the other hand, he also discloses God's faithfulness to humankind. God's good intent in creating human life is to enjoy a faithful relationship with every person. Because of Christ, this intent can now be realized for those who are in him.

The next claim for Christ, that he is *the firstborn over all creation,* is surely one of the most difficult in the New Testament. Of course Paul's claim about Christ's "birth" is not to be taken literally, as Arius did in the early fourth century or as the Jehovah's Witnesses do today. In their antitrinitarian polemic, Arians argued that Jesus was merely the first human being ever "fathered" by God—in a literal sense, the first of a new creation. If they were right, the Lord Jesus would not be God's substantive equal and there could be no Trinity.

Such heresy stems in part from a failure to appreciate the Old Testament background of Paul's expression. Scripture refers to Israel as God's firstborn child (Ex 4:22; compare Jer 31:9; Is 64:8) and so expresses God's election of Israel for salvation and defines its special place in God's redemptive plans. Especially in the Exodus text, the phrase expresses the Lord's faithfulness to Israel, a faithfulness that ultimately ensures its salvation from the evil pharaoh. In Paul's handling of this biblical tradition, Christ and not Israel is cast as God's Son (1:13). God's faithfulness to Christ ensures his resurrection and triumph over death, and in him over all those evil powers that keep a fallen creation captive to spiritual darkness and the consequences of human sins (1:13-14).

It is possible that another ingredient of the background to Paul's use of *firstborn* is the ancient idea of a birthright, which gave the firstborn a privileged status and responsibility within the family (Lightfoot 1879:144-45). Again, if we push this connection too far we risk losing a fully trinitarian theology, for even the firstborn son is not the equal of his father within the household. If Paul had in mind the birthright, it would be only as a metaphor for Jesus' unique and distinctive role within the creation as agent of its salvation. Paul's idiom is better understood through Jewish Wisdom, which he believes is best personified by Jesus (see above). Even as God "created" Wisdom in the beginning (Prov 8:22) by which to create all things (Prov 3:19), so now Jesus is properly understood as God's true template by whom the divine purposes for all things are perfectly revealed.

The next christological formulation (v. 16) only expands and clarifies the cosmic result of God's triumph over evil through the Son. Creation itself contains *all things . . . visible and invisible.* In fact, Paul shares the view of his contemporaries that the cosmic order includes a spiritual realm of *invisible . . . thrones or powers or rulers or authorities* and a parallel but physical realm of *visible . . . thrones or powers or rulers or authorities.* According to Paul's teaching these two realms are fully integrated, so that a spiritual reality lies behind the societal, whether for good (the Spirit of the Risen Christ empowering the church to worship and bear witness to God) or evil (the evil one empowering the enemies of Christ to undermine the church's worship of and witness to God). As a matter of Paul's incontrovertible "theo-logic," all these spiritual powers and their various historical agents have their final destiny in negative or positive relationship to the One in whom *all things were created.*

The NIV incorrectly translates Paul's "in him" (that is, Christ) formula as *by him,* missing the intended force of the phrase. Paul typically uses "in him" or "in Christ" as a metaphor for restored relationships or, even more specifically, the spiritual home of those who belong to Christ, where he (rather than the evil one) rules over them (v. 13). In this particular confession, however, Paul presumes that the destiny of the entire created order—both its spiritual and its physical realms—is linked to Christ's destiny. Further, God's positive verdict on Jesus' messianic work, indicated by the raising of him as Lord Christ, shows that God's purpose for creation will ultimately be carried out (Rev 21:1—22:5).

1:16 Paul's point concerning the relationship between the Lord Christ and God's creation is focused in three interlocking prepositional phrases: *en autō . . . di' autou kai eis auton*—"in him, through him and for him." According to Paul's teaching, which draws on Jewish Wisdom tradition, all the things God has created, whether in the heavens or on the earth, whether visible or invisible, have been fashioned with Christ in mind, achieve their intended purpose through him and now exist for him. Perhaps, as Moule suggests, the effect for Paul's first readers is "to emphasize the immeasurable superiority of Christ over whatever rival might, by the false teachers, be suggested" (Moule 1957:66).

Earlier in this century a fierce debate raged between biblical scholars over the meaning

Christ embodies God's will for all creation; Christ is the content and goal of God's grace, by which God's will is now being brought to reality within history. When the ruling elites of society resist the teaching of Christ, they actually prevent the "good life" from being realized. In whatever form it finally takes, rebellion against God is self-destructive simply because it is at odds with the life-generating resources that God has built into creation. Any secular pretension or humanistic hubris will eventually be exposed as self-deceptive and false, utterly incapable of empowering a person for good. (Hence the recent collapse of Soviet communism.) Claims for national sovereignty or for individual rights, if not subjected to Christ's absolute claim on *all things* and every power, are without any foundation and are surely idolatrous.

Believers must never confuse the secular with the sacred. It is easy to fall into this confusion in the West, especially in America, where public rhetoric often employs a sacred idiom to maintain public conduct that is often secular. The point Paul makes here has less to do with Christ's exalted status than with the consequences of his messianic work, which brought a fallen creation back under the Creator's sovereign reign. To deny Christ as the Lord of God's creation is to deny the redemptive consequences of Christ's death; to reject God's desire to delight in the inherent goodness of creation is to reject the prospect of a new creation of redeemed humanity in Christ.

The next set of christological formulations (v. 17) repeats in chronological fashion the critical relationship between Lord Christ and *all things*. The previous confession stated that the destiny of *all things* is predicated by being in Christ. Similarly, if Christ was *before all things,* and if all things have their beginning *by him* and their purpose *for him,* and if *in him all things hold together* in a coherent and logical way, then

of Paul's phrase *in Christ.* Most view it as a christological formula that envisions Christ's ongoing relationship with the faith community; the debate is over the nature of that union in Paul's mind. Arguments can be divided roughly into two groups. First, as initially articulated by A. Schweitzer and A. Deissmann and later by A. Wilkenhauser, the phrase refers to a spiritual reality—a mystical and transcendent relationship between the church and Christ. Second, as more recently articulated by F. Neugebauer and R. Tannehill, the phrase refers to a more objective reality—an actual participation of the believing community in the Christ event and in its historical results. Conceivably, Paul included both dimensions in his writing; in Colossians, however, the more objective meaning is preferable.

the wise thing to do is to line up under the lordship of Christ in order to enter into God's salvation. As Wright nicely puts it, "No creature is autonomous. All are God's servants (Ps 119:91) and dependents (Ps 104)" (Wright 1987:73).

The final item of the confession's first stanza (v. 18) is clearly transitional from God's first creation to God's new creation, the church. This too alludes to the Old Testament narrative, where the genesis of creation (Gen 1—11) is linked to the genesis of Israel (Gen 12—50). In the biblical narrative these two stories are found together in the book of Genesis, because the story of the one cannot be told without the story of the other: the election of God's people will result in the restoration of God's creation. Likewise, the careful structure of the confession, which locates the initial claim about the church within a stanza about creation, prevents us from assuming that the destiny of the one is somehow distinct from the destiny of the other: both church and creation are "in Christ," and the destiny of each is inextricably bound together because of and for him.

Paul often uses the head-body metaphor when referring to the relationship between Christ and the *church* (O'Brien 1983:57-61). Sometimes Paul uses the body metaphor to express the interdependent relationships among gifted believers within the church (1 Cor 12:10-26). In this context, however, the emphasis is on Christ more than the church: Christ is Lord of the church even as the human head governs the body. Certainly this image of the human body leaves the impression of organic unity between Christ and the church: each is necessary to the other, since a headless body is as useless as a bodiless head (compare Eph 4:15-16).

Perhaps the relationship Paul has in mind stems from his participatory Christology: as members of Christ's body, believers participate by grace through faith in the history of the historical Jesus, from his death to his exaltation. Those who belong to the faith are liberated from the consequences of their sins through participating in Christ's death, and now experience a transformed life through participating in his resurrection.

The critical point to make, however, is that our participation with Christ in the salvation of God takes place in real time. If all things are fashioned with Christ in mind and for his glory (v. 16), and if the church and Christ are inseparable as body and head, then in some extra special sense the redeemed community embodies in real time all that God desires for creaturely existence. Paul resists any theological jargon that might allow believers to speak of their participation in Christ's body without reference to their actual experiences. Christianity is a practical religion, made up of believers who live in and for the restoration of a broken and fragmented world. Our testimony to Christ's lordship is a mended life, made whole again by God's healing grace.

God's Son Is Lord of the New Creation (1:18-20) The second stanza of Paul's christological confession begins with a different point: Christ is *the beginning.* The word *beginning* comes from the same word-family as *rulers* (1:16) and probably carries the same idea: the Lord Christ is at "the beginning of"—or "rules over"—God's new creation, the church, even as he is Lord now over the various elites of God's created order. At times the word carries a temporal meaning, referring to the beginning or first event of a sequence of events. So this claim for Christ's lordship over the church may have a historical aspect: Jesus' death and resurrection begins his cosmic lordship (compare Phil 2:9-11) and inaugurates the new age of salvation's history in him (1 Cor 15:12-28). Paul further expands the confession here by adding the appositional phrase *the firstborn from among the dead.* The new age initiated by Christ's death and resurrection constitutes nothing less than a new order of human life in Christ, the essential ingredient of which is victory over death in its various expressions.

Significantly, Paul recycles the word *firstborn (prōtotokos),* which he used earlier to stake out Christ's status as Lord *over all creation* (v. 15). This word, found in both stanzas, stakes a common claim in two different spheres, creation and church. The histories of God's salvation and God's creation are joined together under the lordship of Christ. God's triumph over spiritual darkness and human sins through Christ results in the restoration of a fallen creation and of sinful creatures, who now share a common Lord. This truth, made real in our common experience of God's powerful grace, will be completely demonstrated at Christ's return.

Of course, this future has a past in the empty tomb of Jesus. Appropriately, then, the prepositional phrase modifying *firstborn* is *from among the dead,* a metaphor for Jesus' resurrection. Since the final phrases of this second section (v. 20) speak of Christ's death, the confession of Christ's lordship over the church's salvation is bracketed by his death and resurrection. According to Paul, these two events constitute the messianic claim that inaugurates the salvation of God's creation. Further, the new life that characterizes the new humanity populating the new creation during the new age of salvation's history is the result of Christ's resurrection (compare Rom 6:4). In that Christ's dying and rising are *past* events, the new creation has erupted in the midst of a fallen creation, and the promised blessings of the new age are now being realized within the history of the church. Since the church's life in Christ is never divorced from creation's life in Christ, the church comes to understand its changed existence within and for the restoration of the world order.

Paul's orientation toward society modifies somewhat the natural conflict over values and convictions between the redeemed community and the rest of the world order (compare Col 3:9-10): conflict gives way to evangelism. As God's new creation, the faith community forsakes the old order but does not live in isolation from it. Rather, believers are called to live in the cultural mainstream as a new humanity and to call into question the old structures of "this present evil age" by its life with Christ and its proclamation of him. The church's incarnation of God's truth in deed and word would have absolutely no effect on other people if believers separated themselves from the lost. Worries about secular contamination only diminish the power of divine grace, which not only transforms believers but also protects them from evil.

The purpose clause that follows, *so that in everything he might have the supremacy,* articulates another result of God's positive verdict of Jesus' messianic mission in the empty tomb. The word the NIV translates *supremacy* comes from the word family of "firsts" (such as *firstborn* in vv. 15, 18) and focuses the purpose of God's new creation: to rank Christ as most important among *all things.* The phrase completes the earlier thrust of Paul's thinking that *all things were created* in him, by him and for him (v. 16), so that the extent of Christ's importance includes *all things* of both old and new orders.

Paul's confession returns to the question of Christ's lordship, but now to clarify what results from his faithful messiahship (compare Rom 1:3), when he "became" Lord by obeying God rather than by appealing to his preexistence (v. 17). But this new emphasis raises a question: how can Christ already "be" and then "become" cosmic Lord? Wright suggests a solution to this paradox in the distinction that Paul makes more clearly in other confessions about Christ, such as the one found in Philippians 2:5-11. There, according to Wright, Paul makes the distinction between a person's natural "right" that is not yet exercised and one whose status is ultimately legitimated by historical fact (1986:75). In this sense, Jesus has always been Lord of all; but as Messiah, by his faithfulness to God his preexistent status was proved valid.

Perhaps a more direct solution, however, lies in the twofold structure of the confession itself. In claiming Christ's lordship over all things, Paul makes a chronological distinction between Christ's preexistent lordship over creation and his postexistent lordship over the new creation. Therefore, while the preexistent Son is *the firstborn over all creation* and is therefore Lord over all things created, his lordship over the church began only after he became *firstborn from among the dead* at his exaltation (see Rom 1:3). With this in mind, we return to the phrase before us, *so that in everything he might have the supremacy,* to understand that *everything* does not refer to the *all things* created as in verse 16, but to all those new things that God's empowering grace continues to re-create within the faith community, beginning with Christ's resurrection.

At the core of the second half of the confession, sandwiched between claims for Christ's resurrection (v. 18) and his death (v. 20), are the redemptive results for humankind that follow from God's positive verdict of Jesus' messiahship. A great deal of scholarly attention has focused upon the meaning of the phrase *for God was pleased to have all his fullness dwell in him*—a claim to which Paul returns in 2:9 in arguing against the "hollow and deceptive philosophy" of his Colossian opponents (2:8). Frankly, this is a very difficult phrase to understand, and virtually every part of it remains contested among interpreters. Yet I think at least two elements should be included in its interpretation. First, Paul's intent is not to defend Christ's preexistence, a point he has already made. Rather, Paul's immediate interest is to confess Christ's lordship over the church. Thus, God's pleasure over Christ's deity explains God's verdict to make him Lord over every aspect of the church's salvation (v. 18;

compare Acts 2:29-36). Second, by positing the fullness of God in Christ, Paul explains why Christ is an effective Lord. That is, God's fullness resides in the exalted Christ so that *through him* all things are reconciled to God.

While these two meanings may help provide the christological focus of this phrase, they do not settle a wide range of other interpretive issues. For example, what does the word *fullness* mean? In what sense does God's fullness *dwell in him* (the exalted Lord Christ)? What is the significance of Christ's *blood* and the nature of the *peace* that it provides the new creation?

Most modern commentators discount any explanation of *fullness* that argues for something other than a circumlocution for God. Actually, verse 19 does not include *God;* the verse's subject is *fullness*—literally, "all the fullness was pleased to dwell in him." Clearly, however, God is the implied subject of *pleased,* since a personal God can experience pleasure and the metaphor *fullness* cannot, and only God has the authority to define the relationship between Christ and the covenant community (compare Rom 9:6-29). But is *fullness* a metaphor of God's nature, as some understand, or perhaps of God's redeeming activity, as others suggest? When Paul speaks of the "grace of God" or the "righteousness of God" in his other writings, he intends the more Hebraic meaning of God's saving action rather than the more Hellenistic meaning of God's saving character. That is, Paul resists reducing God's grace or righteousness to a theological idea; for him God's grace or righteousness refers to God's work within history that transforms people and alters their destiny. Thus in Romans Paul speaks of grace as salvation-creating power and then locates God's righteousness within history (Rom 1:16-17)—first on the cross (Rom 3:22) and then in the actual experiences of the faith community (Rom 5—8). My point is that in a similar way, "God's fullness" is another idiom for divine action. God acted fully in Christ, and nothing of or nothing from God is lacking in Christ's work for us. God's redemptive activity on earth is mediated and God's faithfulness manifested through the Messiah.

This is precisely what God's resurrection of Jesus indicates to Paul. Easter convinced him—initially in his christophany on the Damascus Road—that the cross was neither scandalous nor foolish (see 1 Cor 1:22-

24). In fact, the promised restoration of God's covenant with God's people and then all of creation, ***whether things on earth or things in heaven,*** is finally possible only ***in him*** and ***through him*** (compare v. 16; see Wright 1986:76, n. 3).

The effective outworking of divine grace within history through Christ is further nuanced by the phrase ***dwell in him.*** Hidden in the LXX usage of the word translated "dwell" *(katoikeō)* is a theological, even religious meaning: it is God who "dwells" in the holy place (Jer 7:3,7; compare Mt 23:21; Acts 7:48). In the New Testament, however, "the fullness of God" has come to dwell in the holy person, Jesus, who is the true temple for God's people of the new dispensation (Jn 2:19-21). In his physical absence, the disciples of the risen Christ form a community ***in him*** and are currently the "fullness of God" (see Eph 1:22-23). Thus, the faith community is God's true temple; in its particular life and special history God takes up residence on earth.

Paul's identification of the church as the temple of God (see 1 Cor 3:16-17) is enhanced by the grammatical emphasis placed upon the ***in him*** formula, which the NIV has softened by transposing the formula from the beginning of verse 19 and combining it with ***dwell*** at the end. In my view, Paul's understanding of the covenantal relationship between Christ and the church is encompassed in the ***in him*** formula. Believers dwell in Christ; as a result, they are the real beneficiaries of grace, since Christ is the medium of God's redemptive activities within history.

Indeed, just as this passage confesses faith in the exalted Christ, so must the confessing community define itself as the new humanity that finds its truest, most satisfying life in him. The validity of secular idols is already called into question by the faithfulness of Jesus and his subsequent exaltation as Lord. By dwelling in Christ believers are reconciled with God and can participate in God's triumph. This corporate dimension of the ***in him*** formula is underscored by Paul's shift of focus from Christ to the believers and by his thematic shift from Christ's resurrection to his death. God's resurrection of Jesus simply validates his death as the fulfillment of God's promised reconciliation for all believers who now reside in Christ.

Two different metaphors are used to interpret the redemptive importance of Christ's death—*blood* and *cross.* In a sense, the conflict between

Christianity and Judaism boils down to an interpretation of Christ's death. According to the teaching of Paul, God saves the faithful from the self-destructive consequences of sin through the death of Jesus, God's Messiah. Jesus' death makes it possible to belong to him and to participate with him in the outworking of God's salvation on earth. According to the teaching of Judaism, however, Messiah will not die. Rather, it is faithful (messianic) Israel that suffers and often dies the martyr's death. In light of Israel's experience of suffering, then, religious Jews who anticipate the coming of God's Messiah interpret Scripture as teaching that Messiah will save Israel from its suffering and ultimately from its (i.e., God's) enemies.

While Paul does not emphasize the redemptive value of Christ's physical suffering (as does 1 Peter, for instance), he does emphasize Christ's death, which is even more scandalous. For him, the result of Christ's death is God's salvation, for in his blood and broken body we find our atoning sacrifice for sin. Religious Jews saw Jesus as having suffered the expected end of a Roman anarchist, which simply confirmed their judgment that he was a false Christ and not God's Christ.

We must not gloss over Paul's claims for the redemptive significance of Christ's death. The centrality of the crucifixion for Paul was a radical and intensely controversial claim in his day, though we often take it for granted today. Both metaphors Paul employs in this confession are intended to show the importance of the historical Jesus' execution for humanity's reconciliation with God. *Blood,* then, alludes to the religious importance of his death: blood is life attained by death, and is the priesthood's central image of covenant renewal. The blood of animal sacrifice, shed on the holy days of the Jewish calendar in accord with Leviticus 1—16, was symbolic of eternal life, the promise of God's covenant with Israel. For Paul, Christ's shed blood carries the same significance: the church's covenant with God for eternal life is renewed in Christ's atoning death (see Heb 9—10).

The second metaphor, *cross,* is more political. Although in Galatians 3:10 Paul alludes to the scandal of hanging an offender from a "tree" (compare Dt 27:26), his reference to Christ's cross in his writings challenges the usual Jewish argument that the church's Lord was executed in shame on a pagan cross. For Paul, the irony of this public perception is that Jesus' Roman death only underscored his fidelity to God's purposes (see Rom 3:21-25). Rather than symbolizing his disloyalty to Judaism or to Rome, the cross symbolizes Jesus' loyalty to God. His essential messianic credential is his profound confidence that God will make good on the covenant promise first made to Abraham and Sarah (compare Rom 4). The cross becomes the public symbol of the Messiah's fidelity to God's redemptive promises and triggers, as a result, the disclosure of God's empowering grace within history (see Rom 3:21-22; Gal 2:16-21; 3:22).

The verb *making peace (eirēnopoieō)* expands the meaning of the verb *to reconcile (apokatallassō)*. The community's experience of enjoying "peace with God" (Rom 5:1-5) is the tangible mark of being reconciled with God. It is of further significance that Paul links the peacemaking effect of Christ's death to his *blood.* Of course, this couplet echoes the Old Testament priestly tradition and may foreshadow Paul's later polemic against those who would maintain God's reign on earth by a system of mystical beliefs and ascetic rituals. Paul will argue that God's reconciling grace in the current age is not mediated through formal religious observance but by faith in the faithful Jesus.

Finally, Paul's idiom is inclusive: *all things* are reconciled to God through Christ. In a passage that explores the importance of Christ in terms of God's creation, I am led to understand God's reconciliation of *all things* as encompassing the nonhuman and inanimate worlds, so that "even the stones will cry out" in praise of God (Lk 19:40; see also Rev 21:19-21). While I think it unwise to speculate how God might restore each part of the natural world or whether there are animals in heaven, I also think it unwise to limit God's reconciliation to the human order of creation, for that denies grace its unconditional and universal character.

The New Age (1:21-23) Drawing on a third prophetic typology of salvation from the Old Testament, Paul concludes the confession of faith that provides the theological foundation for his letter. The opening pronoun *you* gives this passage a pointed tone, made personal by Paul's concluding exhortation (v. 23). The language of conversion recalls 1:13-14, thereby bracketing off and providing the focus for the christological confession of 1:15-20: the lordship of Christ gives believers even more confidence that God's rescue operation of lost humanity will be effective.

Such confidence is not always easy. We are often seduced into conformity with the norms and values of our world, which is secular and humanistic, materialistic and cynical. Society's elites seem to control our daily lives and become substitutes for God; our immediate survival at home or in the workplace becomes more important to us than our witness to God's reign. Because of the difficulty of being Christian in a non-Christian world, our incarnation of Christ's victory requires a costly devotion. Yet this devotion is both required and made reasonable by the certainty of our eventual triumph with him.

The images Paul employs in this passage push us beyond conversion toward the future, when we will be vindicated with Christ. In light of this prospect, Paul shifts the reader's focus from Christology to eschatology, from the Lord Christ's reconciling death to the church's entrance into God's kingdom at the end of time. In doing so, Paul rounds out the essential content of his gospel to the Gentiles and readies his readers for the polemic against his opponents at Colosse.

Out of the Old Age (1:21) The images of conversion in this passage highlight the importance of right thinking for making right responses to God (see vv. 9-10). It would be imprudent to think of the unsaved as unthinking or intellectually marginal, or to think of *evil* only in terms of perverted or ignoble behavior. The "evil" in view here is the hubris of unbelief that typically characterizes the best and brightest. They have learned to count on themselves for their security and contentment, and given the public's affirmation of their ability, they find no real need for God's affirmation. The issue is not how much knowledge people acquire or their skill in using it, but how they think about God or about Christ, in whom God's fullness now dwells. A reasoned decision against the truth and values of the Christian gospel and for the falsehoods and fictions of the social order results in a *mind* or intellectual orientation that is *alienated from* the Creator's purposes for "all things." For example, to have a mindset that is *alienated from God* is to learn to think about Christ's death as foolish or even scandalous (compare 1 Cor

1:21 The NIV seems to suggest that wrongdoing corrupts the way one thinks about God: *because* you have sinned, you have become God's intellectual enemies. The reverse is more

1:18—2:5); it is to suppose that we have no spiritual deficit or need to be reconciled with God. In fact, the habits of mind that are formed by rejecting the truth of the gospel result in a life lived as though God does not exist (see Jas 4:13-17).

The process of conversion, then, begins with right thinking about God; and right thinking about God begins with our consideration of the ultimate importance of Christ's death and resurrection. And right thinking about Christ's dying and rising yields a correct response in the *mind* of the reasonable person, which is to depend on God's grace in Christ.

To admit that our experience with God's *shalom* does not depend on our social status or individual talent but solely on God's grace is a conversion from the ways of the world system; it is the way of Wisdom. We should not suppose that this conversion of the mind, important as it is, will come easily to the lost of our world; it requires a paradigm shift in how we function within society. The slogans of secular materialism promise humanity's salvation in terms of self-sufficiency or economic security, technological progress or national sovereignty. According to Paul, God's salvation from evil comes to those who depend upon Christ. And to depend upon Christ is to follow his downwardly mobile way in an upwardly mobile world (see Mk 10:43-45).

Into the New Age (1:22-23) The opening phrase *but now* acknowledges the ultimate importance of Christ's death for reconciliation (as in v. 20). The particular formulation for Christ's death found in this verse is difficult to interpret because it is grammatically awkward. Two important words for the human body are used together: *sōma,* which refers to the whole person in Jewish psychology, and *sarx,* often translated "flesh," which refers either to a particular person's anatomy or to a person's natural opposition to God's purposes. The NIV translation combines the two words to emphasize *Christ's physical body;* this is helpful for three reasons.

First, the emphasis underscores the historical and real nature of Jesus' death and therefore of God's reconciling grace. Second, while I doubt that the Colossian opponents are docetic (denying Christ's humanity and

true to Paul's intent: that is, one's view of the world shapes one's view of God, whether to rebel against God's purposes or to live in conformity with them.

as a result his material solidarity with us), they may well tend toward the theological abstraction (Paul calls it "philosophy" in Col 2:8) that has led to moral asceticism and esoteric beliefs in Colosse. Paul always insists that at the core of the believer's understanding of God is a historical fact—a real person, an ugly execution of that innocent man, his bodily resurrection and ascension into heaven. Likewise, at the core of the gospel is another historical reality—a reconciling God, an atoning death, a new life. Real human sins are actually forgiven and real human lives are actually transformed. In fact, God's reconciling grace is a historical phenomenon, a felt experience. Third, whatever spiritualizing of this event may be found among the Colossian believers, Paul emphasizes the bodily and historical to bring together a human Christ and real human beings into a relationship that has historical results: the physical death of the human Jesus is to save lost people from the self-destructiveness of their sins. What happens to forgiven people has public consequences (compare 2:9)—consequences that take place before our very eyes.

The result of conversion and God's forgiveness of sins through the crucified and risen Lord Christ is the community's future perfection. The infinitive *to present* should be seen as telic (in pursuit of a specific goal): "God's 'presentation' of the Colossians and all believers is a purpose to be accomplished in the future, not a result already achieved" (Harris 1991:59). Of course Paul will argue that this goal has already been achieved as a result of Christ's death; so that believers, who are already "in" the Lord Christ, have already begun to experience the blessings of the future age (see 3:1-4). At issue for Paul is a particular truth about the future of human history: when Christ returns, the faith community will be given transformed bodies because Jesus died and was resurrected bodily (compare 1 Cor 15).

Three distinct metaphors are pulled together by the conjunction *and* to describe the future of the faith community. Together, they constitute

---

1:22 Perhaps there is some interplay between Paul's use of *body* in verse 18, where it is a metaphor for the church, and in verse 22, where it refers to Christ's crucified body. In this sense Paul underscores the participatory nature of the new age of God's salvation: even as Christ's death inaugurates the new age, so also the church enjoys its blessings through its participation in Christ's death through faith in him (cf. Rom 6:1-11).

O'Brien does not find sacrificial language here; rather, he argues that the *find* metaphor qualifies the other two. Thus the text portrays God declaring final judgment at Christ's

the credentials required by God for entrance into God's promised *shalom: holy . . . without blemish . . . free from accusation.* It should not be a problem that Paul mixes metaphors here; he does so often and usually with good reason. In fact, his cultic *(holy* and *without blemish)* and legal *(free from accusation)* metaphors are often found together in the Old Testament, when the prophets speak of a restored Israel's future status before God. Further, both metaphors are hidden in the preceding infinitive *to present;* to present a proper sacrifice to a forgiving God (the cultic sense) and to present an adequate case before a just God (the legal sense) are both eschatological imperatives. God's forgiveness makes both worship (the cultic sense) and a relationship with God possible, since faith accords with God's demand (the legal sense).

In the first half of verse 23 Paul breaks with tradition to address his readers in a more intimate way. His exhortation to them expresses a condition of their reconciliation, which includes both a positive and a negative element. This exhortation has caused problems for those who think of Paul's idea of salvation in terms of God's unconditional grace. However, Paul's understanding of God's salvation is profoundly Jewish and therefore covenantal. The promise of the community's final justification is part of a covenant between God and the "true" Israel. Even the idea of God's faithfulness to a promise made is modified by the ideals of a covenantal relationship: God's fulfillment is conditioned upon a particular response. According to Paul's gospel, getting into the faith community, which has covenanted with God for salvation, requires the believer's confidence in the redemptive merit of Christ's death (as defined in vv. 21-22). And staying in that community requires the believer to keep the faith. Paul does not teach a "once saved, always saved" kind of religion; nor does he understand faith as a "once for all" decision for Christ. In fact, apostasy (loss of faith) imperils one's relationship with God and with the community that has covenanted with God for salvation.

---

parousia that the community is "not guilty" (i.e., *holy and without blemish*) and therefore entitled to enjoy the eschaton, its rightful inheritance (1982:68-69).

1:22-23 Schweizer contends that the eschatological presentation of the community for its salvation is not only *through* Christ but *before him* (and not God) as well, "so that the real goal of Christ's reconciling activity again turns out to be Christ himself. It is he who gives sense and purpose to all that happens. Thus it is for this reason that reconciliation and ministry belong so inseparably together" (1982:93).

So he writes that the community's eschatological fitness holds *if you continue in your faith.*

Schweizer's suggestion that we understand Paul's exhortation in terms of his creative integration of redemptive indicatives (the facts of God's salvation) with imperatives (the responses obliged by God's salvation) is misguided, in my view, because it softens the community's required (and difficult) response to God's grace, which is to keep faith in Christ within an anti-Christian world. The negative ingredient of the passage envisions the very real possibility that the community may indeed *[move] from the hope held out in the gospel,* risking God's negative verdict at Christ's parousia.

Paul's deemphasis of this possibility in his writings is probably explained by his emphasis that God's grace makes the community's faith established and firm. This too, after all, is decidedly Jewish, for God's gift of Torah, like God's gift of Paul's mission among the Gentiles (see vv. 24-27), is to establish the faith of a "true" Israel and secure its future entrance into the promised land (compare Mt 7:24-27).

Despite its great complexity, this passage gives us a wonderful opportunity to reflect on the course of God's salvation. It is something of a road map, tracing the spiritual journey of God's redeemed people from its beginning to its final destination. Thus, verses 13-14 help us understand what happens at the beginning of our spiritual journey, when we are converted to or confirmed in Christ for our salvation from spiritual darkness and death. Verses 15-20 celebrate Christ's current and cosmic lordship over God's creation and new creation, and show why we can be confident, even in the midst of a broken and fallen world, that the Lord Christ continues to mediate the blessings of God's reconciling grace within the life of the new creation, the church. Finally, based on verses 21-23, we are drawn toward the future, the eternal consequences of our

---

1:23 The NIV supplies the preposition *in* to the articular noun *tē pistei* ("the faith"). In the dative case, the noun identifies the place or location in which Paul's readers continue to live. What remains unclear and contested between commentators is whether *faith* refers to the main tenets of apostolic teaching (cf. Jude 3)—thus translated "to remain true to the Faith" (so O'Brien 1982:69; cf. Wright 1986:84)—or to personal faith—thus translated "to persist in the faith" (so Harris 1991:60). The NIV prefers the latter rendering, presumably because it coheres better with its meaning in Paul's other writings.

Paul's use of the words *themelioō,* "establish," and *hedraios,* "firm," may well allude to

reconciliation with God through Christ.

□ Paul's Defense of His Ministry (1:23—2:3)

The central problem we face in studying this passage is to discern its role within the whole composition. Paul does not often write about himself; when he does, it is usually to defend his apostleship or missionary work against opponents within the church. Less often Paul uses autobiography to establish himself as the community's exemplar of piety and teacher of truth. In either case, his self-references are typically narratives that defend the divine origins of his ministry and are carefully worded to show that he is his readers' exemplar and teacher. In the case of Colossians, Paul's defense of his Gentile mission may have the added function of lending support to his Colossian colleague Epaphras, whose status among the readers has been imperiled for some unknown reason (see introduction, under "The Crisis at Colosse").

Besides its apologetical use, Paul's autobiographical passages may also serve a pastoral role. In 1 Corinthians 11:1, for example, Paul encourages his readers to imitate him. With that exhortation he concludes a discussion that illustrates his own missionary work. Here, too, Paul's autobiography provides a useful model of mission. Like Paul, we are sent out by God with a message of reconciliation (see 2 Cor 5:20-21). Our various workplaces, our neighborhoods, our schools, our families are all the places where we labor, as Paul did before us, as missionaries for Christ's sake.

Paul locates his self-defense immediately after the triad of his confessions about God's saving grace (1:13-23). The close literary relationship between Paul's confession and his self-defense is indicated by verse 23, where these initial two parts of his letter's main body are carefully integrated. Their literary relationship makes a critical point in Paul's de-

---

the LXX's use of them for God's "founding" work in both creation and Israel, God's new creation (cf. O'Brien 1982:70). This allusion is especially apropos in light of the preceding christological confession, for Christ is the foundation of each and his messianic work forms the core of Paul's gospel. I am more inclined to see Paul's allusion to Torah's (or even Wisdom's) instructive role in forming Israel's faithfulness to God and thereby ensuring Israel's covenantal blessing (e.g. Ps 119:152). However, this link is perhaps more prevalent in the intertestamental writings of Second Temple Judaism.

fense: in the physical absence of the now exalted Lord Christ, Paul (and perhaps by implication Epaphras) is the current agent of God's salvation-creating grace among his Colossian (and current) readers.

Of course, there is a close relationship between the message and the messenger in the public's attitude toward any ministry. The highly publicized disclosures of the moral and financial corruption of well-known TV evangelists have caused untold damage to the reputation of God within our society. This same point is made often in Scripture, where God entrusts the word of the Lord to trusted servants—a point that Paul underscores. Logically, then, the truth of the gospel Paul advances among the Gentiles, while resting on the trustworthiness of Christ alone, is nevertheless connected to Paul's own trustworthiness.

While certain details of Paul's autobiographical self-defense continue to trouble interpreters, the general outline of this passage is clear. Already in the final phrase of verse 23 Paul begins to speak in the first person about his commission to advance Christ's church among the Gentiles (vv. 24-29). His appeals follow patterns that were familiar in his time and world: his personal experience of suffering (v. 24), his devotion to the Gentile mission (vv. 24-25), his hard work (v. 29) and especially his divine commission to preach God's "mystery" (vv. 26-28). His strong missionary credentials justify the trust his readers place in his ministry and present advice to them.

By including this autobiographical sketch of his mission, Paul shifts the theological focus of his letter from God's salvation (1:13-23) to the church, and from God's Son, in whom salvation is now possible, to himself, through whom that possibility is now proclaimed among the Gentiles. Any religious authority Paul might claim over the Colossians (1:24-29) or any spiritual obligation he feels toward his readers (2:1-3) is based first of all on his commission from God to continue to proclaim the gospel's truth in Christ's name among the Gentiles (compare Acts 9:15-16)

Paul's Suffering (1:23-24) The last half of verse 23 is transitional, shifting the reader's attention from God to Paul and also from the content

Notes: **1:24** The difficult reference to Paul's suffering satisfying what Jesus' lacks is, I believe, an idiom of the Gentile mission. Roger Aus has argued that in Romans Paul's itinerary envisions his expectation that with the completion of his mission—the "fullness

of God's message to the character of God's messenger. The phrase *the hope held out in the gospel* echoes the beginning of Paul's letter, where in 1:4-6 he thanks God for his audience's faith, love and hope—the "fruit" of God's gospel. For rhetorical effect, Paul's echo may well suggest that everything sandwiched in between (especially 1:13-23) is the theological content of the gospel's hope, which the Colossians have *heard and that has been proclaimed to every creature.* As before, the believer's hope for future perfection is based upon what has already taken place on the cross of Christ (see 1:20). The church's future destiny is tied to Christ's. Not only is the faith community reconciled to God by Christ's bodily death, but believers have confidence in their final vindication by participating together in his bodily resurrection (Rom 6:4; 1 Cor 15). In this sense, the church's future hope is not some theological abstraction; it is justified by past events.

The grammar of this verse demands that we place the next two parallel phrases in subordination to *the gospel.* It is God's gospel that is *heard and that has been proclaimed;* and it is the gospel *of which I, Paul, have become a servant.* Paul does not insist that his apostolic office hold the reader's attention, nor is it he who secures the church's hope in the absence of Jesus; rather, the gospel's message is that the crucified and risen Lord Christ justifies human hope. Paul's boast is in him (compare Rom 5:1-11).

Surely public attacks on Christianity are often routed by way of the messenger. We make easier targets than God's grace, and for most of us the integrity of what is proclaimed is measured by who proclaims it. Still, Paul is careful to locate himself under the gospel, as its servant, and talks about himself only after outlining the content of what and whom he has been called to preach.

The gospel is for *every creature under heaven.* The word for "creature" *(ktisis)* refers to every human being and delimits the universal scope of the gospel ministry. In this context, however, it also echoes Paul's earlier claim that the exalted Lord Christ is "firstborn over all creation" (*ktisis;* 1:15). If the Christ Paul proclaims is Lord of creation,

---

of the Gentiles"—Christ will return, and this in turn will bring disobedient Israel back to God (1979:232-62).

then surely the salvation he has effected on God's behalf is offered to every creature as well.

The plain meaning of Paul's words challenges those who limit God's salvation to only a few. The purpose of Paul's christological statements thus far in the letter is to extend Christ's lordship to include everyone and everything. The missionary implication is that everyone outside of Christ must be confronted with this very truth: that even the lost live under Christ's cosmic lordship and by faith can also be beneficiaries of God's grace in him. His is not an exclusive reign; it intends the reconciliation of every creature to God, to rescue all from "darkness" and to fulfill in each person the Creator's good and perfect intentions.

The idea of Paul's suffering, found in the first part of verse 24, should not be separated too severely from his self-understanding as a servant of the gospel. In fact, in the biblical tradition the two belong together: like Christ and the prophets of God before him, Paul is a "suffering servant." Against the biblical background and the memory of Jesus, Paul interprets his suffering as the cost of his servanthood and provides evidence of his devotion to God's call. This impression is intensified by the emphatic way Paul introduces himself here—*egō Paulus,* "I, Paul." Moreover, the ministry of the servant who suffers in obedience to God's call will eventually yield the fruit of God's salvation; that is, the suffering of the servant results in salvation (compare Mk 8:34-8; 1 Pet 2:21-25).

In fact, Paul will return to his servanthood in verse 25 when speaking of God's commission for his ministry to the Gentiles. This may help explain why Paul also speaks of his suffering in terms of his relationship with his Gentile readership: *for you* (that is, Colossian Gentiles) I, Paul, suffered. Since he does not know the Colossian readers personally, never having visited them (see 2:1), it is difficult to understand his words here as an expression of intimacy or personal commitment. Certainly his imprisonment proves his devotion to the wider Gentile mission; but it is primarily his devotion to God that Paul has in mind. God, and not the Colossians, has called him to preach the gospel at the cost of personal suffering. This point is repeated in Paul's other autobiographies, where his service to God is stressed in contrast to self-interest (for example, Gal 1—2).

According to the mythology of the Hellenistic world, the heroic suffering of great leaders at the hands of outsiders was thought to vindicate their integrity, and sometimes also the value of their teaching for the community. Ancient biographical literature often stressed the costliness of virtue and truth. Against this literary backdrop, then, Paul's reference to his suffering may well make two critical points about his intentions for his Hellenistic readers: his gospel ministry proves his faithful service to God, and it proves the value of what he now writes.

What, however, is the plain meaning of Paul's cryptic phrase that his suffering *fill[s] up . . . what is still lacking in regard to Christ's afflictions?* In what sense does the suffering of Christ "lack" anything? And in what sense does Paul's suffering "fill up" what Christ's suffering lacks, if anything? I have argued that here Paul's emphasis is not on God's salvation, as before, but on Christ's church. To the point, Paul is surely not saying that the Lord Christ lacks anything as the messianic agent of God's salvation; nor does he mean that the redemptive results of his death need to be supplemented by Paul. His previous confession of Christ's lordship (1:15-20) and his subsequent assertion of God's forgiveness (2:13-14) testify to Paul's confidence in the sufficiency of Christ's work. Lohse is quite right, then, to object to any interpretation that renders this phrase as a reference to the community's "mystical union" with a suffering Christ, whereby the community is absorbed into and derives spiritual benefit from Christ's passion (1971:69). In fact, Paul rarely speaks in his writings of Christ's suffering (as distinguished from his death) and almost never of Christ's suffering in terms of God's salvation (as the writer of 1 Peter, for instance, does in 1 Pet 2:20-22). The images of a suffering Christ in Paul's writings are usually employed to illustrate and interpret his own suffering as a missionary. Here suffering is exemplary of servanthood, but not expiatory of sin. In this way Christ's suffering is logically parallel to his own; like Christ, Paul is God's "suffering servant"; and like Christ's, his suffering indicates obedience to God's commission.

Most scholars understand Paul's reference to *Christ's afflictions* as a catchphrase from Jewish apocalypticism. In this tradition, Jews understood Israel's suffering as a sign of the last days and a condition for the coming of the Messiah (see O'Brien 1982:76-80). Some even assigned a fixed amount of suffering which, when satisfied, would result in the apocalypse of God's salvation. Israel's suffering, then, was the "birthpangs" of the promised new covenant (compare Jer 31:31) about to become a reality. According to O'Brien, some early Christians, especially within the Jewish church, believed that Jesus' suffering had initiated the "last days" of ever-increasing trials and tribulations (see Mt 24:4-29), when the "true" Israel (the community of Christ's disciples) would suffer for his name (Mt 5:11-12) in order to fulfill this quota fixed by God. With this condition met, Messiah would return in triumph to usher heaven into earth (Mt 24:30-31). If Paul had this apocalyptic formula in mind, then his reference to sharing in Jesus' suffering would indicate that the "last days" of salvation's history have already commenced. In this light Paul's suffering "fills up" what is lacking from what God has assigned the church to suffer.

Paul's phrase, however, is to be taken metaphorically rather than literally. Speaking of completing requisite suffering is yet another way of calling attention to the importance of completing the Gentile mission. In Paul's conception of the Gentile mission, his evangelistic work brings into Israel's number the "fullness of the Gentiles" (Rom 11:1-24) that will trigger the Lord's return to earth and ethnic Israel's return to God (Rom 11:25-26). Even in this passage Paul repeats the root of *to fill* to stress that the aim of his personal sacrifice—*I fill up [antanaplēroō] in my flesh*—is to complete his mission: *to present to you the word of God in its fullness [plērōsai].*

In this letter, then, Paul's imprisonment has come to symbolize his Gentile mission: his mission has resulted not only in countless conversions but also in imprisonment. Yet his personal suffering symbolizes his faithful attention to God's election of Gentiles for salvation and God's commission for him to prepare the Gentile church for the return of Christ. Paul *rejoices,* then, knowing that his ministry will bring God's coming triumph that much closer to his readers.

Of course, Paul's intent in drawing a parallel between himself and Christ may only be to impress his readers that his ministry is in fundamental continuity with Christ's: both are suffering servants, devoted to making God's salvation a reality for every creature.

Paul's Servanthood (1:24-25) In verse 25 Paul repeats his earlier statement from 1:23 that he is a servant (Harris 1991:64). Both times Paul's comment is emphatic: *I, Paul, have become a servant.* His sense of service to God in the ministry of the gospel is his essential identity as a person. In this new formulation, however, Paul replaces *the gospel* with *the church.* This new thematic focus relates Paul's gospel ministry to a particular audience. His work is not removed from real people in real places; he is not an ivory-tower academic, but a pastor who is intent on adapting the gospel message in ways that are useful in the lives of his readers.

As we attempt to follow in the footsteps of Christ, Christian leaders, including pastors, will be tempted to give in to a kind of vocational dualism. On the one hand, to follow Christ demands our single-minded attention to his interests; we are called to serve him and proclaim his gospel. We understand ourselves in terms of our relationship with Christ; we are subject only to him. In the realm of human relations, on the other hand, we remain leaders, in charge of things and expecting unswerving loyalty from those over whose lives we exercise some control and influence. As leaders of people, then, we serve Christ. But is this what Paul means? Isn't he saying that as a leader of Christians he must embody the servanthood of Christ?

The issue is not merely to serve Christ, but to serve *like* Christ. This fashions a different kind of servant leadership—a leadership characterized by setting aside any interest in social standing or political power and submitting ourselves to others in order to share their burdens (see Gal 6:1-10; Phil 2:1-11).

Paul's Commission (1:25-26) The source of Paul's calling is God's *commission.* The word for "commission" is *oikonomia,* which envisions the effective and orderly work of a household or business; it is the same word from which we derive the word *economy.* Paul uses it here in reference to his missionary vocation for two reasons. First, Paul understands his calling and ministry within the context of a "household," God's household (1 Cor 3:10-15; Rom 1:11-12; Eph 2:19-20). He is a servant of and for Christ's church, without personal ambition or any malicious sense of rivalry toward other apostles or even his opponents. Second, Paul understands the tasks of his servanthood as those of a steward or trustee of an organization. (O'Brien uses ecclesiastical terms to define "commission," speaking of it as Paul's call to an apostolic "office" in which he rules over the church; 1982:81.) In this sense, God's commission entrusts Paul with the management of God's household. The "gift of apostleship" (see Rom 1:5) is given Paul to ensure that his stewardship over God's household is spiritually effective (see Rom 1:11). Notice that Paul retains his focus on God to resist the temptation of exalting his own status: the source of and authority for his ministry is God.

The Bible speaks of many heroic people like Paul, whom God commissions and enables to work with great profit in the economy of God's salvation. We should honor their faithfulness without romanticizing their importance to God. Their historical significance is yet another expression of the grace of God, who first rescued them from the results of their sin before commissioning and empowering them for an effective ministry. The true measurement of the effective servant is not intellectual acumen or glib eloquence, committed activism or sincere effort; it is whether the believer has been a faithful and wise steward of God's calling, whatever tasks that may include (see Mt 24:45-51).

Typically, Paul echoes prophetic ways of speaking about his call; no doubt this reflects his discernment of the Damascus Road experience. The formula he uses here to define his task, *to present to you the word of God,* reflects a prophetic missiology: God calls servants to proclaim the word of the Lord to those who have been elected to receive salvation. The sense conveyed is not that Paul's ministry fills in the missing content of the gospel or that his attention to detail makes certain that his audience knows it fully; rather, Paul's particular version of God's word for a Gentile audience completes it in a way similar to his earlier claim that his suffering completes Christ's suffering (see 1:24).

But this interpretation invites a similar question: what does the "word of God" lack that Paul's gospel ministry fulfills? Paul anticipates this question and responds in a parenthesis found in verse 26: *the mystery that has been kept hidden . . . is now disclosed to the saints.* The critical word in Paul's response is *mystery,* the meaning of which continues to

---

1:25-26 For the best popular treatments of Paul's Damascus Road vision of the Risen Christ, see J. Munck 1959 and Stendahl 1977. The consensus of New Testament scholarship is that Paul's experience should be viewed as a call rather than conversion, and that this call is similar to those received by the Old Testament prophets.

Significantly, Paul adds the aorist infinitive *plērōsai,* which is translated *in its fullness,* to further explain *the word of God.* The question remains whether the genitive *of God* is the

be debated. Few scholars today understand *mystery* as a catchword Paul has borrowed from Gnosticism to use here against Gnostic opponents. While he may indeed have his Colossian opponents in mind, including certain elements of their false teaching or religious practice, they are probably not Gnostics (see introduction). Our understanding of Gnosticism, especially of its advanced systems of thought from the second century, has little value in determining how Paul and his first readers understood his reference to *mystery*. Some have suggested that we should understand *mystery* in the context of Hellenistic Jewish apocalypticism, where it referred to God's plan for the future, but most scholars today are not inclined to this interpretation either (even though this meaning would be more apropos as a response to Paul's opponents).

Most commentators place Paul's use of *mystery* in Colossians within the context of Paul's Gentile mission. *Mystery* is apparently used as a catchword for the core convictions of Paul's gospel. But depending on the spiritual crisis facing his readers, Paul emphasizes different theological dimensions of the *mystery* that God has commissioned him to proclaim. For the believers at Colosse, whose crisis stems from their overly Jewish understanding of Christian faith, the central issues, and therefore the substance of the *glorious riches of this mystery* (1:27), are God's election of Gentiles for salvation and Christ's work that makes God's election effective. Therefore, most commentators agree that Paul uses *mystery* as a metaphor for God's plan of salvation for the Gentiles, which is unknown apart from divine revelation. Paul's proclamation of the gospel merely articulates the "mystery" that God has revealed to him, presumably on the Damascus Road. Further, most agree that Paul's usage is more Jewish than Hellenistic and may even be rabbinical. Probably *mystery* refers especially to the particular meaning embedded in biblical texts that is recovered by the interpreter's exposition. The act of interpretation transforms biblical texts into carriers of divine revelation. In

---

object of *word* (the word about God) or its subject (the word from God). Perhaps Paul intends the phrase to include both meanings, since both are apropos for this context: the content of Paul's gospel has been revealed to him from God (cf. Gal. 1:11-15), and its content is about God as well. For the theocentricity of Paul's gospel, see Lemcio 1988:3-17.

this added sense, then, Paul's proclamation of the gospel discloses the *mystery* or revelation of God which had been *hidden* within his Scriptures *for ages and generations* but which God now has enabled him to *disclose* for the conversion of a Gentile people.

God's Mystery (1:27) Groups of Christians still battle each other today to promote the rights or even the salvation of one group over against another. Gender or sexual orientation rather than faith in Jesus Christ has come to determine the believer's status within a congregation. Against a masculine God, then, a feminine God is promoted by some, while for others Christian faith is defined or denied by sexual orientation. In the recent political campaign in America, some conservative Republican believers went so far as to argue that Christian faith and support for Democratic candidates were mutually exclusive! Paul would have no part of such a divisive debate, except to remind all believers that in Jesus Christ many different people have one faith in common (compare Col 3:11; Gal 3:28).

In a similar way, Jewish Christian (and Judaic) opponents of Paul's Gentile mission debated his interpretation of the biblical doctrine of election (see Acts 15:1-21; Gal 2:1-10). Paul taught that even as God had elected Jews for salvation, so also God had elected Gentiles out of the world for salvation. In Christ, Jewish and non-Jewish believers have equal value and access to God, since all ethnic and national barriers have been demolished by Christ's death (Eph 2:11-22). Yet some early believers, recognizing that Christianity began as a messianic movement *within* Judaism, taught that to be Christian meant to remain Jewish. They argued that the Torah laws and the Jewish traditions must be observed so as to maintain the ethnic and socioreligious distinctives of God's people. Paul's response to these Jewish Christian opponents was that God's promised salvation has already been fulfilled by Jesus Christ, and the

---

1:26-27 The background for the word *mystery* continues to be debated. In the thought-world of second-century Gnostic Christianity, one's salvation was determined by whether one knew the divine mystery of humanity's salvation (i.e., the *gnōsis*). Further, this *gnōsis* was linked to a particular teacher, so that "true" Christianity was also linked to that teacher. While many scholars today think that Paul is responding to a competing *gnōsis* and even a particular teacher at Colosse, few now suppose that Paul understands this conflict in terms of a true and false Gnosticism by whose teaching one would enter the salvation of God. Clearly for Paul, we enter into salvation by participating in the atoning death of Christ; and

blessings of God's salvation are now experienced by those who belong to him by faith (rather than by ethnicity or religious observance).

The missiological issue facing every person after Christ, then, is this: How does one enter into Christ, and how does one remain in him in order to participate in the blessings of God's salvation? The short answer given by Paul is *sola fide—"by faith alone."*

Thus Paul begins his summary with the controversial claim that *God has chosen . . . Gentiles* (see also 3:11-12). The story of God's salvation which Paul proclaims begins here: to make *known* to the Gentiles that God is for them too! Paul hinted at this earlier when he wrote that God's salvation was for *every creature under heaven* (1:23; see also 1:20). But he is more pointed here. Official Judaism would not deny God's universal salvation; after all, Isaiah taught that salvation would extend through one restored nation to all nations. Yet according to the prophet, God's salvation of the Gentile nations depended upon Israel: they would be saved only through and because of the faithfulness of the Jewish nation. Even in Paul's day, Hellenistic Judaism was committed to an evangelism program, seeking to convert and proselytize non-Jews. But Gentile converts to Judaism were second-class citizens both religiously and sociopolitically. In light of this religious tradition, Paul's teaching about Gentile conversion is controversial precisely because it is so egalitarian: believing Gentiles and Jews share God's universal salvation equally in Christ.

Gentiles need not go through any Judaic hoops to covenant with God for salvation. The means and hope of their salvation is christological: that *Christ in you* is the only *hope of glory* (see also 2:2). This formulation of the christological core of his gospel, *Christ in you,* reverses the sense of Paul's previous statement that we are "in Christ" (see my commentary on 1:2 and 1:16); here it is Christ who is "in us." At the very least, this reversal of familiar terms calls his audience's attention to Paul's partic-

---

this is what he proclaims according to verse 27. References to "mystery" in Jewish apocalyptic writings are found in its plural form, "mysteries." Such mysteries were granted the community through inspired prophets and seers. Nowhere in this letter does Paul refer to such a revelatory experience, and nowhere do we find the sort of visionary language typical of the seer (as we do in, say, the New Testament book of Revelation).

For a full discussion of the relationship between divine "mystery" and human interpretation according to rabbinical thought, see Fishbane 1986:19-37; Wall 1990:614-16.

ipatory Christology, in which believers participate with Christ in the outworking of God's salvation within history. Such a unity promises Christlike suffering as well as Christlike exaltation (or, in Wright's phrase, "the guarantee of resurrection"; 1986:92).

An additional clue to the meaning of the *Christ in you* formula may be provided by Galatians 1:15, where Paul writes that God revealed the mystery of Christ "in me." Many scholars now believe that Paul is referring here to a personal experience of divine revelation, perhaps on the Damascus Road (see above), by which God disclosed the content of Paul's gospel to him. I suspect that in this autobiographical passage of Colossians Paul may have a similar meaning in mind. That is, the gospel of God's salvation, which proclaims *Christ in you,* is validated by Paul's own religious experience of "Christ in me." In this case, the phrase calls attention not only to the christological message proclaimed to the Gentiles but to its trustworthiness as the "word of truth" (see 1:5, 7).

In the light of Paul's participatory Christology, the community's *hope of glory* is not oriented toward the future return of Christ; rather, we hope to experience the benefits of being reconciled with God *right now* through our present union with the Lord Christ (1:15-20). To hope in the One who is already glorified is to have hope for a transformed today. Paul does not deny the cosmic importance of Christ's Second Coming (see 3:1-4); yet for these readers, whose religion is in retreat from the world, the apostle emphasizes that a vital relationship with the glorified Christ results in a profoundly hopeful orientation toward the possibilities of life on this side of the Lord's parousia.

Paul's Gospel Ministry (1:28) Paul next describes his Gentile mission in functional terms. At this point he reverts from *you* to *we,* perhaps to call to mind his colleagues, especially Epaphras, with whom he shares the gospel ministry. Paul uses three related verbs, anchored by *we proclaim* and expanded by *admonishing and teaching,* which are the "two natural and necessary concomitants of the proclamation of the mystery of Christ" (Harris 1991:72). The word for "proclaim" *(katangellō),* which is used only in Pauline writings and in Acts, refers to the publication of

1:28 The word for "admonishment" *(noutheteō)* is a member of the family of "mind" *(nous)* words. It means to straighten out a confused or immature mind, bringing it into conformity with wisdom. Likewise, the word of "teaching" *(didaskō)* envisions intensive

the gospel for conversion. Lohse calls it "missionary preaching" (1971:77). Yet Paul does not conceive of his evangelistic outreach as the mere proclamation of the gospel for conversion; rather, the conversion of the lost is accompanied by spiritual nurture, admonishment and instruction.[6]

Public gauges of success, whether large numbers of converts or eloquent speech or architecturally elegant sanctuaries, are not effective measures of a ministry's importance. God calculates success by whether a congregation entrusted to the care of a minister is spiritually fed and fit to the end. Paul's gospel not only provides knowledge of God's redemptive mystery but also equips the converted so as to *present everyone perfect in Christ.* The purpose of Paul's Gentile mission is exactly the same as the plan of God's salvation (1:22): the final justification of the saints. His ministry's success, then, can be fully measured only at Christ's parousia (see 2 Cor 3—5).

Paul's Labor (1:29) Toward this eschatological goal, then, Paul *labors,* working hard so that those committed to his spiritual care may be found fit to enter God's eternal kingdom at Christ's return. The church's salvation does not result from divine activity alone. Servants who effectively steward offices and gifts given by God are agents of God's salvation on earth. In this sense, Paul's participatory Christology yields a participatory missiology: believers labor with God to produce salvation. Conversion cannot take place without the *energy* of God; neither can it take place without the proclamation, admonishment and teaching of suffering servants like Christ, Paul and Epaphras. *With all [God's] energy* suggests cooperation between Paul and God for the work of Gentile conversion and instruction.

The order of salvation, then, is covenantal; it is not a spectator sport but a dynamic relationship between God and people from beginning to ending. God works *with* servants of the church, *struggling* with them and *powerfully* working in them to bring forgiveness from sin and the promised life.

Paul's Labor for Colosse (2:1-3) Paul concludes this section on

guidance that replaces intellectual confusion with the stability of truth. All three are idioms of Jewish wisdom, except that Paul's gospel replaces Wisdom as the source of "teaching, rebuking, correction and training in righteousness" that guides people into the good life.

a more personal note: he not only serves the church of Christ (1:24) but "struggles" (in cooperation with God; 1:29) for the congregations at Colosse and Laodicea. Paul's intention is exactly the same as before: to clarify that the purpose of his ministry is to make known to every Gentile, including those at Colosse, *the mystery of God, namely, Christ* (compare 1:27). He does elaborate on the spiritual purpose of his ministry for them: that they may be *encouraged in heart and united in love* and may have *complete understanding . . . and know the mystery of God, namely, Christ.*[7]

In Paul's Jewish psychology the *heart* symbolizes human volition rather than human emotion; the hard decisions of an embattled life are made by the believer's *heart,* fortified and matured by *the mystery of God.* Paul's gospel ministry strengthens the Colossians against false teaching so that they are able to make decisions that please God. The word translated "united" *(symbibazō)* means literally to be "knit together" and refers to an action that naturally follows after (if not also from) a fortified *heart.* That is, the purpose of Paul's ministry (presumably his proclamation of the gospel, and his pastoral admonishment and instruction; 1:28) is corporate: that the congregation weld well together in mutual love.

The truth of one's message is discerned in a very practical way, then—by whether or not a loving community is formed. False teaching or even a wrong emphasis often creates factions, with the result that the gospel's ministry is undermined. A Christian witness to God's grace is too difficult to maintain in a graceless society without the loving support and firm resolve provided by a people. Paul's use of the body metaphor for the church (compare 1:18; 1 Cor 12; Eph 4) implies this same lesson.

The NIV links the next couplet, *understanding* and *knowledge,* with the first couplet, *encouragement* and *unity,* as Paul's overarching purpose for the Gentile mission. But rather than taking these couplets as describing the congregations that resulted from Paul's campaigns, it seems best to understand them as describing the evangelistic campaigns themselves. Harris, for example, interprets the two couplets as compris-

2:2 O'Brien prefers to understand the word translated "encouraged" *(parakaleō)* by the NIV as "strengthen" (1982:92-93), thereby stressing the intended result of Paul's ministry.

The ending of verse 2 was corrupted during scribal transmission. The exact grammatical relationship between *God* and *Christ* remains unclear. Some textual variants, for example,

ing the specific objectives of Paul's ministry (1991:81) and perhaps even of this letter to them. If anything, Paul's earlier petition for "knowledge and understanding" (1:9-10) seems to indicate that the congregation will be spiritually healthy only if they know the gospel that Epaphras first preached to them. That is, the qualities of the productive minister are reproduced in his congregations.

In this light, the genitives used by Paul in this passage to modify *understanding* ("complete") and *knowledge* ("the mystery of God"; compare 1:27) are particularly important. In the first case, *complete* translates *plērophoria* (literally, "full accomplishment"), another in the family of *plērō-* words that Paul has already used (see 1:9 and 1:25) for his aim to teach the congregation a fuller, more complete understanding of the gospel: to fill in what spiritual competencies they lack. In the second case, the phrase *mystery of God* supplies the core content of the complete gospel—*namely, Christ.*

Clearly, verse 3 is parallel to verse 2 in thought. The idea contained in the phrase *full riches of complete understanding* is virtually repeated in the following phrase, *all the treasures of wisdom and knowledge,* so that the idea of *mystery* finds a parallel in the word *hidden.* Significantly, sandwiched between these two parallel phrases is their focal point: *Christ, in whom* all these mysterious riches and hidden treasures of God's mystery are disclosed by the preaching of Paul's gospel. Remember that for Paul the biblical Jew, the mysteries of God's treasured salvation lie hidden within Scripture and are mined by exegesis; and for Paul the Christian missionary, the proclaimed faith is a christological monotheism, and so the wonderful riches of our faith are both deposited and drawn through Christ.

Simply put, spiritual maturity results from knowing Christ. The distinctive emphasis in this letter on *wisdom* (1:9, 28; 2:3, 23; 3:16; 4:5), *knowledge* (1:9-10, 27; 2:2-3; 3:10; 4:7-9) and *knowing* (1:6; 2:1; 3:24; 4:1, 6, 8), especially linked to Paul's proclamation of Christ, is no doubt made with Paul's Colossian opponents in mind. They too are concerned with

extend the ending to view Christ as God, so that the *mystery of God* disclosed is that Christ is God. Others expand the name Christ into a christological confession. The NIV accepts the critical reading and rightly translates "Christ" as epexegetical, identifying Christ as the sum total of God's mystery.

ideas, but their "philosophy" is not centered by the teaching of and about Christ (2:8) and therefore is "hollow and deceptive," incapable of forming the spiritual life of the Christian congregation (2:6-7).

PAUL'S ARGUMENT AGAINST CHRISTLESS THEOLOGY (2:4-15)

To this point in the main body of his letter, Paul has reminded his readers of the essential ingredients of the gospel (1:12-23) they first heard from Epaphras (1:6-7), and has defended his authority to admonish and teach his readers in its light (1:24—2:3). Having laid this foundation, the apostle is now ready to attend to the situation that has occasioned his correspondence—the false teaching that threatens the faith of the Colossian believers.

Paul's response to false teaching typically contains two parts. First, he identifies the theological errors present in a particular congregation and draws out their negative implications for faith and life. For Paul, the problem with bad ideas is that they result in distorted notions of Christ and what it means to follow him. Second, he argues against these errors in light of the foundational convictions of his gospel ministry, usually introduced at the outset of a letter. This, then, is the fabric of Paul's letter-writing: to clarify a problem along with its spiritual and moral consequences and to articulate the proper response to it in light of the readers' own understanding of the "word of truth."

Following this pattern, Colossians contains two sharp discussions. The first discussion is theological (2:4-23): Paul challenges the legitimacy of the theological convictions that underlie the competing understanding of Christian faith in Colosse. The second discussion is mainly ethical (3:1—4:1): Paul draws upon moral tradition *(paraenesis)* to describe the character of Christian life that is now imperiled by the false teaching.

The polemical and theological discussion is divided into two subsections, each presenting an argument against a principal ingredient of the false teaching. In 2:4-8, the apostle introduces the first problem that threatens the readers' faith. I call it sophistry: the use of an elegant vocabulary in *fine-sounding arguments* to *deceive* an unsuspecting audience (2:4). According to Paul, certain Christian teachers at Colosse promote a *philosophy* of religion that consists of *human traditions* and centers on *the basic principles of this world* (2:8). Paul responds to this theological error in 2:9-15 by restating two central claims about Christ on which this congregation's faith has been properly constructed: (1) Christ is the *fullness of the Deity . . . in bodily form* (2:9; compare 1:19), and (2) he is *the head over every power and authority* (2:10; compare 1:18, 20). On this christological tradition (rather than *human traditions*) the community can participate with Christ in God's forgiveness of their sins (2:11-15).

In our day, as in the ancient world, people often measure the value of what others say by how well they say it. Even within the church we put great stress on a person's academic credentials, as if a Ph.D. granted one a corner on heavenly wisdom. The result is that we learn to value elegant systems of church dogma that are held together by sophisticated and learned arguments. In the life of many congregations, faith has become so intellectualized that its relational, experiential dimension has been bleached out. Certainly it is important to think through carefully what one believes and why. Yet many of my students come to university with strongly held convictions about Christ but without the experience of a vital relationship with him. Knowing *what* to believe has replaced knowing *whom* to believe.

In the pastorate and in academia, I have often found that when faith consists only of ideas, without practical experience of their truthfulness and usefulness, it is easily shattered when it comes up against competing ideas. Biblical faith is very concrete, rooted in the teachings and work of a person, Jesus of Nazareth, and embodied in personal and social relationships. Thus, when one's understanding of Christian faith centers on a collection of elegant, even powerful ideas at the expense of an experience of God's love, it quickly becomes an idolatry: the idea of God replaces a life-transforming relationship with the Lord.

So in 1 Corinthians Paul warns his readers that the reign of God is not a matter of eloquent, educated talk but of Spirit-empowered walk (1 Cor 4:18-21). To know Christ as the "wisdom of God" (1 Cor 1:30) and to acquire "Christ's mind" from the Spirit (1 Cor 2:14, 16) rather than the "philosophy of this age" (1 Cor 1:20) is the measure of true Christianity. Paul is not against education; rather, he opposes a Christianity that elevates academic ideas about God above our spiritual relationship with God in Christ.

The second subsection of Paul's theological polemic begins in 2:16-19 with his clarification of a related theological error. I call it ascetic piety: the denial of physical comforts as the mark of true devotion to the Lord. Apparently, there is at least one important parishioner in the Colossian congregation who has assumed the role of a "spiritual umpire" (see 2:18), making judgments about what constitutes authentic Christianity. This person's code of conduct is based on what people eat and drink and whether they observe the holy days of the Jewish calendar (2:16, 21). Paul claims these regulations, like the *human tradition* that informs the *deceptive philosophy* (2:8), are nothing more than "human commands and teachings," and their effectiveness is based on an "appearance of wisdom" rather than the truth of the gospel (2:22-23).

According to Paul, wisdom, whether true or false, is measured by its results. Wisdom is true if it produces a community that worships and bears witness to God in its shared life. Thus, in 2:20-23, Paul's verdict on self-righteous asceticism is negative: when measured by the "reality" of Christ's death (2:17, 20), this form of Christian spirituality "lacks any value" whatever (2:23). Paul's Christianity is practical; decisions believers make about their spiritual well-being must be aimed toward getting into the proper place ("in Christ"), where God's grace empowers growth and worship (see 2:7). Relying on carefully thought-out ideas or rules of abstinence rather than on what God has already accomplished for us in Christ is at least imprudent, because it imperils the present results of Christ's work in us.

□ The Error of Sophistry (2:4-8)

Paul's quarrel is not with academic philosophy per se, nor is it with anyone who drafts persuasive and learned arguments to advance the gospel truth. Paul himself is well educated in these matters and often appeals to philosophical ideas and uses sophisticated arguments to explain the gospel more effectively (see Acts 17:16-34). Rather, Paul opposes those whose learning is used to advance falsehoods as gospel

Notes: **2:4-8** R. Horsley has argued that in 1 Corinthians, Paul is writing against a perception that Christian teachers such as Paul and Apollos were leaders of "wisdom cults." Much like today, in Paul's day a wisdom teacher would gather a following that adhered to his "wisdom" and supported him financially. Adherence to a teacher became synonymous

truth. He opposes any philosophy devoid of Christ that claims to teach about the spiritual order of God's creation and reign.

Notice that Paul shapes his initial statement of the problem as an inverted parallelism (ABB′A′), presumably for rhetorical effect. I will follow this same pattern in my exposition of this passage. The problem of sophistry is introduced in verse 4 (A) and repeated in verse 8 (A′), thereby bracketing its essential solution which is introduced in verse 5 (B) and repeated in verses 6-7 (B′). The effect of this parallelism is to relate problem and solution as two integral parts of a coherent polemic, making Paul's argument easy to follow.

The Deception of Words (2:4) As Paul introduces the content of the false teaching which he will argue against, he bids his readers remember what he has just said about his divine commission and Gentile mission (1:23—2:3). The opening phrase *I tell you this* reminds his readers that the commentary that follows comes from one who has been commissioned by God (1:25-26) to "teach and admonish" them (1:28—2:1). His autobiographical statement implies that *his* instruction (rather than that of the false teacher) should form the theology of Colossian Christianity.

Even in his opening thanksgiving, Paul's petition (1:9-10) hints that the problem facing his readers is that they have trusted outsiders for the "word of truth" about God's grace. Paul has in mind a particular kind of deception—the fast line and smooth talk. People are conned every day by appearances. We are easily deceived by those who seem nice and sincere, who look good or who provide us with appropriate references and credentials. The false teacher in Colosse is a con artist who uses Christian clichés and slogans to deceive immature believers.

The two words Paul selects to introduce the first error, *deceive (paralogizomai)* and *fine-sounding arguments (pithanologia),* share a common element, *logos,* or "word." Paul's first emphasis is what congregational leaders say and teach. Ironically, the second word is usually used in the positive sense to characterize compelling and convincing *argu-*

---

with religious zeal (1977:224-37). Something like this may also be in view in Colosse. There is some evidence in this passage that a specific teacher is in view, a person who is advancing the "philosophy" that some have apparently been attracted to with religious fervor.

ments. Here, however, especially when coupled with *deceive,* the word takes on a pejorative sense, characterizing arguments that seem persuasive but upon closer analysis are actually facile, lacking in both christological content and spiritual effect (see 2:8).

The validity of such judgments is measured by two criteria: (1) whether the content of the teaching fits with what the apostles teach about Christ, and (2) whether the resulting behavior fits with what the Spirit empowers believers to be and to do. The reports Paul has received about the Colossian situation (whether from Epaphras or some other source) have apparently convinced him that what is being taught there fails on both scores. He makes this clear in what follows.

The Trustworthiness of the Messenger (2:5) Paul has a personal stake in this controversy. He is well aware of his own tenuous status at Colosse: he has never visited this congregation and does not have firsthand knowledge of the falsehood he is addressing in this letter. His opponents may well counter, "What does Paul know about our situation, anyway? What gives him the right to speak so pointedly about it?"

Nevertheless, Paul promises that although *absent from you in body* he is *present with you in spirit.* This intriguing connection between his bodily absence and spiritual presence, which reflects his apostolic self-understanding, reflects his understanding of Christ, who while absent in body continues to be present with us through his Spirit. For this reason I am inclined to take Paul's statement of his spiritual presence quite literally rather than as a metaphor for his personal support. The *spirit* of his apostleship, not unlike the Spirit of the Risen Christ, is alive and active through available writings or remembered sermons and continues to minister to congregations where he is now bodily absent (see my comments on 4:7-9). It may be that Paul's discernment of the Colossian crisis is the result of intercessory prayer, when his *spirit* is illumined by Christ's Spirit (see Rom 8:26-27) quite independently of others' reports and letters. In this sense, prayer has enabled Paul *to see how orderly you*

2:6 The phrase *Christ Jesus as Lord* does not appear anywhere else in Paul's New Testament writings. Actually, the NIV obscures Paul's grammar, which combines an articular *Lord* in apposition to *Christ Jesus.* Literally, the phrase reads "Christ Jesus, [who is] the Lord." In Colossians Paul makes this his essential claim about Jesus (so 1:15-20), which forms the core of the gospel proclaimed to the Colossians and accepted by them as "the word of truth" (1:5).

are and how firm your faith in Christ is.

Maintaining an *orderly* and *firm* faith is necessary for the community's nurture (compare 1 Cor 14:33, 40). Some commentators suggest that these are characteristics of a battle scene and so of an embattled congregation. Yet Paul expresses *delight* in their already orderly and firm faith, probably because he is *present* with them *in spirit;* and while Paul's tone throughout this section is harsh toward his opponents, it remains gentle toward his readers.

The Trustworthiness of His Message (2:6-7) By repeating the main point of the previous verse, Paul adds to its meaning and importance. The expression *received Christ Jesus as Lord* probably does not refer to a conversion decision. In fact, I doubt that Paul would think of conversion, much less salvation, as conditioned upon a personal declaration of Jesus's lordship. Rather, the word *received (paralambanō)* suggests the passing of a sacred tradition from one group of believers to the next. Given Paul's earlier references to Epaphras (1:6-7) and to his own mission (1:23—2:3), this phrase probably refers to the spiritual heritage of his Colossian readers, who *received* their theological understanding, confessed in 1:13-23, from Paul's Gentile mission and particularly from Epaphras. This is their tradition, their sacred heritage, the religious roots that continue to mark out the boundaries of their life together in Christ. Significantly, Paul makes this point in the indicative mood—that is, what they have received from Epaphras indicates the fact of their conversion to Christianity.

In contrast, the next phrase, *continue to live in him,* is stated in the imperative mood, asserting the behavior that logically and necessarily must result from the theological conviction that Jesus Christ is the Lord of all things. Among aboriginal people in Australia, males go on a "walkabout" as part of their rite of passage into manhood: they travel alone across their land to become familiar with it and thus a part of it. The Greek word for *live (peripateō)* literally means to "walk about." Accord-

---

The NIV translation nicely picks up a subtle point reflected by Paul's grammar. The tense of the imperative *to live* is present, and when following an indicative verb in the aorist tense *(received)* this implies a continuing action or reality. The point Paul is making, then, is that the result of Christ's lordship (1:15-20) is a life of unbroken fellowship *in him.*

ing to Paul, our trust in the received gospel of God's grace through Christ results in a "walk about" in him; we become familiar with him and a part of him. The apostle often sets indicative statements about God's salvation next to imperative statements about our response to God in order to show their close, even logical relationship. To embrace the truth about God's Christ is to live in him.

Our passage into Christ transforms the way we live. The four participles that follow in verse 7 express four characteristics of the Christian's "walk about." Each is stated in the passive voice because each is given by God's grace rather than acquired by human effort. The first two, *rooted and built,* are metaphors of growth, envisaging the dynamic character of Christian nurture, while the second two, *strengthened . . . and overflowing,* are metaphors of worship, envisaging the spiritual results of devotion to God. The two couplets are naturally related, since the nurture of Christ's community is facilitated by corporate acts of worship, when it is taught the faith it has received and offers its thanksgiving to God.

The Deceiving Philosophy (2:8) Having reminded the Colossians of the importance of his apostolic "spirit" (2:5) and of the christological traditions they have received from him (2:6-7), Paul returns to restate the problem of sophistry in a more urgent way (see 2:4). He begins with the warning "Take heed!" or, as the NIV puts it, *See to it.* The peril of sophistry is that believers can be taken *captive* by an eloquent teacher who advances a sophisticated *philosophy* that is nevertheless *hollow and deceptive* in spiritual effect: the *human traditions* on which it is based compete against the christological traditions of the gospel. The philosophy in view draws upon *the principles of this world* and is therefore contrary to the apostolic "spirit" of Paul within the community, which reminds his readers of the Christ-centeredness of God's salvation.

The verb *take captive (sylagōgeō)* is found only here in the New Testament and suggests an illegal kidnapping. The word sounds very much like *synagogue,* and Wright suggests that Paul intentionally chose

2:7 *The faith* is articular, no doubt referring in this case to the content of Christian belief rather than the act of believing. In this sense, Paul says that divine grace works within the context of worship to increase the community's understanding of the faith that it has accepted as true.

2:8 Most translations, including the NIV, blunt the force of the opening phrase *See to it*

this rare word as a "contemptuous pun" to warn believers not to be taken in by a philosophy with roots in the esoterica of Colossian Judaism (1987:100). In addition, Paul may use this verb to recall the conversion motif of 1:13, where he spoke of salvation as God's rescue operation. The peril of the Colossian error is thereby highlighted: believers, who are rescued by God's saving grace from darkness and brought into the light, are now threatened by an enemy that seeks to recapture them and enslave them once again to the darkness of false teaching. In fact, the word *darkness* is used elsewhere as a metaphor of false teaching that closes the mind to the gospel truth (see Jn 1:5).

To be taken *captive* by a *philosophy* need not mean to accept a form of truth (that is, "philosophy") that is inherently flawed. Rabbis, for example, spoke of biblical teaching as "philosophy," because philosophy helped them organize biblical teaching into coherent and meaningful systems of truth. Paul himself has nothing against "love of wisdom," which is what *philosophy* literally means (compare 1 Cor 1:30). In this letter's opening thanksgiving, Paul agreed with other ancient philosophers in contending that "the word of truth" will produce good fruit (1:5-6). Yet now he uses the word more precisely to denote a system of integrated ideas that is promoted as gospel truth but whose result is *hollow and deceptive*—that is, spiritually useless.

My son, who works with computers, uses a slogan—"garbage in, garbage out"—to label ineffective programs. If you do not feed information to a computer in the proper format or language, then even the most powerful computer will be unable to run your program and find your solution. In the same way, even though a philosophy consists of fine-sounding arguments, if its content is garbage it will not produce workable solutions to the daily struggles of faith and life. According to biblical Christianity, true religion is measured by what it produces as much as by what it teaches (see Jas 1:26-27; 2:14-26).

In the case of the Colossian congregation, the troublesome philoso-

---

that no one. According to Harris, Paul's use of the imperative *blepō* ("See to it!") and *mē tis* ("that no one"), when followed by the future verb *estai* (which is not picked up by the NIV), is exceptional and "tends to make the danger more imminent and the warning more urgent" (1991:91).

pher is advancing a system of wisdom based upon *human tradition*—a phrase that Paul will use again in 2:22 to describe the ascetic morality that is also being promoted among the Colossians. Now, whether it is the source of a religious philosophy or a moral code, a sacred tradition is not a bad thing. As a Pharisee, Paul had been steeped in oral and written religious memories from his youth. As Christ's apostle, he continues to speak of those traditions as a witness to Jesus Christ in order to mature faith in him (2:6; compare 1 Cor 11:23; 15:3). The problem lies rather with a particular kind of tradition which is not sufficiently christological in content. Paul contends that if a congregation's religious heritage does not depend on Christ, its source must be human imagination rather than divine revelation. The yield of such a tradition is finally spiritually useless.

The phrase *basic principles of this world* is more difficult to interpret; the meaning of *basic principles (stoicheia)* remains unclear. In context, the word is Paul's rubric for the content of the *hollow and deceptive philosophy.* Luther thought that *stoicheia* was a Pauline pejorative for Jewish law, since Torah-observance was equated in his own experience with works righteousness, and works righteousness with human rather than heavenly merit. More recently, Banstra has come to understand Paul's use of *stoicheia* in the context of Jewish Wisdom. In this light, the false philosophy teaches that *this world* is ordered by impersonal forces (such as natural laws); thus, to be reconciled with God means to live according to these forces (Banstra 1964). The codes of conduct, even the spirituality, that might result from such a natural philosophy would have seemed excessively secular for Paul. With this in mind, Reicke argues that the meaning of *stoicheia* is best discerned in the context of Hellenistic Judaism, where it is used of angelic mediators of divine revelation, whether in writing Scripture or through religious experiences such as visions or oracular speech (Reicke 1951:259-76). If Reicke is correct, Paul's reference to *stoicheia* would indicate that his Colossian opponents say their sophistry is validated by angelic sources.

2:8, 20 Many sectarian religions in the ancient world were dualistic and taught that the natural order conspired against the spiritual order. These groups were marked by esoteric ideas, and asceticism (a rejection of the material and physical) typified their communal ethos. For this reason, Schweizer contends that Paul's use of *stoicheia* has earth's four basic

With most commentators, however, I prefer to understand *the basic principles of this world* as referring to earth's four basic elements (earth, water, air and fire) and so to translate *stoicheia* as "elements" rather than "principles." The erroneous philosophy at Colosse may well have taken shape within the larger milieu of religious thought in the Hellenistic world. The Greeks commonly divided all things into an invisible spirit world, generally considered good and sacred, and a visible material world, generally considered frivolous and profane. A version of Christianity shaped within this religious environment would tend to understand devotion to Christ as a negative response to earth's elements—that is, as an ascetic lifestyle, which demands strict injunctions against the earth's elements (see 2:21).

Paul probably uses this phrase, then, as a vague reference to this feature of dualistic religion, which denies the material world as "worldly" and spiritually counterproductive (compare 2:18, 20). In fact, ascetic conduct is an external index for measuring a person's spiritual status. Within the community, the result is an ethos of legalism and judgmentalism in which spiritual vitality is diminished by the terror of breaking a strict moral standard.

This same tendency toward moral asceticism continues to influence conservative Protestant Christianity as well as many modern religious movements, where spirituality is excessively inward, the private reserve of one's feelings and intellect, and has little positive to do with one's public life (see introduction, under "Paul's Message for Today"). For Paul, Christ's lordship over all things material and spiritual (1:15-20) produces a worldview in which our spiritual devotion is integrated with our material obligations. There is no division between "spirit" and "body."

Whenever Christ's lordship over all things pertaining to life and faith is diminished, the result is stunted spiritual growth that can even imperil one's salvation (see 1:23). In fact, the practical results of a religious philosophy like that found at Colosse are a moral asceticism (2:20-23)

---

elements in mind (Schweizer 1988:455-68). If this word represents the *basic principles* of the *hollow and deceptive philosophy* at Colosse, his attack would be against a version of Christianity that fails to celebrate Christ as Lord over the physical order of human life.

that actually rejects God's creation as bad, and a visionary mysticism that replaces life in Christ with visionary experiences of angel worship (2:18). Such a spirituality makes the experience of God's liberating grace a real impossibility.

□ Paul's Response to the "Philosopher" (2:9-15)

In responding to a philosophy or system of truth devoid of any Christology, Paul returns to two core convictions found in his opening confession of the Lord Christ (1:15-20). The first claim is that Christ is the personal and complete revelation of God within history (2:9-10; compare 1:19). The second claim is that Christ rules over every other power within God's created order (2:10-15; compare 1:18). When we embrace these two christological convictions, Paul says, we participate with Christ in the abundant fullness of God's salvation.

Christ Is God Within History (2:9-10) The first formulation of Christ's lordship claims that Christ embodied *all the fullness of the Deity* and that he did so *in bodily form.* Clearly, Paul intends to challenge any requirement that Christians go through other "spiritual powers" to get to the exalted Christ. Our access to the exalted Christ in heaven is immediate and direct, and through him we have the attentive ear of God Almighty (see Heb 4:14-16). If we are "in him," we belong to One who is fully God and require nothing else.

The word Paul uses for God *(theotēs),* translated "Deity," is distinguished from another word *(theiotēs)* used often by ancient philosophers when referring to something or someone "divine." The distinction is

---

Notes: **2:9-10** Scholars have long debated the circumstances that gave rise to an incarnational Christology within earliest Christianity. Of course, to confess that Jesus is fully God says nothing about how the church came to recognize him as such—especially since he never confessed himself to be God. Dunn has recently argued, not without criticism, that earliest Christianity's understanding of Jesus is already envisioned by the different Christologies within the New Testament itself, and he assembles a logical, orderly progression of New Testament thought that culminates in the Wisdom Christology of Colossians and Hebrews along with the Word Christology of Johannine formulations—the most "mature" thinking about Jesus found in the New Testament (see Dunn 1980). These biblical statements about Christ constitute the raw material for a fully formed incarnational Christology, articulated some four hundred years later at the Council of Nicea.

As with every other doctrine of the church, the changing environment of the emerging

important for understanding Paul's Christology. Christ is not "divine" in the sense that we speak of superb food as "simply divine" or of virtuous individuals as "godly." Christ is much more than a superb person of godly virtue. Paul asserts that Christ Jesus is God *in bodily form.*

We may well presume that Paul's point underscores a practical theology: by taking on human form in the person of Jesus from Nazareth, God, who is neither human nor limited by history, has become a human participant in world history. Through the person of Jesus, God is able to disclose more perfectly and intelligibly the Creator's kind intentions for all things.

Paul expands the traditional formulation (1:19) by adding the adjective *bodily form* to underscore Jesus' humanity as the definitive historical and personal repository of divine revelation. The Messiah is neither a theological idea nor the subject of Christian proclamation; he is the historical Jesus of Nazareth in whose personhood the truth and glory of God are fully embodied. Not only is Paul's epistemology (source of knowledge) christological, but his anthropology (view of human existence) is christological as well: Christ discloses God's perfect and good intentions for every human being. Thus, in him God's salvation-creating grace is at work to bring about ideal humanity in all who believe on him. A philosophy that is Christless is also hopeless, since without Christ a new humanity is a real impossibility.

Because I do not locate the teaching of Paul's Colossian opponents within early Christian or Jewish Gnosticism, I am inclined to disagree with modern efforts to define *fullness* in philosophical (see Lohse 1971:100) and Gnostic (see Houlden 1977:190) ways. More likely, Paul's

---

church gave impetus to a developing understanding of Christ and his continuing significance. New challenges to faith probe and trigger new reflections on old ideas, resulting in a deepened, fuller comprehension of God's truth. Some speculate, for example, that Hellenistic religions, which often promoted an "immortal man" as savior, prompted the earliest believers to think and speak of Jesus in a similar way. Others suppose that the philosophical environment of Paul's world, which viewed the world as existing in "two stories," shaped the conviction that the risen Christ mediates or bridges God's unseen, eternal world and humanity's seen, temporal world. In his incarnation Jesus discloses the truth about the eternal God within a temporal world. Even today, the new circumstances and dilemmas of modern life often aid us in recognizing new dimensions of Jesus' importance, which strengthen our faith.

point is Jewish and theological. *Fullness* in the Old Testament speaks of God's presence—for example, when the prophets say that God's "glory" or presence "fills up the earth" (see Is 6:3). In this sense Jesus is the presence of God within history. The prophets sometimes locate God's glorious presence in the holy city of Jerusalem or in its temple's sacred "holy of holies." If Paul's use of *fullness* follows the word's Old Testament use, as I suspect it does, then he may well be asserting that the very presence of God is posited in the body of Jesus, which is God's temple (Jn 2:19; Mk 14:58). Additionally, I suspect that Paul uses *fullness* quantitatively: that is, all of God is "fully" present in Christ Jesus. In no other person at no other time in the course of human history are God's truth and empowering grace so completely embodied and so easily recognized as in the Lord's life and work.

Yet how are we to understand the present tense of the verb *lives?* That is, how does the exalted Lord Christ *continue* to embody deity? Quite literally, Paul may be suggesting that the humanity of the historical Jesus continues to define his posthistorical, heavenly existence. While this is a possible meaning, Paul's point seems to me more metaphorical. The idiom of this passage is clearly confessional and doxological, recalling his earlier poetic statement about Christ (1:19). In this less literal sense, the historical results of God's triumph in Christ "continue on" in the community of believers. In support of this interpretation, Harris rightly argues that the verb is a "timeless present tense" and refers to the permanent residence of deity in the living Lord (1991:98). Thus, while the incarnation is a historical event, limited by the space and time of Jesus' life and messianic mission, its consequences are embodied by those who "live on" in him. Christ lives, therefore we live.

The church's ongoing experience of Christ's exaltation is envisioned in the first half of verse 10, where Paul underscores the practical importance of God's incarnation in the person of Jesus Christ. What difference does the incarnation make to the believer's life, since the community has *been given fullness in Christ* (see Eph 1:22-23)? The missiological value of Paul's statement is self-evident and crucial to his argument: in the absence of the historical Jesus, the church is now the personal presence of God within history and therefore responsible for mediating his revelation and redemption to the world.

Yet here Paul also links the *fullness* of God with the newness of life; thus, as we become alive through faith in him, our humanity is made more complete. By the work of grace, every good intention of the Creator for the creature is realized *in Christ.*

The deity of Christ is a nonnegotiable article of Christian orthodoxy; to deny it is to reject what stands at the core of our faith. But to confess this article of faith without then providing an explanation of what it means or why it is essential for Christian nurture is to exchange the Colossian sophistry for another. And to confess the full humanity of Jesus without really believing it is simply dishonest. We must never suppose that the mere verbal confession of truth is what counts; our confessions of faith must be fleshed out consistently and responsibly in our lives (see Jas 2:18-20). Paul's brief commentary on Christ's incarnation, although cast in the idiom of Colossian Christianity and without the critical awareness formed by the church's subsequent debate, nevertheless provides us with a biblical model to guide our thinking about Christ's deity.

Paul emphasizes two points in claiming that Jesus Christ is God incarnate. First, Paul asserts that the incarnation has to do with the humanity of Jesus: he is the "Deity bodily." I do not think that Paul uses the phrase ontologically, as a reference to Jesus' divine nature. Rather, in response to the mystical and world-denying tendencies of the Colossian heresy, he uses it to demystify and "rehistoricize" Jesus. Jesus is not only the risen and exalted Lord Christ; he is the Jesus of history, whose bodily death (1:22), bodily resurrection (2:11-12; 1 Cor. 15:35-49) and bodily exaltation (3:1) have real importance for real people. Paul knew that only by considering the Jesus of history can believers truly comprehend God's true and good intentions for our own life and work. Christianity is not a religion of theological or christological abstractions; it is, in Wesley's words, a "practical divinity."

Unfortunately, many interpreters miss Paul's emphasis on Jesus' humanity and suppose that the incarnation has mostly to do with Jesus' divine nature; his humanity is collapsed into his deity, so that he really isn't human after all. In this way we fall prey to the old docetic heresy: Jesus' messianic ministry gives the appearance of humanity but is actually effective for our salvation only because he is God and not really human. Following this conviction, his perfect love for others and sinless devotion to God are viewed as somehow inevitable; being God, he could do nothing but love God and God's creatures perfectly. Further, his atoning death as a blemish-free sacrifice for sin is viewed as the result of his deity rather than his absolute and requisite obedience to God. These docetic conclusions make Easter not so much God's vindication of Jesus' servanthood as the verification of his divine nature.

Surely this perspective on the incarnation is wrong-headed. It fails to make sense of the Bible's four authorized biographies of Jesus, each of which portrays him as God's obedient servant-Son. Docetism also makes irrelevant Jesus' essential demand for us to follow him, to be his disciples. How can humans follow after someone who isn't human? Further, to embrace Christ's deity at the expense of his humanity is to misplace God's work for Christ's. When Christ is no longer Christ, the fundamental and compelling importance of Christianity's messianic roots are forever lost. With Peter (Mk 8:29, par.) and Martha (Jn 11:27), we first of all confess Jesus as Messiah, whose death and resurrection inaugurated the new age of God's salvation. Moreover, we must always distinguish between God and God's Messiah in the work of salvation. In interpreting Scripture we must remember that both Jesus' self-understanding and Paul's Christology were God-centered: both were christological monotheists whose central belief was that God saves humanity from the destructive results of sin through and because of the results of Christ's life, death and resurrection.

Even here in Colossians, with its keen emphasis on Christ's preexistence and cosmic lordship (1:15-20), Paul sees the pattern of salvation as centered in God's saving grace. It is God who rescues us from darkness and forgives our sins (1:13-14), and it is God who is reconciled with us in Christ (1:21-22). The importance of Christ for Paul is his relationship to God as the Messiah: by his obedience to God, "even to death on a cross," God's promise of salvation has been fulfilled for all those who believe.

Second, Paul insists that the incarnation has to do with the covenantal nature of God's salvation. With the possible exception of Philippians 2:6-8, Paul's conviction that God has taken human form in the man Christ Jesus does not lead him into any profound theological reflection on the nature of the relationship between preexistent Christ and God. Paul is not as preoccupied as we are with how the three members of the Holy Trinity are related to one another. His interest in relationships is far more practical; he explores how the members of the heavenly Trinity are related to the earthly church and how they covenant together to bring about the church's salvation within history. In fact, here the confession that the *bodily* (and not preexistent) Lord Christ is the *fullness* of God naturally implies that people found in Christ by faith also participate in the *fullness* of God's purposes embodied in Christ (compare Eph 1:22-23; 4:13). By virtue of being in Christ by faith and with him for the outworking of God's salvation, the church is re-created by God's grace and brought into conformity with the Creator God's good intentions for human life.

Thus, to confess that God was in Christ Jesus *bodily* is to claim that God continues to be in the community covenanted together in Christ Jesus. For Paul, the church is the continuing and living body of Christ, in which the fullness of God now dwells. This practical orientation toward the incarnation, which moves the debate from the nature of Christ's being to the source of the church's salvation, challenges the sophistry in both Colosse and today's church.

Christ Is Lord over History (2:10-15) Paul's second christological argument is a more direct response to the Christless philosophy in Colosse: Christ *is the head over every power and authority* (2:10). Paul is here alluding to his earlier confession that Christ is the head of God's new creation, the church (1:18). In expanding his earlier claim, Paul includes *every power* under Christ's lordship. He has in mind certain spiritual authorities, probably angelic (see 2:18), because the Colossian heresy contends that God's rule over the church is mediated by angelic agents. Paul's logic is convincing: if the Lord Christ rules over these authorities, who in turn supposedly mediate the human-divine relationship, then he is the ultimate mediator of God's rule (compare 1 Tim 2:5). Worship is due him alone. To suppose that any other devotion is required for salvation slights the centrality of the Lord Christ: for God's salvation is by him and is entered into only through him.

While few people today view the world as the ancients did, Paul's commentary on Colossian sophistry remains pertinent. Many of us so elevate our spiritual authorities, whether pastors or religious leaders, that we come to depend upon them and are devoted to their teaching to the exclusion of all else. When our focus is thus moved from Christ's lordship, the formation of authentic Christianity becomes impossible. In effect, the church is decapitated and rendered spiritually dead. Rather than proclaiming their pet project or special wisdom, pastors must teach their congregations about the Christ to whom they are submitted.

Circumcision by Christ (2:11) The implication Paul draws for his Gentile readers (that is, those who were once *dead in sins and in the uncircumcision of your sinful nature—2:13*) is centered on the Jewish practice of *circumcision*—a symbol of identity with the people who are covenanted with God for salvation. The word translated *putting off (apekdysis)* has the sense of stripping off one's clothes. In this case, it is used in parallel with "to circumcise" to create the harsh (and therefore vivid) image of stripping off the flesh (or foreskin) of the penis, done by the rabbi during circumcision. Thus, Paul is able to make a bold contrast between Jewish and Christian identity. In some quarters of Judaism, Gentile converts were made to endure physical circumcision; in the Christian faith the same rite of passage is *done by Christ,* who "cuts off" the *sinful nature* (literally, "the body of flesh") of those *in him.* Paul has made this same christological point with different words and images in 1:13-14. There, the rite of passage is into the Son's kingdom, where redemption is found because God has forgiven our sins and rescued us from their consequences.

In this more polemical setting, Paul recasts this christological point in order to contrast Judaism and Christianity. Some commentators speculate that Colossian Judaism, whose mysticism many think influenced the false teacher (see introduction, under "The Crisis in Colosse"), taught that the act of circumcising the Gentile convert to Judaism triggered the activity of heavenly *powers and authorities,* which resulted in the convert's mystical passage into the covenant community. It is possible that Colossian Judaism has influenced the teaching of Colossian Christianity, and that Paul is challenging a similar belief and practice among these believers.

2:11 Some commentators suggest that the grammar of this difficult phrase refers rather to Christ's body and, by implication, to his death. In this sense, Christ performs the act of

Against this teaching, Paul redefines *circumcision* as *done by Christ* rather than *by the hands of men* (compare Rom 2:28-29), so that Gentile converts to Christianity may have renewed confidence that their membership in the covenant community is by trusting in Christ's death and resurrection.

Alive with Christ (2:12-13) Thus, membership within the true Israel of God is conditioned upon faith in the Risen Christ, whose trustworthiness is vindicated by *the power of God.* According to Paul, membership in the community covenanted with Christ for God's salvation has always required faith in God's power over sin and death (see Rom 9—11). Sarah and Abraham believed that God had the power to bring human life from sterility (for the purposes of procreation, both were "as good as dead"—Rom 4:19-21); and Christ also believed that God would raise him from the dead. Such faith results in the revelation of God's salvation-creating righteousness (Rom 3:22). This kind of faith in the power of God is the condition of maintaining membership in the covenant community (1:23).

Paul's reference to God's *power* provides the setting for him to speak of the believer's *baptism* as the rite of passage into Christ, since this is where God's power is found. He continues to contrast Judaism and Christianity by showing that Christian baptism and Jewish circumcision (2:11) have a similar purpose: marking the covenant of a people who belong to God rather than to the *powers and authorities* (2:15). Paul is concerned that in Colosse certain liturgies have been vested with divine power and have become substitutes for trust in Christ's work. For this reason, and without denying the more formal and sacramental meaning of baptism, he emphasizes its spiritual significance for Christians. In fact, he says, circumcision has a similar meaning. Thus, the "true Jew" is the believer whose identity is fashioned by the Spirit's "circumcision of the heart" rather than by Judaism's "circumcision of the flesh" (Rom 2:28-29). In this view the Spirit, not formal religion, is the agent of God's covenanting grace. Likewise, for Paul the "true Christian" is the believer who is baptized by the Spirit into the redemptive results of Jesus' death

spiritual circumcision on the cross. The NIV, however, takes Paul's analogy in a pejorative sense; thus, "flesh" *(sarx)* refers to sin nature rather than human flesh.

and resurrection (see Rom 6:4; 1 Cor 12:13).

In alluding to baptism here, Paul is not referring to a specific rite or liturgy that may mediate divine grace or be its visible sign. While such a notion may be in the background, baptism here is principally another metaphor for Paul's participatory Christology. It signifies that believers participate with Christ in the outworking of God's salvation within their history. While the agent of the believer's baptism, as of the circumcision of the "true Jew," is the Spirit (rather than the church), there are outward and visible results of joining Jesus in his death and resurrection (which is not the rite of baptism itself). Even as Christ's death (1:20, 22), burial (2:12), resurrection (2:12) and exaltation (2:13; 3:1) are all historical and public events, so also are their results in the lives of his disciples.

In this passage, then, Paul uses a sequence of three passive verbs in combination with the prefix *with (syn)* to chart the community's participation in Christ's redemptive work: by God's empowering grace, we have been *buried with him (synthaptō), raised with him (synegeirō)* and finally *made alive (syzōopoieō) with him (syn autō).* Those who are baptized into Christ because of their confidence in the redemptive results of his messianic work participate *with him* in those demonstrative and life-changing results. This is hardly the stuff of mystical religion!

Triumph over the Opposition (2:13-15) The foil for Paul's description of what results in the lives of those who participate in the Christ event is Jewish Torah (or law). According to Acts, the religious crisis provoked by Paul's Gentile mission has to do with both circumcision (see Acts 15:1) and Torah observance (see Acts 15:5; 21:20-21, 28). The two are principal symbols of Judaism's covenantal theology. Circumcision is the public expression of a family's faith in God's rule and is required for getting into the community covenanted with God for salvation (see above), while obedience to Torah is required for staying in the community. Opponents to Paul's mission inside and outside the earliest church did not protest the fact of Gentile conversion; rather, they

---

2:14 The word for the Mosaic law (Torah) is not used here. Rather, the phrase used by Paul, *written code, with its regulations*, suggests that he has in mind the various rabbinical commentaries on the Torah rather than the Torah itself. Paul, himself a devout Jew, understood that Torah reveals the holiness, righteousness and goodness of God (Rom 7:12; compare Rom 2:12-16). Properly interpreted, then, Torah becomes the "law of faith" in

were displeased that Paul did not require Gentile converts to become Jewish as well as Christian.

Perhaps the false teacher in Colosse is demanding that Gentile converts to Christianity follow Judaism's pattern of proselyte conversion. Accordingly, the Colossian "philosopher" may argue that while faith in Christ (perhaps even indicated by one's circumcision; see Gal 2:3) gets the believer into the covenant community, observance of Torah and tradition *keeps* the believer in. To be a true believer, then, requires two conversions—to Christ and to Judaism, which together maintain the church's social identity and religious practice. Of course, such teaching goes against Paul, for whom the only condition for Gentile membership within the Israel of God is faith in Christ. To stipulate any other membership requirement is to demote the work of Christ and its result: that God *forgave us all our sins.* Paul has translated the Jewish significance of circumcising the Gentile convert into christological terms for Christians (2:11-13), and he will do the same for Torah observance (2:14).

According to Paul's gospel ministry (see Acts 15:19), the Gentile convert is obliged to identify with Christ by faith alone. Getting in and staying in the church are conditioned upon faith in Christ's faith expressed *by the cross* (compare Gal 3:22-25; Rom 3:21-25). On the cross of Christ, God has *canceled the written code, nailing* there *its regulations,* which legislated payment on the debt of our *sinful nature* and *opposed* the Gentile mission, since the law made a relationship with God even more difficult for non-Jews (see Eph 2:11-18).

Paul recycles the important catch phrase *powers and authorities,* which before spoke of Christ's cosmic lordship over all powers (1:16; 2:10), to express here God's final, decisive verdict against all competing powers. Because of Jesus' messianic death *by the cross,* these anti-God powers are *disarmed . . . made a public spectacle of* and *triumphed over.* These verbal metaphors roughly correspond to the chronology of Christ's death, burial, resurrection and enthronement (2:12-13; 3:1), dur-

---

Christ, since Christ fulfilled the law's demand on the cross (Rom 3:27-31; 9:30—10:4). Therefore, Torah does not contradict Christ but bears witness to him, and must not be used by the church to diminish him in any way or to cause the alienation of Gentile believers from God's salvation. In Paul's mind, this tendency in Colosse must be replaced by the proclamation of the gospel for the Gentile mission.

ing which he disclosed and brought about God's triumph over sin and death. The NIV translation envisions this verdict as the result of military victory—a common image of God's triumph over the anti-God kingdom in Jewish apocalypticism (see Rev 19:11—20:10). Paul's images, which he draws from his background in apocalyptic Judaism, compel the reader to conclude that any ruling elite that challenges God's reign has already been humiliated on the cross.

Wright has argued for a more concrete and political understanding of the *powers,* especially in this passage. Christ's death humiliates Roman and Jewish authorities, civil and religious, who conspired together to execute Jesus and who continued to undermine the work of his church (1986:114-16). In this same sense Christ's resurrection vindicates his *political* innocence, humiliating in turn those who executed an innocent man (see Lk 23:4, 14, 22, 41, 47).

With Wright, I do not think the phrase *powers and authorities* necessarily envisions a demonic kingdom, even though it refers to an entity clearly antagonistic to God's purposes. But against Wright, I think Paul may be speaking of certain *Christian* (rather than Roman or Jewish) *powers and authorities,* perhaps those in Colosse who some have come to depend on for spiritual vitality. It is the most subtle kind of corruption to depend on anyone or anything other than Christ to mediate God's reign within the church (see 2:8). If this is the case, then Paul's message is clear and pointed: Christ has replaced any other spiritual authority, whether angelic or human; God's promised salvation is now mediated through Christ alone. The apostle's admonishment is that his readers nurture a spirituality that depends upon the lordship of Christ, as Paul (along with Epaphras and others) proclaims and exemplifies.

Colossians 2:4-15 is an important passage for us today. The seductions of the false philosophy that enticed Colossian Christians away from Christ are similar in substance to several popular movements within the contemporary church (see introduction, under "Paul's Message for Today"). In particular, we should share Paul's concern for "fine-sounding"

2:15 The NIV has provided an alternate reading for the final phrase of its translation of verse 15. Rather than *triumphing over them by the cross,* the alternate reads "triumphing over them in him." The phrase in the Greek *(en autō)* is ambiguous, and its translation rests on which antecedent the translator prefers, whether *the cross* in verse 14 or the *autō* in verse

words (2:4) that seem orthodox but are actually Christless and shaped by the myths and values of humanistic culture (2:8). The success of the prosperity gospel, which legitimizes materialistic greed by Christian language and selective proof-texting, is but one example of how secular ideas have found a home within the church. Even more blatant an example comes from the Republican Party convention in my home state of Washington, where the religious right demonstrated around a portrait of Jesus praying before the Liberty Bell—as though Christ himself stood behind the political platform of a particular wing of a secular institution!

In his article announcing "the return of Spiritism," Marvin Olasky comments that the promise of "warm and fuzzy spiritual feelings" draws even mature believers from the "dull, pedantic preaching" of mainstream Christianity into more trendy but contentless religious movements. Olasky laments the current "era of frivolity" which helps to shape believers, leading them to tolerate and even encourage the self-centered precepts and easygoing demeanor of popular religion. He exhorts church leaders to stress the importance of "Christ-centered worship that is oriented to the glory of God rather than to the needs of men and women" (Olasky 1992:24).

Similarly, Paul calls for the formation of a critical mind that is rooted in apostolic teaching (2:5-7), necessary to discern truth from falsehood. He also makes the essential criterion of discernment what is claimed for Christ Jesus (2:9-10). To the extent that Christian worship and witness are determined by something or someone other than Christ, they will fail to produce a congregation that participates with Christ in God's salvation (2:11-15).

Paul's concluding caution about the *powers and authorities* (2:15) also provides us with a biblical commentary on the church's participation in America's therapist culture. The Blys and Bradshaws of the public arena and the movements they sponsor have become our principal interpreters. Those who treat the human spirit, often with occultic and fraudulent strategies, have great "power and authority" in American life

---

13, which reaches back to Christ in verse 11. Commentators are split on this matter; however, in following a general rule of grammar, I prefer the nearest antecedent, *the cross*, and therefore favor the NIV's translation. In any case, the theological difference between the two grammatical possibilities is nil (so also Harris 1991:112).

today. This is nowhere clearer than on public television, where various specialists in popular psychology with their quasi-religious notions of self-fulfillment attract large audiences, including many supportive Christians. More and more believers bring their problems, even their desire for spiritual well-being, to their Christian therapists, seeking psychological answers to spiritual questions. More and more of our preaching proclaims the gospel of a secured and serene psyche rather than of forgiven sins and reconciliation with God.

I do not deny that in certain cases therapy is required for healing, yet I believe that our growing dependency on therapists too often reflects our failure to depend wholly upon Christ. More attention to the spiritual disciplines (such as personal prayer and Bible study, corporate worship and witness), which nurture one's relationship with the Lord, and less attention to psychological analysis (which nurtures one's relationship with self) will ultimately promote the wisdom and peace to empower a more contented humanity.

PAUL'S POLEMIC AGAINST CHRISTLESS ETHICS (2:16—4:1)

□ The Error of Ascetic Piety (2:16-23)

Sociologist James Davison Hunter, in his recent book on evangelicalism, characterized historic evangelicalism as "world-denying." In order to draw more sharply the social borders that distinguish the orthodox from all others, evangelical believers tend to draft creeds of right belief and codes of right conduct that oblige them to abstain from certain foods (such as alcohol) and practices (such as dancing or extravagant dress) that mainstream believers consider spiritually harmless. Ascetic and austere expressions of one's devotion to Christ are thought by evangelicals to be useful in bearing witness to Christianity as an alternative to the values and convictions of the surrounding secular order. And to a certain extent this is a correct perception. Paul has already stressed in his opening thanksgiving prayer (1:3-12) that the gospel produces the fruit of transformed character, a changed people who know what is true and live according to it. Faith should expect moral results.

The problem Paul addresses in this passage, however, is the legalistic submission to such regulations, such that observing them can even replace a congregation's devotion to Christ. What results is often called "self-righteousness": one's devotion is measured by how drab and dreary one's Christianity is! The arrogant sloganeering that asserts that the simpler the lifestyle, the greater the holiness, does not wash with Paul. For him, the mark of true religion is not a rigorous compliance to rules of self-denial, but faith in Christ and a life in his Spirit (see Rom 14:13-18). What finally defines the borders of true Christianity is "being in Christ," where God's grace transforms a people into an alternative faith community. Any definition of Christianity that substitutes regulations of self-denial for self-transformation by the grace of God is spiritually impoverished and finally useless.

Accusation Without Foundation (2:16-17) The second section of Paul's theological polemic envisions a particular person who apparently is acting as a spiritual umpire, watching to see whether the community observes certain holy days and complies with certain dietary regulations and using these things to determine the quality of their devotion to God. In response, Paul issues here the first of two negative commands (imperative + *mē*): Do not let anyone judge you. The verb for *judge (krinō)* is often used of God's final judgment, and it may be that the community's fitness for the new age (even the church's hope for participation in it) is determined in their minds by food and celebrations. The list of these celebrations, which includes *a religious festival, a New Moon celebration or a Sabbath day,* is fairly typical (compare Hos 2:13; Ezek 45:17; Jubilees 1:14). Since the list encompasses annual festivals (such as Passover or Yom Kippur), monthly meetings (such as the New Moon celebration) and the weekly observance of sabbath, it is evident that Paul's opponents required a rather comprehensive obligation. Moreover, within Judaism most of these celebrations were intended to help the community look forward to Messiah's deliverance of Israel from its suffering and to its entrance into God's promised shalom. Thus, for the Christian to participate in these Jewish celebrations was tantamount to a denial of Jesus' messiahship. In addition, the dietary rules that accompanied the holy days had a social (as much as a religious) role: to publicize the community's distinctiveness as a separate people. To eat particular foods and not others symbolized their particularity within the world order. This function also detracted from Christianity's single social marker—its faith that Jesus is Lord Christ.

I should emphasize again that Paul's objection is not to religious celebration per se, and probably not even to a congregation's public expression of worship that borrows from the traditions of Judaism. Rather, Paul's primary concern here is any observance that does not concentrate the celebrants' attention upon Christ's importance for salvation. To observe a Jewish calendar of worship seems foolish to Paul when it does not celebrate Jesus as Lord Christ (compare Lohse 1971:115-16). He argues that it elevates an eschatological *shadow* (that is, Jewish worship's anticipation of God's salvation) over its *reality* (that is, the future blessings of God's salvation already experienced by those *in Christ).* Paul does not employ this shadow-reality dualism—a motif of Hellenistic Judaism—to deny the truth about God's promised salvation that is expressed by Judaism's worship on holy days or in eating patterns; rather, his purpose is to assert that the Messiah has already fulfilled the promise so that the reality is present, not future. Paul is not anti-Jewish; but he is opposed to those who appeal to Jewish practice to measure and even replace the core convictions of the Christian faith.

Righteousness Without Relationship (2:18-19) The second command expands the first: *Do not let anyone . . . disqualify you for the prize.* The verb *disqualify (katabrabeuō)* literally refers to the negative decision of an umpire (Harris 1991:120). Apparently, the person Paul has in mind monitors the congregation's readiness for final justification *(the prize)* and decides against it when the believers' conduct does not accord with the rules of Jewish celebration (2:16) and asceticism (2:21). But in this case, Paul seems more interested in the sort of self-righteous spirituality that is typically required by such a person. The NIV obscures the modal sense of Paul's phrase *thelōn en* by translating it "delights in"; better is the RSV's "insisting on" the attributes that follow, *humility and*

Notes: **2:18** An element of interpretation of the cryptic phrase *the worship of angels* is grammatical, specifically the nature of the genitive *of angels.* If *of angels* is an objective genitive, then the *angels* are the object of the community's worship. While this interpretation is grammatically possible, it is unlikely for lack of historical evidence. If *of angels* is a subjective genitive, then the *angels* are themselves the worshipers—presumably of God. This reading supports the most likely solution: Paul has in mind the importance placed upon angels as a higher order of being with a more direct access to God than humans. For some,

the worship of angels. The NIV further obscures Paul's point by adding *false* to the Greek word for *humility (tapeinophrosynē).* From his perspective, the false teacher certainly does not require a false humility from believers! This word for *humility* may carry a technical meaning for particular expressions of humility, such as fasting. From Paul's perspective, what makes this demand for humility seem false and even foolish is that it is not motivated by devotion to Christ. A believer's humility, whatever form it takes, is proper only when it boasts in what God has accomplished through Christ (compare Rom 5:1-11). Without Paul's perspective, the various outward expressions of one's inward piety are judged arrogant and *unspiritual;* at day's end, they represent human efforts to attain what God has already granted us in Christ.

The other item, *the worship of angels,* has prompted much scholarly discussion (Francis 1975). Wright outlines three possible interpretations (1987:121-22). First, Paul may have in mind actual liturgies of angel worship, borrowed from either pagan or Jewish religious practices. Apparently these liturgies were followed by some Colossian believers for their spiritual formation. If so, Paul would have surely considered such worship idolatrous. Few scholars, however, subscribe to this interpretation; there is simply too little evidence from the ancient world that angels were worshiped either by pagans or Jewish believers. The second possibility is a variation of the first: Paul uses the phrase ironically. Some believers spend so much of their time speculating about angels (as though they worshiped them!) that they have little time left to serve Christ in more practical ways. I doubt that Paul denied that angels exist; rather, in this view, his concern is with a highly speculative and mystical doctrine of angels (angelology), one of the "human traditions" that make up the Colossian "philosophy" of religion (see 2:8). Third and most likely is that Paul has in mind a teaching that focuses on the angelic worship of God. J. B. Lightfoot, for example, contended that *humility* and

---

this has made their worship logical.

Many scholars have examined the phrase *goes into great detail* to explain the importance the false teacher attached to *the worship of angels.* The Greek term used, *embateuō,* refers to a careful consideration of some claim or perception in order to gauge its truth. In this sense, then, visions of angels worshiping God were described in precise detail as models or means of acquiring the truth about God.

worship of angels belong together, so that the sort of *humility* expected of the spiritually mature believer presumed that God was too holy to be worshiped directly. Only the angels that populated God's throne room had direct access to God; thus the community's worship of God must be mediated through them (1876:222).

Following Lightfoot's lead, I suppose the spiritual umpire could have thought that Christian worship of God is mediated through angelic beings and that worshipers are required to have visionary experiences of angels occupying the heavenly throne room—visions rather like those in the book of Revelation and in ancient apocalyptic literature generally. Thus, according to this view, an extra special visionary experience, which is then verified by its description in *great detail,* complements religious observance to create an esoteric Christianity composed of *idle notions.*

One result of this orientation toward religion is the formation of an elite, who alone possess insider information about the mystery of God (1:24-27) and who alone know the path that leads into salvation (1:13-14). Such arrogance disposes of the need for an apostle like Paul, or even of Christ's Spirit, to mentor the congregation's spiritual well-being (compare 1 Cor 1—4).

Returning to the head-body metaphor (see 1:18), Paul now restates his great emphasis on believers' participating with Christ in the liberating results of his messianic work. In doing so, Paul summarizes his objection to a preoccupation with esoteric experience, which when combined with countless regulations detaches the faith community from its Lord just as decapitation severs the head from the body. Even as the head and body must remain attached for strength and growth, so must Christ and the church remain intimately related one to the other. The believer's experience of God does not require visions of angels worshiping God; rather, it is an experience of intimacy with Christ, the real sensation of his purifying love for us and within us that *causes [us] to grow.*

Religion Without Results (2:20-23) Once again Paul uses the difficult but important catchword *stoicheia,* translated "basic principles," to call attention to his opponent's preoccupation with the four basic elements of earth (see 2:8), which make up the very things not handled, not tasted, not touched. From the beginning of his letter, Paul has underscored the importance of relating the material world to the spiritual: the one should always bear witness to the other. Indeed, in the next passage Paul will again admonish his readers to understand the "earthly" in terms of the "heavenly" (3:1-4). This integration of spirit and heaven with matter and earth provides the foundation for Paul's ethical program (3:5—4:1), where the moral emphasis falls on transformed relationships rather than the regulations of ascetic piety.

Perhaps it is prudent to point out that Paul's concern is not so much that a Christian's spirituality be abundantly "worldly"; rather, he is concerned that the rigors of Christian devotion not be viewed as means for acquiring God's grace. In fact, our devotion to God should include a measure of self-denial (compare Mk 8:34-38) coupled with a resolve not to conform to the norms and values of secular culture. However, these virtues are the fruit of participating with Christ in the salvation of God. Our rejection of middle-class materialism and our embracing of a simple lifestyle, then, constitute a positive response to Christ's lordship rather than a negative response to a world we suppose is inherently evil.

The Rules of Wrong Religion (2:20-21) Paul reminds his readers of an accepted fact (*ei* + indic): *you died with Christ to the basic principles of this world.* The moral response of true religion does not consist of codes having to do with earth's elements, even if we are denying ourselves the use of those elements (compare 2:8). In fact, Paul will go on in chapter 3 to describe the moral life of Christian faith in terms of codes of human virtue and relationships.

Colosse's spiritual umpire has been teaching that spiritual maturity is reflected more by the believer's self-centered asceticism than by transformed relationships. Logically, Christians who place greatest priority on otherworldly experiences will tend to deny the value of this world, even (ironically) to emphasize its denial. In Colosse, where some equate spiritual maturity with otherworldly visions of angels, certain religious behaviors give concrete expression to their world-denying orientation. Thus, it is claimed, the mature believer will abstain from certain foods (2:16) or activities (compare 3:5-11): *Do not handle! Do not taste! Do not touch!* Such are those who are not yet liberated from the *basic principles* by affirming in practice the lordship of Christ over earth and its elements.

Paul may well be mocking actual prohibitions used at Colosse, probably to express religious (*do not taste* certain foods) and social (*do not touch* certain people) commitments. While the background of these prohibitions is not known, it is not difficult to find similar sayings in both Jewish and pagan literature of Paul's day (for these see O'Brien 1983:149-50). Again, the problem for Paul is not really the idea of religious asceticism; he even encourages certain ascetic practices on occasion (compare 1 Cor 7). Rather, his primary concern is what religious motivation prompts this lifestyle and whether it ultimately enhances the believer's relationship with Christ and neighbor. Clearly, he believes that submission to these moral codes tends to denigrate Christ's redemptive work and promote enmity between believers. They simply do not have much spiritual cash value.

The verb *submit* (*dogmatizō,* from which we get "dogmatic" and "dogma") in this context means to submit to certain official decrees or legal obligations, presumably in order to be freed of some debt or to keep from being indebted (and worse). If this debt is owed to something or someone other than Christ, then such devotion is wrongheaded. Further, we may presume from Paul's teaching that to encourage legalism, as such codes surely do, is to discourage the grace that is available to all who have *died with Christ.*

The Results of Wrong Religion (2:22-23) Paul further justifies his criticism of Christian asceticism through a twofold appeal to common sense. First of all, he says, any rule of faith that is based on prohibitions such as those listed in verse 21 could not possibly be effective, because they are based on things (such as food) that *perish.* Why determine the eternal by the temporal? This seems as foolish as idolatry, which substitutes what is created for its Creator. Further, perishable items lack eschatological value, since they belong to the world order that will perish at Christ's return. Second, this same ascetic rule of faith is *based on human commands and teachings.* Not only are the prohibited commodities perishable, but their disposition is determined by human patterns ("dogma") of consumption (such as etiquette), whether ascetic or hedonistic.

To conclude his polemic against the champions of Colossian philosophy, Paul returns to his initial concern (2:4) over any purportedly wise teaching in a cultural environment that responds favorably to "fine-sounding arguments." When one scratches the surface of such teaching and finds that it fails to insist on the Lord Christ's singular importance, Paul asserts, the church must condemn it as "hollow and deceptive" (2:8). Any Christless version of truth has no redemptive value. Likewise, the *regulations* of ascetic piety have no redemptive value because they too are based on *human commands and teachings* (2:21-22; compare 2:8) rather than on Christ. They too *have an appearance of wisdom* (compare 2:4) in a religious environment where self-denial is honored, but in reality *they lack any value in restraining sensual indulgence.*

Paul's final word is "flesh" *(sarx),* which the NIV takes in its pejorative sense, "sin nature." When coupled with his earlier phrase *treatment of the body (sōma),* Paul's criticism is ironical: a legalistic concern to abstain from bodily indulgence will result in a concern for the physical that is actually "fleshly," lacking in any spiritual value. Not only does legalism demote the importance of divine grace, it also focuses primary attention on the physical "what" rather than the theological "why." In this sense self-denial is actually counterproductive for faith.

Perhaps in reaction to a culture dominated by impersonal technology, today we hunger more than ever for a personal experience with God. Yet because of technology, we have also come to expect the spectacular even in the ordinary routine of life. Technology makes life easier for us. More and more Christians seek spectacular experiences of God; we demand "signs and wonders" that will make our lives easier. God is just another name for technology. Paul would brook no compromise with any religious philosophy that promotes a spectacular brilliance or a mystical experience as the badge of an abundant spirituality (see 2:16-18). He would interpret our current emphasis on personal, dramatic religious experiences as a threat to the centrality of the congregation's relationship with Christ and the spiritual disciplines that fortify that relationship (2:19).

This passage is also an important corrective to any version of Christianity that is world-denying (2:20-23). If Christ is Lord over the created order (1:15-18), his people should be actively engaged in transforming all things to accord with the Creator's good intentions for them. Ironically, believers who legalistically follow codes that deny or limit interest in the material or sensual are routinely seduced into another kind of *sensual indulgence*—one that replaces selfless devotion to Jesus with self-centered concern over the proper handling of those very natural elements he rules as Lord.

□ Paul's Response to the "Spiritual Umpire" (3:1—4:1)

Paul's second response to the teaching that threatens Colossian faith offers a description of the Christian life in four parts. After introducing the essential structure of his ethics (3:1-4), Paul goes on to characterize what a life in Christ is not (3:5-11) before then describing what characterizes life in Christ both within the congregation (3:12-17) and within the home (3:18—4:1).

Paul draws his ethical materials from the Jewish synagogue. On the surface, there is really nothing distinctively Christian about avoiding the vices enumerated in 3:5-11 or pursuing the virtues of holy living referred to in 3:12-17. Moreover, the household code enlisted in 3:18—4:1 generally arranges the various relationships within a family according to prevailing standards, even those found within the pagan world. For Paul, the moral *content* of the believer's life has not changed with the coming of Christ. The will of a good and holy God did not change with Christ's coming. The real issue, therefore, is one of moral *competency:* believers are made capable by God's grace to do God's will (compare Rom 12:1-2). The contrast between vice and virtue that Paul draws in this passage is yet another, more moral way of speaking of the believer's conversion. In this sense, then, we can speak of Pauline ethics as "missionary ethics," since virtuous character presumes conversion, and conversion presumes the preaching of the gospel.

When God rescues us from the kingdom of darkness and transports us into the kingdom of God's triumphant Son, the natural result is for us to "put off" vice and "put on" virtue. In this sense, Pauline ethics is descriptive of transformed life rather than prescriptive: the logical, even expected yield of "being in Christ" is to live in accordance with God's will (Wall 1979). The indicatives of God's salvation are fully integrated with the imperatives of Christian existence, so that Paul does not speak of one without the other. To embrace the truth about God's grace is to receive God's grace and to be empowered for living according to God's will (1:9-10).

Of course I am tempted to make excuses for my disobedience. Most of us appeal to the frailties of our fallen humanity or the utter secularity of our culture to explain why we do not follow Christ. Worse, we may construct a theology of grace that considers perfected love of God and neighbor a real impossibility for us; divine grace is not able to transform us into new creatures after all! This is precisely what Paul argues against. For him, the problem with bad theology is that it creates a faulty perception of the real world. The real world is not the marketplace or the town square, fashioned by secular lies and selfish pretensions, but "the kingdom of the Son" (1:13), which is defined by "the word of truth, the gospel" (1:5). The Son's kingdom is the real world because only there will God's grace redeem us from our broken condition to remake us into new persons (3:10) in the image of the One who created us.

Paul also presumes, with other religious Jews, that bad theology will have its moral effect. Already we know that the sophistry championed by some in the Colossian church has resulted in a spurious holiness which supposes that "false humility and . . . harsh treatment of the body" (2:23) constitute a worshipful response to God. In Colosse, then, the issues at stake are not only a false theology that replaces the redemptive importance of Christ's work with "spiritual beings" and "human traditions," but ethical matters as well.

For this reason, I am inclined to interpret Colossians 3:1—4:1 as an integral part of Paul's polemic, setting forth the moral flip side of his theological argument against the "hollow and deceptive philosophy" that threatens the Colossians' confidence in Christ as the only mediator between God and humanity. While the cast of this part of the letter is less polemical, I think Paul has shaped the timeless truths of his moral exhortation into a specific response to the Colossian crisis.

The Foundation of Pauline Ethics (3:1-4) The language of this passage reflects the cosmic idiom of Colossian Christology (compare 1:15-20), and the ideas it expresses are thoroughly Pauline. Three of these ideas are especially important for understanding his moral instruction.

The first is discerned from the grammar of the passage. As elsewhere in his writings, Paul integrates indicative verbs (those indicating facts) with imperative verbs (those that demand something of the reader). Many scholars have recognized the importance of this grammatical relationship for Paul and have explored its significance. In my opinion, the interplay between indicative and imperative moods of the same verb within a passage expresses the logical connection between what one believes and the way one lives (compare "walk by the Spirit" in Gal 5:16, 25). If we trust what Paul proclaims to be true—that the indicatives or facts of God's salvation are found in Christ Jesus—then we also must trust that God's grace will transform us so that we are able to live in accord with God's perfect will. Our minds are *in fact* renewed to know God's will; our sin nature has *in fact* been "crucified with Christ" and replaced with the Spirit of the Risen Christ. The result is that our vices are exchanged for virtue. For Paul, the transformed life is the moral result of our participation in Christ's work and helps to validate our public confession that he is indeed God's Christ and creation's Lord.

Thus, Paul begins chapter 3 with an indicative statement: *you have been raised with Christ.* He expands its eschatological implications with two other indicative statements: (1) *your life is now hidden with Christ in God* (v. 3) and (2) *you also will appear with [Christ] in glory* (v. 4). Yet these indicative statements about the facts of God's salvation for those who are *with Christ* surround and focus the critical imperative statement: *set your hearts on things above* (v. 1), which is then repeated for emphasis, *set your minds on things above, not on earthly things* (v. 2). Paul's point is this: the natural, even logical, response to our participation in Christ's triumph—indicated by where he now sits *at the right hand of God*—is to exchange *earthly* (or secular) for *heavenly* (or sacred) norms and values. This exchange of the secular life for the sacred constitutes for Paul the central moral reality of the new life; and he envisages it practically in various codes of Christian conduct that he lists

---

3:1-4 For an excellent discussion of the dualistic tensions in this text both spatially (between heaven and earth) and temporally (between present and future), see Lincoln 1981:122-30. Lincoln's conclusion is that the "hiddenness" motif envisions the believer's present life with Christ, which is hidden in heaven from those on earth. Thus, the corresponding "revealed" motif envisions the future glorification of the believer at Christ's pa-

and develops in 3:5—4:1.

Paul's ethical teaching does not belong to the "two-story" moral universe characteristic of many ancient and modern religions; he does not consign moral good to one story (heaven) while consigning moral evil to another (earth). Ethical conduct for him must embody monotheistic faith. There is a morality that pervades all of creation, because there is one Creator. In this light, believers must integrate their "yes" to the norms and values of God's reign with the decisions they make in response to moral dilemmas. The sorts of persons we have become in Christ and the kinds of actions we now take as his disciples must always reflect what and in whom we believe. Ethical choices can not be divvied up into private morality, rooted in values between "me and thee," and public morality, rooted in another set of values between "me and we." The work of grace is inside out, so that private matters of the heart are always fleshed out in the public actions of the body. For the Christian, the marketplace, the town square and their ruling elites are under the lordship of Christ too.

Behind this moral integration of our private and public lifestyles stands the more encompassing spiritual integration of the visible and invisible worlds. Paul taught that God's triumph over sin and death in Christ has already been realized invisibly in heaven and therefore must also be realized visibly on earth. The moral frustration we often feel as believers, when we know what to do but are unable or unwilling to do it, is explained by this spiritual reality: our actual experience of the final triumph of God's grace over human sin awaits Christ's return (see Rev 12:10-12). Paul's exhortation to *set your hearts on things above, where Christ is seated at the right hand of God* (3:1) in order to "mind" his reign on earth envisions a profound confidence that Christian praxis engages the immoral values of "this present evil age" in a battle that has already been won by the exalted Lord Christ (see Rom 12:2; 13:11-14; Gal 1:4-5). Perhaps Paul's point parallels the more familiar idiom of the

rousia. In this sense, "the 'hidden-revealed' motif in connection with the believer's union with Christ demonstrates that the dynamic of this relationship is the dynamic of the history of salvation and the true heavenly-mindedness remains rooted throughout in that history" (129-30).

Lord's Prayer: "Our Father in heaven . . . your will be done on earth as it is in heaven" (Mt 6:9-10).

The second emphasis of Pauline ethics is discerned from the literary structure of this opening passage. The christological foundation for ethics is made clear by the four explicit references to Christ in 3:1-4, all of which are located at the center of the passage. Especially important in my view is the coupling of an article with each of Paul's four references to Christ. This grammatical strategy is quite unusual and may well stress the decisive importance of Christ for what follows (see Harris 1991:136).

The last two references to Christ in verses 3 and 4 form the center of an inverted parallelism and thereby give readers a visual aid to confirm Christ's central importance for life:

3: (A) Your life *(hē zōē hymōn)* . . . (B) with Christ *(syn tō Christō);*

4: (B′) When Christ *(hotan ho Christos),* (A′) who is your life *(hē zōē hymōn).*

This foundational conviction of the moral life is fleshed out in what follows (3:5—4:1). This passage includes three codes of Christian conduct (3:5-10; 3:12-16; 3:18—4:1), each of which concludes with a summary statement of Pauline ethics (3:11, 17; 4:1). These three summary statements include a christological confession that recalls the central importance of Christ's lordship for the community's obedient response to God's will.

The third emphasis of Pauline ethics is the vital relationship between Christ and God, which Paul envisions in the critical phrase *your life is now hidden with Christ in God* (3:3). Paul returns to this theme in 3:17 to conclude that whatever is done in Christ's name and through his power must finally be an offering of thanksgiving to God (see my comments on 3:17). If doing God's will has a christological foundation, it has a theological aim: to bring glory and pleasure to God. Thus, the new life is provided its content by the knowledge of "the image of its Creator" (3:10) and its incentive by the community's call as "God's chosen people" (3:12).

The "theo-logic" of this perspective has already been set forth in Paul's earlier confession, which gives thanks (1:12; 3:16-17) for God's rescuing us from our self-destructive sins (1:13, 21), reconciling us by Christ

(1:22) and placing us in Christ (1:13), where we are forgiven by grace (1:14) and transformed for the good (1:22). A proper understanding of Paul's realized Christology is that our participation with Christ in death and resurrection positions us with the people—the true Israel—that God has covenanted with for salvation. The community's changed life, which has exchanged vice for virtue and alienation for reconciliation, is the byproduct of God's grace; it also constitutes hard evidence that the new creation that God promised through the prophets is now being fulfilled in the life and history of God's people.

The Ethical Demand: Aim at the Things Above (3:1-2) The opening statement claims that the faith community has been resurrected with Christ, even as it has already died with him (compare 2:20); the believers *have been raised with Christ,* who *is seated at the right hand of God.* The latter phrase alludes to the Davidic Psalm 110:1, where the king of Israel is promised victory over his enemies. In this new setting, where Messiah has replaced David as King over kings, the exaltation of Christ is interpreted as his triumph over God's archenemies—sin and ultimately death (see Rev 20:11-15). Not only does Paul reclaim the importance of Christ's exalted status as Lord over all creation (1:15-20), but he reclaims the significance of the church's participation with him in his exaltation: we share in Christ's triumph over sin and death.

In this commentary I have called the Christology of Colossians "cosmic" because of its keen stress on Christ's lordship over all things that make up God's creation. From the beginning of his letter, Paul has developed the theological implications of this conviction in response to the false teaching in Colosse. He is now prepared to draw out its implications for Christian discipleship. Paul has also stressed the church's participation with the cosmic Lord Christ in the results of God's salvation within history. Holy living is one of these results; and we can be confident of this prospect because Jesus is Lord of all.

The apostle's opening statement introduces the aim of discipleship: the pursuit of *things above, not . . . earthly things* by the proper set of our *hearts* and *minds.* This exhortation draws from Paul's prior polemic against the confusion in Colosse about the "things above." The Colossian philosophy's attention is indeed set on heavenly things, but on angels rather than on Christ, supposing that they rather than he are the conduit to God. The moral result is a distorted concern for *earthly things* (see 2:16-23). Actually, to focus attention on Christ rather than on "basic principles" results in a truer discernment about *earthly things.* Paul is not asking us to forsake any interest in *earthly things;* to do so would result in a different version of the asceticism he has just condemned in 2:20-23. He is rather saying that when our spiritual devotion is properly focused on the Lord Christ and his unique relationship to God (as the Son who sits *at the right hand of God* in heaven), we will be able to see the value and role of *earthly things* more clearly from God's perspective.

We tend to think of the moral life in terms of either its rules or its overarching vision. If we define morality by certain rules of conduct, then we view the person who obeys these rules as moral. For example, if we establish that telling the truth is a rule of right conduct, then the person who tells the truth is moral. If, on the other hand, we define morality by the characteristics of a moral world, then we tend to view the person who possesses these same characteristics as moral. For example, if we agree that a moral world is just and compassionate, then the person who is capable of just and compassionate conduct is moral.

In my view, Paul's ethical teaching flows from a moral vision rather than moral rules. He is less interested in "doing" codes of rules, although he provides them, than he is in "being" Christian. To be a Christian is to be able to do God's will (see Rom 12:1-2; Eph 2:8-10). Paul was raised in an ethical monotheism, Judaism, which prescribed in great detail how to please God through one's behavior. But his Gentile mission roots Christianity in the indicatives of God's salvation, not its imperatives; it is a religion of divine grace, not human merit. Paul realizes that to know codes of right conduct without having the moral capacity to act on them gets us nowhere. The moral issue, then, is not whether one complies with some prescribed code but whether one is the sort of person who is able to be moral. If one has moral character, then one will act morally.

For Paul, morality is first of all being in Christ, which nurtures the

---

3:3-4 In Revelation John's vision of salvation is not finally concentrated by a place, the new Jerusalem, but by a people, the Bride of the Lamb (Wall 1991:243-60). It strikes me that the hope of many American believers, especially those without much socioeconomic power—like the Colossians, who are "insignificant ex-pagans from a third-rate country town" (Wright 1986:133)—is the future realization of their materialistic dreams: in heaven

capacity to see the things above. If "to seek" *(zēteō)* after the exalted Lord Christ envisions the "practical pursuit of spiritual goals" (Harris 1991:138), then "to set the mind" *(phroneō)* emphasizes the seeker's spiritual capacity to accomplish those spiritual goals. Without being in Christ, the faith community has neither the right goals nor the transformed character sufficient to pursue God's goals in any case.

I would contend that the genius of Paul's ethical teaching is not the various codes he provides to describe the moral life. They contain nothing new; in fact, Paul's Judaism offered a much more comprehensive morality than did his Christianity. Indeed, Torah had already codified God's will. For Paul the problem is practical; it has to do with the sorts of persons we are and whether we are actually able to do God's will. Thus, Paul's moral innovation stems from his christological monotheism. His claim is that in Christ we not only are forgiven and redeemed by God but are also transformed into new persons, capable of knowing and doing the will of God. Nothing less than a moral revolution was triggered by the death and resurrection of Jesus!

The Theological Fact: Living with Christ in God (3:3-4) Remember that Paul's vision of Christian life grew out of his understanding of Christian faith. With his theological assertion *For you died,* Paul returns to 2:20 to clarify the community's christological ethics. Having died and risen with the Lord Christ (3:1), believers "mind" the *things above* (where we find the exalted Christ) simply because Christian *life is now hidden with Christ in God.* The deeper logic of this poetic phrase is inescapable: since we have already participated with Christ in his death and resurrection, we have been *hidden* in the *things above,* in God's "things." So we can really do nothing but "mind" the *things above,* since we are part of the heavenly whole! In this section of his letter Paul will set down no more important an ethical principle than this: that in Christ we should expect victory over sin, since in our new-creatureliness we now have the capacity to obey God. Paul will expand this idea in verses 3 and 4.

---

we will finally win the lottery! Paul's hope, like John's vision, is not for a wonderful *place* where we will finally have every "thing" we did not have on earth; rather, it is for a wonderful *existence* in which persons and relationships with God and one another are perfected and God's good intentions for creation are realized.

Paul uses the verb "to hide" *(kryptō)* in connection with "the mystery of God's salvation" which God revealed to him and commissioned him to preach among the Gentiles (see 1:25-26; 2:2-3). As I said earlier regarding his use of this "hidden-revealed" motif, Paul seeks to draw attention to certain claims previously made by his Scripture. According to Jewish teaching, the plan of God's salvation was to be kept hidden as a mystery until the messianic age, when its revelation would announce the beginning of universal peace, promised by God through the biblical prophets.

Paul's use of *hidden* here recalls this same motif, with its implications for his Gentile mission, and vests it with moral content. Implied in what he says is that believing Gentiles are *now hidden with Christ in God,* further exposing the error of claiming that to become Christian the Gentile believer must also become Jewish. From other New Testament writings (especially Acts 15 and 21) we know that Jewish believers were generally concerned that Gentile converts not carry their old moral baggage into their midst, where it might corrupt their lifestyle and disqualify them from God's blessing at Christ's return. The Colossian error distorted this Jewish concern. Paul's response in Colossians is that Gentile believers are *with Christ in God* and therefore reside in a place other than Judaism, a place where divine grace will transform them into a new creation, capable of doing God's will.

Paul also links his realized Christology with his futuristic eschatology. The result of participating with Christ in his death and resurrection is *also [to] appear with him in glory. Glory (doxē)* is another apocalyptic motif that is closely associated with heavenly existence. In Paul's modification of Jewish apocalypticism, Christ's death and resurrection constitute the true apocalypse of God's salvation; Christ's faithfulness has already resulted in God's triumph over humanity's sin and death. Christ's future return, then, marks the inbreaking of God's heavenly triumph upon earth; the future manifestation of glory will be the full realization of what God has promised the covenanted community on earth, within history and within its transformed life. Paul may well be offering a tacit commentary on those who are overly concerned with *earthly things:* the perfection of creation (earthly things) at Christ's coming will be enjoyed by those who are vitally concerned about "heavenly things." God's new creation, the church, will then enjoy the best of both worlds!

The Community's Conversion from Vice (3:5-11) When someone restores an old car, it is not enough to simply paint over the rust. Even if the paint is of highest quality, the rust will soon reappear and if not quickly treated will destroy the car's body. The rust must be removed and rusted parts replaced before the car is painted.

God's grace is similar in that it enables us to get rid of "the old self" before restoring our capacity to live in accord with the Creator's intentions. This is the logic of conversion; and that logic is envisioned by this passage, which casts its first ethical exhortation in negative terms: *put to death* immorality and *rid yourselves* of it. Sin is where God's grace begins its work by rescuing sinners from the "dominion of darkness" and its destructive ethos. And those who have died and risen with Christ to a new life (3:1-4) have already put to death those things that are opposed to that life (compare Rom 6:4-11). The moral imperative, then, is to become what one has already become in and with Christ. In negative terms, if vice has been crucified with Christ, then vice must be crucified by those in him.

End Sexual Immorality (3:5-7) In introducing his moral program, Paul has located his essential moral principle to "mind the things above" somewhere between his realized Christology (3:1) and futuristic eschatology (3:4). His opening demand, *therefore,* cues the reader to the dynamism between "the already and the not yet" that will continue to frame his description of the moral life: to *put to death . . . your earthly nature* is to avert *the wrath of God [which] is coming.*

The NIV obscures Paul's intended meaning by the phrase *your earthly nature.* In the Greek, this phrase literally reads "the limbs that are upon the earth" *(ta melē ta epi tēs gēs)* and probably refers to people's body parts or "limbs" (compare Rom 6:13, 19; but see Lohse 1971:137). The literal sense seems especially apropos here in a catalog of vices involving sexual organs (however, see O'Brien 1982:176-78). Putting body parts to death should not be viewed as a vow of celibacy, or worse, of castration (to become, in Jesus' words, a "eunuch of the kingdom"—see Mt 19:12); Paul has already chided those who would inflict pain on the body to gain favor with God (2:23). Rather, understood in the light of 3:1-4, this exhortation refers to the radical transformation of the believer's mind, which brings a new way of understanding the body. Thus, in 1 Corinthians 6:12-20 Paul outlines a new perspective on human sexuality that comes from a new perspective on the body, not only as an instrument to be used for God's glory rather than for sexual perversion (1 Cor 6:19-20) but as the place of God's final justification: the body will be raised incorruptible (1 Cor 6:17; 15:35-49).

Because the human body has eschatological value and the prospect of a transformed body is critical to Paul's conception of hope (compare 1 Cor 15:42-54), the reader should expect the subsequent caveat *the wrath of God is coming* (compare 1 Cor 6:9-10). *The wrath of God* is a familiar eschatological catch phrase and refers to God's judgment on a fallen creation. According to Romans 1:18-32, God's eschatological wrath is already revealed within human history whenever we refuse God's good for creation. God's wrath withdraws the grace that prevents people from doing what is best for them. Thus, we are allowed to act in self-destructive ways (Rom 1:32). As a future prospect, God's wrath reclaims creation for its Creator by utterly destroying the old order of sin and death (see Rev 21:1-4). God does not single out particular sins for special displeasure; rather, the need for salvation is indicated by sin's self-destructive tendencies.

Where salvation has begun for those in Christ, the old has given way to the new, vice has given way to virtue. Eschatology yields to soteriology with its moral result: the community's conversion to the new age is indicated publicly by a change of lifestyle. Those in Christ no longer live *in the life you once lived.* The shift in verb tense from future (v. 6) to aorist (v. 7) underscores that a real change has taken place in the past, with results into the present and future. Unfortunately, the NIV obscures the inverted parallelism in verse 7, which emphasizes that the new life or walk (B) marks a change from a life "in these immoral ways" (A). Literally, the verse reads: "in these ways" (A) "you used to walk" (B), "you once lived" (B′) "in these ways" (A′). The repeated formula makes Paul's critical point: to live in vice rather than in Christ means to exist in a "dominion of darkness" where evil forces and powers shape a self-destructive life in rebellion against God's good intentions for the creation.

Paul lists five sins to illustrate: *sexual immorality, impurity, lust, evil desires and greed, which is idolatry.* Scholars have variously located the ancient source for the lists of vices or virtues that are found throughout the writings of Paul (see O'Brien 1982:179-81). Since rabbis used such lists to guide the moral formation of young Jewish children, it is likely that Paul had memorized them in his Jewish catechism. Because no single list is found in Paul's writings, it is also likely that he adapted both their content and their form to address particular situations. Some have argued that he uses lists of virtues and vices to illustrate the moral byproduct of belief or unbelief rather than to respond to specific situations. While the vices and virtues selected by Paul have general application, in most cases he modifies them to have special significance for his first readers. Again, his point is not to prescribe a code of conduct which must be obeyed if one is to be fully Christian. This would oppose Paul's core ethical conviction: that the Spirit of the Risen Christ has replaced "written codes" in the new dispensation of God's salvation (Rom 7—8; 2 Cor 3). Paul lists moral virtues or immoral vices in order to describe the effective yield of God's transforming grace in the believer's lifestyle (Wall 1979).

In the case of Colossians, Paul constructs his lists in response to the rules imposed by the spiritual umpire (see 2:20-23). Because such rules "lack any value in restraining sensual indulgence" (2:23), in the absence of a vital relationship with Christ they may actually result in sexual vices. The problem Paul envisions is christological rather than moral per se. Colossian believers are tempted to submit to rules of self-denial as a substitute for devotion to Christ, and sexual perversion is a symptom if not a result of this heresy. According to Paul, the church's participation in the results of Christ's work extinguishes the behaviors that rules of ascetic conduct have no power to deny. In fact, such codes "lack any value," Paul says (2:23), not because they produce illicit passions but because they are ineffective in ending them.

The final vice, *greed,* which Paul clarifies as *idolatry,* seems out of place in this catalog of sexual sins. Perhaps the best explanation of its meaning proceeds from reading the list backwards as a chronology of sexual sin. *Sexual immorality* (that is, *porneia,* which usually refers to sexual relations outside of marriage) is the byproduct of *evil desires* (natural sexual desire corrupted by sin), which more specifically are *lust.*

This process from lust to sexual immorality has its source in *greed (pleonexia),* which literally means "to crave more" or to covet what one does not have (O'Brien 1982:182-83). In Jewish teaching *greed* is often combined with *idolatry,* because whatever is the object of greed (in this case, more and better sex) has replaced God at the center of one's life (compare Jas 4:1-12). If Christ is Lord over all things, then the disciple's passions are brought under control and centered by "minding the things above." The result in the believer's life reproduces the Creator's good intentions for humanity.

Especially at a time when many mainstream churches wrestle with Christian ethics, Paul's advice guides our response toward issues of human sexuality. Today, the tragic results of sexual dysfunction are every day's news: AIDS, sexual harassment in the workplace, increasing promiscuity, adolescent pregnancy, confused gender identity, and pornographic depictions of both women and children. Paul's lists of sexual perversion or of sexual purity set moral boundaries around our sexuality—what accords or discords with God's will. The lists describe, then, the fruit of God's character-creating grace in a person's life: sexual purity is evidence of fellowship with God. Yet the lists also describe sexual patterns that reflect God's original intentions for creation (compare Rom 1:18-32). The aim of grace as it transforms human existence is to restore humanity to a time when God's good purposes for human beings were carried out purely. The lists describe the kind of sexual revolution that will bring humanity back from sexual chaos into harmony with the Creator. The result of this sexual revolution in Christ is an alternative moral culture.

End Impure Speech (3:8-9) Paul's second vice list (which also includes five sins) begins with a familiar eschatological idiom, *But now.* "But now" that the new age of God's salvation has begun because of Christ, you must get rid of vice. As before, the church's imperative, *you must rid yourselves,* is linked to the indicative of God's salvation: since God has forgiven us our sins and redeemed us from their consequences (see 1:14) and since God's reconciling grace has liberated us from accusation and sin (see 1:22), we are to live a vice-free life. In this case the sins are social and not sexual, and deal primarily with speech that reveals hatred toward others and usually results in broken fellowship.

James reminds us that the real issue at stake when people talk with each other is not so much the verbal transmission of ideas, but how those ideas affect human relationships for good or ill (Jas 3:1-18). Thus, if our speech is informed by heavenly Wisdom and thus characterized by purity (Jas 3:17), then relationships are put at peace and the community can await God's "harvest of righteousness" (Jas 3:18). If, on the other hand, our speech is informed by earthly wisdom and is thus "of the devil" (Jas 3:15), then relationships are destroyed by "bitter envy and selfish ambition" (Jas 3:14) and the community finds "disorder and every evil practice" within itself (Jas 3:16), thus imperiling its entrance into a future *shalom* (Jas 3:2; 1:4). Similarly, the purpose of Paul's second list is to remind the reader that God's grace does not fixate upon the individual. Christianity is not a cult of the individual! Rather, God's grace transforms a people who live in right relationship with one another. To end *anger, rage, malice, slander and filthy language,* and to *not lie to each other* repairs relationships.

How this fivefold catalog of social vices is relevant to the Colossian situation is difficult to say. Perhaps we should take our clue from the emphasis Paul places on the final vice: *do not lie* (*pseudomai,* lit. "to speak falsehood"). Paul's earlier polemic against the errant philosophy focused on two contrasting claims: the gospel is "the word of truth" (1:5), and the competing philosophy is "hollow and deceptive" (2:8). Since the measure of the message is its fruit, Paul implies here that the philosophy has resulted in a weakened capacity to resist sexual and social vice.

Many of my non-Christian students reject the compelling claims of the gospel because their experience with Christians has not been very convincing. Christians' slandering other Christians does not constitute solid evidence for a gospel of reconciliation. Congregations that are angry with each other are not solid evidence for a loving God. Christians who claim to love the Lord and then lie or cheat to get ahead or to live extravagantly do not provide convincing evidence to the non-Christian world that God's grace makes much of a difference in one's life.

The essential point of this section is this: the missionary Paul is mindful that fundamental changes in how we use everyday language or in our attitudes toward human sexuality are the most compelling evidence for the truth of the gospel we confess. Incarnation is critical to proclamation; without the first, the second seems as hollow and deceitful as the Colossian philosophy seemed to the apostle.

The End of Vice (3:9-10) Once accepted and rooted, the gospel will have its moral effect. Vice is rejected and rooted out *since you have taken off your old self . . . and have put on the new self.* Paul makes his point more vivid by using verbs for taking off and putting on clothes—another metaphor of change. As we grow up, we learn why and when it is important to change our clothes: either because they are dirty or because they are inappropriate for a new occasion. Paul's choice of metaphors draws from Jewish teaching, where dress symbolizes the character of a community's relationship to God: taking off vice and putting on true devotion to God is a change of spiritual clothes proper for the Jewish way of life. Likewise, Paul says, God's grace has made sin inappropriate for our new life in Christ.

It is necessary for a new humanity to put on new clothes of holiness. Several commentators understand the "old-new" motif in terms of Paul's "Adam Christology." Frequently in his writing Paul alludes to Adam to typify a particular response to God: Adam is a type of rebellious humanity, who need God's salvation (Rom 5:12-21) but whose sin prevents God's grace from having its redemptive effect. Christ, whose response to God is obedience rather than rebellion, is the "second Adam" (1 Cor 15:45-49; Phil 2:5-8); he is a type of believing humanity who have been redeemed. In this light Paul uses the words *old (palaios)* and *new* (either *neos,* as here, or *kainos,* as in 2 Cor 5:17) to express the transforming power of God's grace over sin for those in Christ.

The phrase *new self* does not mean Paul is focusing on personal ethics at the expense of a corporate understanding of the new life. While morality requires individual responsibility and character, Christianity is not a cult of the self-sufficient individual; it is a way of worship and witness for an entire people of God, a "new humanity." *The new self,* then, is a metaphor for a congregational and relational whole. Individuals who respond to God's call by confessing Jesus as Lord and are subsequently transformed by God's salvation-creating grace become members of a people in whose life and history God's transforming power is at work. For Paul, then, the critical decision for any individual is how to become a member of God's people in Christ. The primary fruit of an individual's faith is how the believer relates to others who belong to the congregation of God's people.

For this reason, some scholars have understood "taking off old and putting on new" as an allusion to Christian baptism (Wright 1987:138-39). The verbal ideas are stated as aorist participles, which indicates that Paul has in mind an event of singular, unrepeatable importance, such as conversion and the baptism of the new believer into Christ's transcendent body (see 3:1-4). But for Paul, this union with Christ is not quite so mystical. The great achievement of the Christ event is God's victory over the evil forces that prevent human beings—God's greatest creation—from enjoying what God intended us to be and to do.

Paul extends the meaning of his first metaphor by a second: *which is being renewed in knowledge in the image of its Creator.* The ethical renewal of the *new self* is nothing less than the complete restoration of God's very good purposes for human existence, which were left unrealized because of the Fall. Paul is absolutely confident that the deepest longing of the human spirit can now be satisfied in Christ. Paul has already indicated that this is the aim of God's reconciliation (1:22) and so of his own evangelistic ministry (1:28). The community's hope for perfection in the Creator's image rests on the knowledge that Christ is "the image of the invisible God" (1:15) and the very embodiment of God's intentions for humanity (2:9). In this sense, to "mind the things above" is to know that those who already have participated in Christ's triumph are now being *renewed* in his image—the pattern of moral transformation the Creator has established for all humanity. Paul's conclusion would not be lost on his readers: a Christless religion based on "human traditions" and mediated by "spiritual beings" is powerless to renew people, because it transmits a false knowledge of God's moral pattern for the new age.

The New Way in Christ (3:11) The christological foundation of Paul's ethical teaching is sharpened by this first of three important conclusions to his moral codes (also see 3:17 and 4:1). The first part of this passage describes the "new humanity" that accords with *the image of the Creator: Here* (that is, in Christ) *there is no Greek or Jew, circumcised or uncircumcised, barbarian* (uncultured non-Greeks), *Scythian* (the most remote and savage non-Greeks), *slave or free.* This is a Pauline "Magna Carta" of the sort we find in Galatians 3:28. The sociology of the faith community found in Christ is egalitarian. The meaning of this statement for the Colossian believers is similar to its meaning for the Galatian believers: the gospel doesn't confer on one class of people a higher value than any other. God doesn't play favorites; God saves us all in the same way and for the same end. Thus, the divisions Paul draws here represent religious (Jewish) and cultural (Hellenistic) classes (see Wright 1987:139-40). Paul may be responding to the elitism promoted by the false teaching in Colosse, whose "fine-sounding" arguments, "traditions and regulations" have had greatest appeal among the educated (and perhaps Jewish) middle class. In Christ all believers are equal, regardless of social class.

Armed with a faith founded on this conviction, the Wesleyan revival of eighteenth-century England helped to fashion social and political reforms on behalf of the working-class poor that have been carried through to this day. John Wesley had in mind the transformation of all life, spiritual and societal, on the basis of the gospel. The gospel claimed that the poor and powerless were the equal of the ruling-class rich; the love of God gave value to society's marginal members within a world whose greed and indifference victimized them. Within a Wesleyan "society" the least and the last had a voice and a vote for the first time. This empowered them and provided them with a new vision for all of society. The Wesleyan revival and countless other evangelical movements bear witness to the truth of the gospel, which reorders the way our relationships are viewed; the grace of God transforms the way life is lived.

The concluding formula, *Christ is all, and is in all,* echoes the confession of 1:15-20 and once again lays claim to Christ's lordship over the new order. In Schweizer's words, "Christ is the measure by which everything is to be defined" (1972:200); he is "all that matters" (Harris 1991:154). This is the firm conviction of the new humanity—those who have already "taken off" the fallen order and "put on" the good intentions of the Creator which they have begun to realize in Christ.

The Community's Conversion to Virtue (3:12-17) The tone of Paul's moral exhortation changes from negative to positive as he shifts his attention from pagan vice to Christian virtue. This shift of emphasis reflects the natural movement of conversion out of darkness into light. In the previous passage Paul addresses the community as a "new self" because with Christ they have put to death the "old self" and have risen to newness of life. In this passage Paul defines Christian character rather than prescribes rules to obey. For him, morality is a matter of what sort of person one becomes in Christ, where one "puts on" the capacity for doing the good that God has willed. *Therefore,* believers are transformed by the working of divine grace into people who have the character to do God's will. This new character results in and is clearly demonstrated by transformed relationships within the church (3:12-17) and the home (3:18—4:1).

Be Holy (3:12-13) Significantly, Paul calls the community *God's chosen people, holy and dearly loved.* In doing so, he identifies this largely Gentile congregation with God's Israel and Messiah, who were both *chosen* by God's gracious initiative for salvation. Because the terms for God's salvation had taken on an ethnic and nationalistic hue within Paul's world, his statement is religiously and politically controversial. In fact, according to the Old Testament (Deut 4:37; 7:7), God called Israel out from among the Gentiles for salvation and chose them to be a "holy" people (compare 1:2), the object of God's extra special love. But the mystery ciphered for Paul and central to his gospel for the Gentiles (compare 1:24-26) is that God has chosen them as well.

Paul's doctrine of election carries implicit moral content, since some Jewish believers within the earliest church argued that Gentile converts to Christianity should behave like Jewish proselytes (the Gentiles who had converted to Judaism). As I suggested earlier in the commentary, perhaps the ascetic and liturgical codes imposed by the spiritual umpire express this Jewish concern for Paul's Gentile mission (see 2:16-23). If so, this allusion to a biblical people, inclusive of Gentiles, recalls an ingredient of his argument against false teaching. The point is this: not only are Gentiles chosen by God for salvation, but they have also been included by God in a new creation and empowered by God's Spirit to bear witness to the Lord in their daily lives (compare Acts 10:45).

The moral result of salvation in the life of God's people is holiness. The catalog of traditional virtues illustrates the character of holiness that grace creates in us: *compassion, kindness, humility, gentleness and patience.* I am not convinced that a careful study of each word can tell us much more about this list (however, see O'Brien 1982:198-201). Paul's point seems to me more general and impressionistic: he fashions a list of five virtues to illustrate his conviction that the five vices of the previous two lists (3:5-8) have been overturned in Christ. According to his gospel, such a moral reversal is the "fruit" of conversion (1:9-11). Appropriately, then, each virtue is cited elsewhere by Paul, who typically alludes to the Old Testament's description of God's saving activity now completed through Christ. Moreover, O'Brien concludes that "each of the five graces with which God's elect are to be clothed shows how Christians should behave in their dealing with others, particularly with fellow-believers" (1982:201).

In addition, reconciled relationships within the faith community bear witness to God's triumph over society's corrupting influence. In this sense, changes within us and between us serve an evangelical purpose: people become convinced that the gospel is true when they see its fruit in the lives of believers. Thus in Galatians, Paul writes that the Spirit produces a compassionate community capable of complying with the "law of Christ" which bids believers to bear each other's burdens (Gal 5:22-23; 6:3-5). The mark of true Christianity for Paul is how well believers care for others, even those outside the "household of faith" (Gal 6:10).

The virtues listed in Colossians include words that carry a profound emotional content referring to how one feels when responding to another in need. Luke uses the word *compassion (splanchna)* to characterize the good Samaritan's sympathetic response to his needy neighbor (Lk 10:33) and again for the forgiving father's happy reaction to his prodigal son's return home (Lk 15:20). Holiness is not exclusively defined by acts of private devotion; rather, it pertains to public occasions when the community can express its status as God's chosen people through concrete responses to those who are last, least, lost and lame among us. For Paul, our personal salvation is always embodied in our public relationships (see Eph 2:11-22).

Paul himself seems to have specific situations in mind for practical application. First, how does a congregation of believers, made holy by

God's grace, respond to a troubled relationship in which each tends to revert to "vice," maintaining grudges and fueling old rivalries? To *bear with each other* means to "put up with" persons who rub us the wrong way. This does not suggest that we are simply cordial towards difficult neighbors in a detached way; rather, Paul calls us to be vulnerable to grace in order to achieve newfound intimacy where hostility once existed. Indeed, the measure of divine grace is what Wesley called "social holiness." *Compassion, kindness, humility, gentleness and patience* are the very characteristics of the congregation's life.

The second occasion is dealing with abusive people who need our forgiveness when our emotional tendency is to "pay evil for evil" (see Rom 12:17-21). The holy response, prompted by grace, is to forgive. As beneficiaries of the Lord's forgiveness, we know from our own experience how and whom to forgive. Wright suggests that Paul's exhortation *forgive whatever grievances you may have against one another* echoes the teaching of Jesus (see Mt 18:21-35; Wright 1987:142). Actually, Paul's emphasis is different though complementary. In Matthew the disciple is exhorted to forgive in order to be forgiven; we secure God's forgiveness by forgiving others (Mt 6:12, 14-15; 18:35; compare Lk 11:4). Paul gives the same exhortation but roots it in the community's experience of already being forgiven. Rather than a condition of God's forgiveness as in Matthew, forgiveness for Paul is a response to God: we forgive because we are already forgiven. Rather than a requirement for entering into God's salvation as in Matthew (Mt 5:20; 7:21-24), forgiveness is in Paul's teaching a result of Christ's death. Paul emphasizes the believer's liberation from evil forces and factors that prevent our reconciliation with God and with other people.

Be Loving (3:14) Just as Paul earlier gave special emphasis to the evil of telling lies (3:9), he now singles out *love* for special emphasis. Love for others is the reverse of dishonesty toward others, and such a reversal of character marks one's entrance into Christ and the new age of God's salvation. I remain convinced that though vice and virtue lists were a common literary convention of Paul's day, he always composed his lists with a specific congregation in mind. So his exhortation to love others has particular meaning for the Colossian situation, especially since here Paul expresses such a familiar concern in a unique way. Elsewhere he writes that love is the all-encompassing moral principle (Rom 13:8-10; 1 Cor 13; Gal 5:14). On this occasion, however, he writes that *love . . . binds [all these virtues] together in perfect unity.*

Lohse interprets this summary phrase to mean that love produces a moral perfection that distinguishes those who endure to the end and receive salvation at Christ's return (1971:148-49). Yet Paul's idea of perfection is not ethical (as it is perhaps for Matthew—see Mt 5:48) but eschatological. That is, perfection is not so much the goal of moral formation, so that the church's unity with God is the result of moral maturity. Rather, *perfect unity* is a property of God's grace, which perfectly unites the church "with Christ in God" (3:3) and prepares it for Christ's return (1:22, 28). Of course, Paul's Jewish opponents at Colosse challenge this definition; they see Christianity, like Judaism, as an ethical monotheism, and they believe that moral perfection is required by God. Against them, then, Paul's exhortation to *put on love* presumes a different moral calculus: *love* is the fruit of faith in Christ (3:1-4) rather than compliance with codes constructed by human tradition (2:20-23; compare 2:8).

Be at Peace (3:15) As love between people must reign in the faith community, so also must *the peace of Christ rule in your hearts.* According to Jewish psychology, the heart is the location of volition; one's entire life is guided by what takes place in the heart. If *the peace of Christ* rules the heart, then every decision made and every action taken will have the quality of peace. Yet Paul expresses this prayer for peace as a corporate prospect: *as members of one body you were called to peace.* So love characterizes the community's public life, and peace characterizes its internal life. This being so, every collective decision and action that comes from the community will have the character of peace.

But what does Paul mean by *peace?* First, peace comes from the Lord Christ and conforms to the results of his death and resurrection. Paul uses the same root verb for *rule (brabeuō)* that he earlier used of the spiritual umpire who has threatened to "disqualify" *(katabrabeuō)* any convert who fails to observe ascetic religious practices (2:18). The result

3:15 The phrase *the peace of Christ* is grammatically ambiguous. The genitive *of Christ* might simply identify the exalted Christ of 1:15-20 as the heavenly source or location where

in this case is moral and spiritual frustration (2:22-23). In sharp contrast to Paul's opponent, Christ's spiritual umpiring promotes peace within the community. Second, the meaning of *peace* comes from its Old Testament use. While Paul elsewhere speaks of the spiritual and interior dimensions of *shalom* (Rom 5:1-11), the biblical prophets used it as a comprehensive word for God's full transformation of the covenant community's situation. God chooses Israel for salvation (v. 12) and calls Israel to peace. Thus, when Jeremiah, with whom Paul closely identified, denounced the false prophets of Israel, he claimed that their teaching could not produce peace and should be viewed as "deceptive words" or "lies" (Jer 7:4-8; 23:14). Truth produces peace, while lies produce spiritual and moral frustration.

Further, if Christ rules over the community as Lord of all things, the peace he gives no doubt extends beyond the inward experience of reconciliation. Addressing the Colossian setting, Paul perhaps feels it necessary to extend the meaning of *peace* to include the material: the Lord Christ's rule ends any need for asceticism, which not only denies the physical but, in the case of the Colossian "philosophy," abuses it as well (see 2:23).

Be at Worship (3:16) The final characteristic of the community's life is its worship of God. The worshiping community expresses its devotion to God in two ways: instruction and celebration. Paul's exhortation to *teach and admonish one another* echoes the earlier description of his own ministry (1:28). Paul's ministry aims to produce congregations that will continue his ministry of the gospel elsewhere (compare 2 Tim 2:2). Here, however, he is careful to ground the community's teaching in *the word of Christ.* This phrase has many possible meanings. It could refer to a body of Christ's teachings that circulated within the earliest church. The idea that the word should *dwell in* the community may suggest that Paul has in mind the Spirit of the Risen Christ rather than a written collection of Jesus' sayings. In fact, the close correspondence between the ideas of "wisdom" and "Spirit" in Paul's writing (compare 1:9-10) may justify this conclusion. Especially given that the "wis-

---

this peace is found and secured. Better, I think, is to view *of Christ* as a subjective genitive, indicating that the risen Christ is now in a position to give *the peace* to his disciples on earth.

dom" of false teachers (2:23) has been contrasted with wisdom found in Christ (2:3), the wisdom motif may be used here with polemical bite: only when Christian teaching is led by the Spirit of Christ, which is mediated by the gospel of Paul (1:9) and not the errant philosophy of his opponents (2:4-8), will truth be made known.

Just how Christ's Spirit conveys this word to his people, whether by prophetic utterance or by intellectual illumination, is unclear. In my opinion, however, the phrase *the word of Christ* compares favorably with Paul's earlier phrase "the word of truth" (1:5), which refers to the gospel of grace (1:6). In this sense, then, what is taught to the worshiping community by the Spirit conforms to the gospel learned from Epaphras, preached by Paul and envisioned in this letter's arguments and advice.

The second expression of the community's devotion to God is the celebration of salvation by the singing of *spiritual songs with gratitude in your hearts to God.* Paul's set of words for congregational singing, *psalms, hymns and spiritual songs,* "describe the full range of singing which the Spirit prompts" (Lohse 1971:151). Yet lists in Paul's writings tend to be illustrative rather than technical; his purpose is to impress his readers with an important point rather than with precise prescription. Thus we do not gain much by trying to differentiate among *psalms, hymns and spiritual songs* (for this see O'Brien 1982:209).

Paul's point is that songs complement teaching in worship. In the Christian liturgy, hymns often clarify the great themes of biblical exposition and prepare parishioners for proclamation and sacrament. In early Methodism, for instance, Charles Wesley's hymns provided the context for understanding the theological contribution of his brother, John Wesley. And what interpretation of the magisterial Reformation is better or more convincing than Luther's "A Mighty Fortress Is Our God"?

The second reference to *hearts* in this context no doubt is intended to couple the community's experience of *shalom* (3:15) with its worship of God. Worship is a natural response that springs from a community filled to the brim with its actual experience of God's peacemaking love.

3:16 The grammar does not make clear how Paul intends to link the singing of *psalms, hymns and spiritual songs*—all dative—with "teaching." Harris (1991:169) comments that the datives could express the form of the teaching: Christian teaching is conveyed "by means of" what is sung. On the other hand, the datives might characterize the circumstances

Thus, the effective purpose of worship is not experiential but rather the interpretation of and response to our heartfelt experience of divine love. In this sense, the phrase that the NIV translates *with gratitude (en chariti)* reflects the community's only response to the grace *(charis)* of God, which is proclaimed in their teaching and admonishment (compare 1:6) and celebrated in their singing.

I have noticed a disturbing trend among my students, many of whom come from devout families and growing churches: they are biblically illiterate and therefore spiritually fragile. In many congregations worship has become a spectator sport, geared to a generation fashioned by the slick tricks of the media. The "feel good" experience has replaced the hard discipline of knowing God in spirit and truth. The church's vocation in the world is to be of and for God, and this is a difficult and often costly calling. Christians today must have minds as tough as nails, able to cut through the vapid secularism and materialism of our world with the "word of truth."

Every believer today is under siege; the church's witness—even its faith in God—is threatened by the norms and values of a pervasively anti-God world. To support and direct God's people for their daily battles, preaching must be informed by a rigorous study of biblical texts. The church's teaching ministry must help its members understand all of life through a scriptural filter. If we are to know the truth and the demands of God's reign and to better understand the deceits of our anti-God world, so that we are prepared to worship and bear witness to the Lord, our congregations need to gather closely around the Scriptures.

The Beginning of Virtue (3:17) Paul's summary of his discussion of virtue is similar to his summary of vice (3:11) in two ways. First, both affirm that the whole of Christian life, *whether . . . word or deed,* derives from the *Lord Jesus.* By minding the "things above," the community finds that it has good reason for *giving thanks to God the Father through him.* Second, both continue Paul's polemic against false religion. Lohse suggests that the phrase *in the name of the Lord Jesus* was formulated to

---

surrounding the teaching: Christian teaching is complemented by what is sung. O'Brien contends for the former (1982:208-9), but with most translators and on the basis of church tradition, my preference is the latter.

encourage the conviction that "the Christian's entire life is placed under obedience to the Lord" (Lohse 1971:152-53). Any rule of faith that disregards the centrality of the Lord Christ for Christianity's self-understanding cannot result in proper worship of and witness to God. Further, our active worship to God comes *through him [Christ]* alone—not through our congregational leaders or religious rituals and rules. This closing formula, which places the community in relationship to God through Christ, reminds us of what Paul said earlier in 3:3: the community's hope for salvation is viable only if its "life is hidden with Christ in God."

Virtue Illustrated by the Christian Family (3:18—4:1) God's grace also results in changes within the home. Martin Luther referred to the Bible's instructions on family life as *Haustafeln* (literally, "household tables")—codes or "tables" of rules that guided behavior in the home. In Luther's day, as in our own, meals were a family's focal point. Meals are occasions for gathering family members together, perhaps for the only time during the day, for conversation and celebration. In such close quarters relationships are set in bold relief and are either nurtured or undone because of things said or actions taken. Most of what is said around a meal is not rehearsed. Questions raised are often unstudied and expressed with passion. So if a sense of order is to be maintained, family members must be guided by overarching principles of conduct. Without rules, family conversation can erupt into angry arguments that produce hard feelings and broken fellowship.

In Paul's world, codes of household rules were commonplace. Both religious and nonreligious populations realized the importance of familial relations for the well-being of the whole society. For Christians, who believe that every person is created with the image of the Lord Christ in mind (see 1:15-18), the similarity between scriptural and secular codes is not surprising (see 3:9-10). Whether pagan or Christian, reason-

---

3:18—4:1 Bible scholars continue to disagree over why the New Testament household codes of Paul's world agree with those of Roman society. Most agree that such conformity actually arose out of social conflict between the church and other institutions. Such conflict was largely based on disagreements in social values between believers and outsiders. In this climate of unrest, created by Christianity's radical social values, some scholars are inclined to view the *Haustafeln* as accommodations required to survive, while others view them as

able people observe that a certain order to social relationships, especially within the family, contributes to the common good of humankind. In Western countries, nearly every week some national magazine publishes yet another report that makes this point, typically stated negatively: the decline of the family is the surest barometer of the decline of the culture. So it makes sense that comparisons of the various *Haustafeln* in the New Testament (such as Eph 5:21—6:9; 1 Pet 2:13—3:7) with those found in other ancient works show that the early church's teaching about the family generally conformed to its social world.

With closer scrutiny, however, we should find critical differences between the secular and Christian worlds and between their codes for family conduct. For example, Paul calls his readers to observe his code for reasons that are both christological (3:18: *as is fitting in the Lord*) and eschatological (3:24: *you will receive an inheritance from the Lord*). That is, his reasons are religious and not societal. Further, the egalitarian sociology of God's people (see 3:11) is radically different from the hierarchy and patriarchy of the Jewish and Roman worlds. Where the new age has dawned in Christ, people are valued as equals regardless of their station or role. The believer's way of seeing has been transformed by divine grace, and this renewal of the mind has resulted in a new sense of being and a new capacity for doing. In this sense, then, calls to submit to or love another mean something very different for the believer than for the nonbeliever. In fact, Paul, who teaches that God's grace works within the community to produce a distinctively virtuous life (3:12-17), would no doubt argue that without our participation with Christ in God's saving work the intent of such household rules is corrupted so that they produce only vice (see 3:5-9).

Tragically, our churches provide numerous examples of dysfunctional families in which abuse has been justified by a distorted interpretation of Paul's household codes. Wifely submission is taken to mean the sub-

---

illustrations of the church as an alternative to the social order. I share the latter view that the subtle distinctions between the *Haustafeln* and the non-Christian household codes of Paul's world are intended to clarify how family relationships within the church are at odds with the dominant models of family life found elsewhere in the Roman world (Wall 1988:272-85).

jugation of the woman's whole being to the man; husbandly love is taken to mean the man's condescending care of the woman. The abuse promoted by such interpretations has led many believers to disregard Paul's teaching as irrelevant and too misogynistic for today's liberated environment.

Part of the problem with this perspective is exegetical: what plain meaning does this text have within the context of the whole composition and its point of origin? In the case of Colossians, we must assume that the household code it contains has an integral role in Paul's composition and expresses his concern for the readers—that is, he uses this household code to address the crisis in Colosse. With this in mind, two exegetical questions face us: First, what has Paul said to this point in his argument against his Colossian opponents that prepares us to understand this household code? And second, why does Paul include it in his description of the Christian life?

Paul's general concern stems from the deeper logic of his gospel, introduced in the opening thanksgiving: ideas about God are embodied in action toward others, and only the truth about God's grace can produce holiness and peace in human lives. In this light, Paul has made three critical points in his description of the Christian life.

First, Christian morality is properly motivated by mindfulness of the "things above," where the enthroned Christ is found (3:1-4). When people confess Christ's lordship over all creation (1:15-20), they will resist the separation of morality into compartments, one spiritual and the other material. The values of God and the norms of God's reign, which Jesus incarnated during his messianic mission, inform all spheres of the church's conduct. In this sense, the believer's public conduct, whether in word or deed, will be at odds with the values of the secular order, whether at work or at home.

Second, Christian morality is set within the new creation (3:9-10), an egalitarian community (3:11), which has "put to death" by God's grace all vices that result in death rather than life and therefore undermine God's purposes for creation.

Third, the new life that characterizes the faith community now hidden with Christ in God (3:1-4) bears witness to God through Christ by word and deed (3:12-17).

The Christian family is the proving ground for life in Christ. If the gospel about Christ has been accepted and the truth about God's grace affirmed, relationships within the home will be transformed. There, where intimacy is sought and goodness expected behind doors closed to the pressures of the secular order, our truthfulness in public confession will be found out. Paul no doubt realizes that what happens in the home validates what has happened in the heart.

Paul adapts a traditional moral code of family life for a Christian congregation and so implies that the empowering grace found in Christ also is found in the Christian home. Family members who are in Christ continue to live with each other but in new ways.

Paul's description, however, remains somewhat selective and idealistic. For him, morality expresses God's grace; and he never speaks of grace to excuse sin but always to describe victory over sin. He doesn't list all the exceptions, nor does he describe the difficulties facing the Christian family in an anti-God world. Further, his understanding of the home is shaped by a culture that devalued women and children and often treated household servants no better than animals. The unqualified demand for wives, children and servants to *obey* reflects in part the social realities of Paul's world.

Some say that he did not seek to reverse these social arrangements because he thought the end of the age was imminent; others say that he was simply too conservative—too much a Roman citizen—to threaten Rome's social institutions. That may be. However, I prefer to understand Paul's moral teaching as visional. For him, the transformation of the mind by God's purposes disclosed in Christ produces a new way of looking at social and spiritual realities. Thus, while he retains the current social institution (that is, the "family unit"), he replaces its secular focus with a recognition of the lordship of Christ and the hope of God's coming triumph in him. What is central to this passage is Paul's call for an intellectual reorientation (repentance is exactly that!) toward relationships within the home such that the way family members treat one another is transformed.

For example, if a wife sees herself as subservient to her husband, she will allow him to dominate and even abuse her. If, however, she views herself as Christ's disciple and her husband's equal in Christ, her understanding of submission will be changed: she will submit herself to her husband in the same way that Christ submitted himself to God. The result is that God's salvation will have its full effect (see 3:10; Eph 4:12-16). Being made equal in Christ will radically alter the way two disciples relate to each other as husband and wife. The result will be the woman's elevation within the Christian home and the end of her abuse there (see commentary under 3:18-19), and this in turn will be a witness to a misogynistic world.

The student of this passage should not think that Paul is responding to abusive relationships within the Christian homes of Colosse; there is no evidence whatever to support this conjecture. Rather, this household code is another important example of Paul's desire to make the gospel practical for life. If the Colossian philosophy moved the congregation toward intellectualism and asceticism, Paul may have included this *Haustafel* in Colossians to check the drift toward irrelevancy. The Christian gospel has to do with the way we live our daily lives; to embrace its truths is to bear its fruit "in every good work" (1:10). For most of us, truth comes closest to home in the family; here is where the fruit of the gospel is most vividly and vitally known.

Wives and Husbands (3:18-19) The first two rules of Paul's household code, *Wives, submit to your husbands* and *Husbands, love your wives,* are joined with the command to act toward each other in ways that are *fitting in the Lord.* The "careful balance" between wife and husband envisioned by Wright (1987:147) assumes the woman's equal value within the community that belongs to Christ. The issue at stake is not gender but how disciples, whether male or female, are oriented toward the Lord. Thus, secular notions of submission, whether feminist or patriarchal, must be set aside and replaced by notions of how Christ submitted himself to God. Likewise, condescending notions of love must be replaced by a love like Christ's for his neighbors.

According to Colossians, whatever else we may suppose about Christ's submission to God, we cannot think of Christ as God's inferior. He is, after all, "the image of the invisible God" (1:15), "the fullness of the Deity . . . in bodily form" (2:9). Moreover, Christ's devotion for the church is expressed as an intimate union between the two: Christ is "in" every disciple (1:27; 3:11). So the female disciple participates with Christ in God's salvation to the very same extent that the male disciple does. Whatever the social hierarchies being promoted by the spiritual umpire in the Colossian congregation, they do not accord with the nature of human relationships between those believers in Christ (see 3:11).

More important to our exposition of this controversial passage is the meaning of the Christian phrase *as is fitting in the Lord* that Paul adds to the code. The verb *fitting (anēkei)* refers to any act considered "proper" or suitable for its subjects. That is, the propriety of the wife's submission to her husband or of the husband's love for his wife is gauged by the new realities found *in the Lord.*

Two integral aspects of Paul's Christology that are emphasized within Colossians provide content to this added phrase. First is the exaltation of Christ as Lord "over all things"—the universal effect of God's triumph over sin and death through him. To worship Christ as Lord is to acknowledge that God's promised salvation has already been fulfilled for those "hidden with Christ in God." Second, however, is the community's participation with Christ in the real results of God's triumph over sin and death. Not only is God's triumph demonstrated in the death and resurrection of the Lord Christ, but in him God's people now experience transformation from vice to virtue and from death to life. In this sense, then, actions "proper" for those who live in the Lord Christ must bear witness to God's triumph. Specifically, actions between husband and wife must show forth the new creation that has begun with Christ. In the larger context of Paul's moral exhortation, then, both the wife's submission and the husband's love are characterized by the virtues of 3:12-14, while marital relationships that belong to the fallen world are characterized by the vices listed in 3:5-9.

Paul's exhortation to Christian husbands not to *be harsh with* their wives recalls their conversion from vice to virtue. Surely the verb rendered "harsh" (*pikrainō;* literally, "to embitter") is the opposite of a "binding love" (3:14; see O'Brien 1982:224) and, like all vice, results in broken relationships (see Heb 12:15). Perhaps Paul's phrase recalls the Deuteronomic code (Deut 29:18), where "bitter poison" within the community is said to result from idolatry; Paul lists idolatry with the vices of the old order (see 3:5). However the wife submits and the husband loves, both actions must bear witness to the new life they share as codisciples in Christ.

Why then does Paul retain the rhetoric of the old order, which seems to place wives in a hierarchical relationship to their husbands? This question carries an even greater force given the egalitarian character of relationships within the church (see 3:11). In recent years some Christian feminists have questioned Paul's resolve in these matters; he seems to equivocate on matters female. Perhaps his apparent ambiguity on male-female relations stems from his missiological praxis: the preaching of the gospel must accommodate its audience if it is to be heard and responded to (1 Cor 9:19-23). Paul's use of hierarchical language may well be rhetorical rather than sociological; his desire is to convey a new pattern for family relationships which is best communicated in "old wineskins." By so doing, the theologian Paul is not commending the old or even suggesting that old and new patterns for marriage can possibly coexist in God's kingdom. Clearly, he views the church as the new social order within the old fallen world. However, as a missionary he knows that social conflict, which is inevitable when the new and old clash (see Rom 12:14-21), constitutes a crisis for the hearing of the gospel.

Crosscultural communication is a missiological imperative! What would have been the missiological result of asking husbands to submit to their wives, when both the religious and secular establishments of Paul's day agreed that wives should submit to husbands to maintain the "proper" (and natural) order of things? I speculate the practical result would have been unfavorable, with the ministry of the church shoved out toward the margins of the cultural mainstream. Then the gospel would simply not have been heard.

Naturally, Paul wants the relationship between Christian wives and their Christian husbands to embody the lordship of Christ for all to see. Obviously, this is impossible when marriages are abusive, or when one spouse is prevented by the other from realizing God's good intentions in the Lord Christ (as in 3:5-11). Should a Christian wife continue to submit uncritically to her husband if it results in personal abuse (the vices of 3:5-9) rather than in spiritual maturity (the virtues of 3:12-15)? I think not. Should the measure of a husband's love for his wife be whether her devotion to the Lord Christ is strengthened and God's interests (rather than her husband's) for her life achieved? I think so. In

Christ, God shows no favorites; God is for both husband and wife, and in equal measure (see Wall 1987:276-85).

Parents and Children (3:20-21) The Greek word Paul uses for "children" is *tekna,* which refers to young children living at home. While it is certainly not unusual to find instructions for dependent children in ancient household codes, Paul's version is quite extraordinary because he treats even dependent children as Christ's disciples. This is clearly the intent of the incentive clause *for this pleases the Lord,* which I think applies equally to fathers. The relationship between parent and child is centered on their common devotion to the Lord. The word translated "pleases" *(euarestos)* is always used in the New Testament of conduct that accords with God's will (even though outside the New Testament it often identified socially aware behavior). Perhaps Paul brings together both meanings and adds the object *the Lord* to press the point that social propriety within the Christian family is determined by the Lord, not by the dominant values and typical behaviors of the surrounding secular order.

If Jesus Christ is Lord over all things (1:15-20), and if the believing community has already triumphed with him over the powers of darkness (1:13-14), then what is "proper" between the child and parent is finally construed on the Lord Christ's terms rather than on society's. Neither the child nor the parent should hold the other hostage to society's values and expectations. Neither should seek self-justification in terms of what is "pleasing" to or expected of their own peers. Parents often project their ambitions or those of their friends on their children, trying to remake them in the image of their personal failures. But parenting is a sacred task; as disciples of Christ, Christian parents seek to raise up children in the image of the One who is "Deity . . . in bodily form."

The elevated value of children within the faith community is also evident in Paul's admonition to fathers that they are not to *embitter their children, or they will become discouraged.* Parenting within the Christian home requires a balance: maintaining the children's obedience without alienating them from the faith. Paul does not deny that young children require parental guidance. In fact, O'Brien notes two important differences between Paul's exhortations that a wife submit to her husband and that a child obey the same person. First is the change of the verbal idea from submission *(hypotassō),* which only sometimes means obedience, to the more explicit word for obedience *(hypakouō).* Second is the change of verbal voice from middle, which implies that the wife's submission is voluntary, to an active imperative, which implies the child's unquestioning obedience (O'Brien 1982:224).

However, Paul is no doubt aware of the potential for child abuse in communities that require strict compliance to parental authority, where the rod is not spared lest the child be "spoiled." What often results is not redemption but the obliteration of a child's self-esteem (which quite possibly is one meaning of the word *discouraged;* see Wright 1987:148-49) and bitterness toward the parent and the parent's faith. Demanding obedience without love, or conditioning love upon obedience, imperils the child's formation, because it alienates him or her from all nurturing relationships with God, family and community (see 3:14).

While children are to obey both parents, only the father is admonished against harsh treatment of his children. Why not the mother too? Rather than a normative statement about God's order (so Wright 1987:148), it probably is better viewed as an accommodation to the Roman world (so O'Brien 1982:225), where the father was vested with primary authority over the household. No doubt Paul realizes that personal authority in any sphere—even his apostolic authority within the Gentile church—is easily corrupted into coercive and abusive authoritarianism. It is always tempting for the one whose word is final to speak that word in self-serving ways. In this sense, then, the incentive clause to do what *pleases the Lord* bids fathers to reverse the Roman notion of power. Rather than defining the parent-child relationship in terms of his power over the child, the father who is first of all Christ's disciple is to become servant of his children (so Mk 10:42-45). Paul's exhortation to fathers, then, envisions Christian discipleship in two ways: Christian fathers consider the tragic consequences of overly harsh discipline, and they replace coercive power with empowering service of their children.

Slaves (3:22-25) Let me begin my commentary on this particular unit of the Colossian *Haustafel* with a caveat, especially for American

---

3:22-25 For a discussion of the social background of the Roman institution of slavery, see my introduction to Philemon in this volume. In fact, Paul's letter to Philemon concerning

readers: Do not read Paul's instructions to Roman slaves as though their status and experience were the same as those of antebellum American slaves. While they share the general similarity that all slaves are mastered by their owner, to link these two slave institutions without regard for their vast dissimilarities will lead to distorted interpretation (see my introduction to Philemon; "Slavery in the First Century").

Scholars are sometimes puzzled that Paul devotes so much of the Colossian code to slaves. Two different times, surrounded by five different reasons, Paul exhorts slaves to obey their masters. Why this emphasis? Two general solutions to this exegetical puzzle are often advanced. One is that Paul is responding here to the social world of the Colossians. Commentators who prefer this option suppose that Paul is responding to a congregation made up of slaves and slave owners, both of whom have been shaped by a society that promotes slavery in order to maintain Rome's economic and military viability. Another explanation is that Paul emphasizes the slave-master motif in this letter to illustrate his core ethical proposal to "set your minds on things above, not on earthly things" (3:2). In this second explanation, Christian slaves are viewed as representatives of God's people; they represent every believer's vocation, which is to serve God.

On closer scrutiny, however, we see that Paul's expansion of the code primarily concerns the Christian slave's essential moral dilemma, especially in the workplace: What does it mean to serve two masters, one on earth (that is, the company or the boss) and another in heaven (that is, the Lord Christ)? In my opinion, this is exactly the dilemma that continues to face all workers who serve the Lord: Who is it that reigns where we live and work? Especially in the workplace, is our primary ambition to have a career and to move ahead in competition with other workers? Like Jesus, who posed the dilemma of "two masters" (see Mt 6:24; par.), Paul presents a clear exhortation: the true disciple, who might have both earthly and heavenly "masters," must follow the lead of a mind set on "things above."

The central challenge for slaves, which Paul repeats, is to *obey your*

---

his slave Onesimus provides Paul's own commentary on Colossians 3:22—4:1.

earthly masters in everything. Again, Paul's admonition conforms to traditional moral teaching in the ancient world, which demanded that household slaves utterly obey their employers. Such hierarchies were viewed as critical to the social and economic order. So *whatever you do, work at it with all your heart.* Again, however, Paul retains the form of the prevailing social institution but changes the reason for it: to bear witness to the Lord Christ. In fact, Paul is convinced that a christological orientation will transform even our ordinary tasks into acts of worship, moving us to do our work even better.

The moral issue at stake is what motivates a person to work well. Most of us bunch our reasons under two general headings: either we enjoy a good working relationship with our boss or company, or we expect to derive some personal benefit from our work. Paul comments on both reasons. On the one hand, the daily chores of household slaves, often difficult and sometimes dehumanizing, are motivated by *reverence for the Lord;* Christian slaves work as though *working for the Lord.* Paul's instruction does not go as far as 1 Timothy 6:1, which makes the master the object of the slave's respect; nor does he suggest, as does 1 Peter 2:18, that masters can sometimes be harsh (but see 3:19). Rather, Paul's concern is to mind the "things above" rather than "earthly things"; thus Christian workers are not motivated by their *earthly masters,* whether to *win their favor* or to work *for men* (compare Eph 6:5-8).

Whether we punch in and out on time or whether we appear competent to our coworkers and bosses is not at stake for those who think of work as an act of worship. To work in order to bring pleasure to God is sufficient motivation to be faithful stewards of our talents and opportunities.

Workers are also motivated by the prospect of payment for their labor. In this case, Paul says faithful slaves *know that [they] will receive an inheritance from the Lord as a reward.* The inclusion of this eschatological motif in the code is unique among New Testament *Haustafeln* and is therefore exegetically significant. Most slaves in the Roman world received meager rewards: by law they could own little and inherit nothing. Therefore, Paul is speaking ironically here, perhaps to call attention to an earlier claim made about the gospel. In introducing his commentary on the false teaching in Colosse, Paul notes that the gospel (1:27-

28) produces the "fruit" (1:6; compare 3:1-4) of "hope" (1:5) for a heavenly "inheritance" (1:12). Heavenly profit is based on faith, not social class; it is paid to those who serve Jesus Christ, whether the servant is powerful master or powerless slave.

James Hal Cone, an important African-American theologian, has said that black spirituals celebrated visions of heavenly reward to affirm what it means to be fully human in an earthly context where love, justice and liberation were rarely realized. From the gospel stories the slaves knew about God's love and justice; they spoke of their heavenly home as the place where they would finally and fully experience these truths. To mind the "things above" is to hope for an inheritance that reverses socioeconomic conditions on earth, where many people are oppressed and denied humanity. Significantly, the spiritual songs of American slaves were mostly composed in the fields of hard labor rather than in the churches of earnest worship. They expressed the real reason slaves continued to work well in spite of terrible treatment: they minded the One above in the confident hope that he realized their true value and would one day give them back their humanity. In this limited but profound sense, they shared a rich *koinōnia* with their Christian counterparts in ancient Colosse.

And Masters (4:1) Paul completes the Colossian *Haustafel* by turning his attention to slave masters. Already he has described the sociology of the community located by God's grace in Christ, which makes "slave and free" equal because they are both in Christ and he in them (3:11). It should not surprise the reader, then, that Paul promotes an alternative understanding of the Roman institution of slavery. The gospel does not necessarily seek to reverse the social arrangements between slave and master; in this case, Paul does not exhort the master to emancipate the slaves (however, see Philemon). Rather, his instruction is for the master to provide slaves *with what is right and fair*—something any virtuous person would do (compare 3:12). Although other codes in the ancient world also encouraged the humane treatment of slaves (see O'Brien 1982:232), the issue for Paul is where one finds the moral competency to do what the code outlines. The requisite virtue to do *what is right and fair* belongs to the "new creatures" found in Christ.

However, Paul's teaching also presses the christological incentive behind such behavior: *you know that you also have a Master in heaven*—mind the "things above"! The relationship between earthly masters and the heavenly Master provides the moral impetus for just treatment of household workers. Further, if the phrase "Master in heaven" alludes to 3:1-4, as most commentators suppose, then it conveys an eschatological meaning as well. According to the Jewish moral tradition, inhumane treatment of slaves would bring down the Lord Almighty's wrath on Judgment Day (compare Jas 5:1-5). According to Paul's teaching, a relationship with Christ transforms all earthly relationships, including those between masters and slaves. So the Christian master, transformed by God's grace, will naturally treat slaves fairly and will therefore "appear with [Christ] in glory" (3:4).

□ Benediction (4:2-28)

The concluding section of each of Paul's letters contains his benediction, typically expressed as a prayer or doxology. Ancient writers usually added various greetings, specific instructions and general exhortations to their closings. Paul is no different, although he baptizes these literary conventions with the distinctive phrases of his Christian ministry. Appropriately, then, Paul's goodby to the Colossian believers includes exhortations concerning their evangelistic work (4:2-6) and internal relations (4:7-17), before concluding with his benedictory doxology (4:18).

While this concluding passage has an eye to the situation facing his Colossian readers, it actually falls outside of the letter's main body, where Paul addresses the audience's spiritual crisis more directly and pastorally. In my opinion, then, we should not understand these verses as part of Paul's polemic against his opponents. They rather reflect his general interest in the spiritual well-being of any congregation under his care, regardless of the particular problems it might be facing. His exhortations in this letter's benediction convey a universal message, then, equally valid for any congregation. Yet this passage is also interesting because it provides us with a window into earliest Christianity and offers an intriguing model that clarifies the dynamics of congregational life.

Notes: **4:2** Lohse argues that the participle *being watchful* should be translated as an independent command to agree with the preceding imperative: "Devote yourselves to prayer and be watchful and thankful" (1972:164). However, agreeing with the NIV, I think

Paul's Evangelistic Concern for Outsiders (4:2-6) Paul's opening exhortation is framed by two imperatives, both of which convey his deep concern to evangelize the lost. The community that God has called out of the world for salvation by the gospel (see Rom 10:8) is called in turn to preach that gospel; evangelism is the church's vocation. The work of evangelism includes prayer (4:2-4) as well as proclamation (4:5-6)—a point already highlighted in the letter's opening words (1:5-9). In fact, this concluding passage connects well with Paul's opening thanksgiving (1:3-12). So Paul's exhortations to pray for the church's mission (4:2-4) and to be wise toward outsiders (4:5) form a sort of bookend, paired with its opening thanksgiving, bringing into even clearer focus the purpose of the letter's main body. That is, Paul's interest in correcting the errant philosophy concerns the church's vocation; the Christless teaching and ascetic morality of the "hollow and deceptive philosophy" (2:8) threaten the church's evangelistic mission to outsiders.

The Ministry of Prayer (4:2-4) Paul is first of all concerned with his readers' prayer life, and he commends three characteristics of effective prayer to them. The opening imperative, *devote yourselves (proskartereite),* is frequently used regarding prayer in the New Testament (especially in Acts: 1:14; 2:42, 46, etc.) and suggests a gritty determination not to give up until God's response comes (compare Lk 18:1-8). The second phrase, *being watchful,* may imply a perspective toward the future, when Christ returns and God will answer every prayer fully. Most commentators are inclined not to find a futuristic meaning in this phrase because of Paul's emphasis in Colossians on a realized eschatology; but I disagree. Paul's opening thanksgiving is grounded in the congregation's future hope (1:5) and restated as the aim of his Gentile mission (1:22, 28). The congregation is called to pray in the confident expectation that it will be made acceptable before God at Christ's return (Schweizer 1982:172). In addition, the word for *watchful (grēgoreō)* modifies and intensifies Paul's exhortation to pray, calling for vigilance or alertness to petition God for all that agrees with God's eschatological plans. In the immediate context, persistent and vigilant prayer is an ingredient of the

---

it best to take this participle as circumstantial; that is, watching for the future return of Christ characterizes the devotion required in fervent prayer (O'Brien 1982:237).

church's evangelistic mission: believers must pray that those in need of God's salvation be converted before Christ returns.

The third characteristic of prayer, *thankful,* suggests two possible meanings. A thankful prayer expects God's answers (see 1:12; Wright 1987:152). Since this exhortation concerns the church's evangelistic mission, a thankful prayer also acknowledges that salvation finally belongs to the Lord and is the work of God's grace.

The more specific object of the congregation's intercessory prayer is *that God may open a door for our message.* The meaning of the "opened door" metaphor is debated among scholars (see Wright 1987:152). Elsewhere in Paul's writing the image refers to the occasion for conversion granted by God through the preaching of the gospel (1 Cor 16:9; 2 Cor 2:14; compare Acts 14:27). No doubt this is the primary meaning intended by Paul here. But Paul may well have placed this phrase in an inverted and parallel relationship with the next two phrases, *so that we may proclaim the mystery of Christ, for which I am in chains.* If this is the case, then the church's message is more specifically *the mystery of Christ* (compare 1:26-7). Thus to pray for an "opened door" is to pray that Paul's prison door be opened by God's grace so that he will be "given another chance to preach" God's gospel (see Lohse 1972:165).

The transition from the plural *our message* to the singular *I am in chains* no doubt is intended to underscore the difficulty of Paul's personal situation. While he is called by God to *proclaim the mystery of Christ,* he cannot do what he *should* because he is in prison. In effect, then, the community prays that God's will be done on earth as it is in heaven: that God open the door of Paul's prison, setting him free to reveal *the mystery of Christ,* which is that Christ is for Gentiles too, and that he is the "hope of glory" for them as well (1:27).

The Ministry of Proclamation (4:5-6) Paul's second imperative to the Colossians is to *be wise in the way you act toward outsiders.* The word *outsiders* generally refers to non-Christians (1 Cor 5:12-13; 1 Thess

4:4 The Greek particle *dei* is better translated "it is necessary" rather than the NIV's *as I should.* The NIV softens the force of Paul's probable intent to recall his earlier apologia in 1:24—2:3, which is tied to this exhortation by *proclaim* (*phaneroo;* translated "disclose" in 1:26). Paul's earlier use of this verb is coupled with "mystery" to express the particular purpose of Paul's ministry: to make the full word of God known among the Gentiles (1:25-

4:11-12). In rabbinical use, however, it may include believers who stand outside correct teaching. Perhaps Paul has both groups in mind, including those persuaded by the false teachers along with the lost of the world, since the ministry of evangelism includes both. Moreover, he would have been especially concerned about the negative effect immature believers have on the lost. Since we authenticate God's salvation by our lives and words, we can either impugn or enhance God's reputation by bad or good example (Lohse 1972:167). How many non-Christians justify their unbelief by testimonies of a Christian's hypocrisy! To excuse our sins by referring to our spiritual immaturity or by pointing out the Lord's perfect love will simply not do. In Christ's earthly absence, the church remains the conduit of the word of truth on earth, for good or for ill. If we remain in vice and despair, without any indication that God's grace makes a difference, who but the fool will believe the claims of the gospel? For this reason Paul calls us to life grounded in a wisdom that knows God and remains committed to the trustworthiness of the gospel (1:9-10; compare 1:28; 2:3; 3:16).

With respect to the ministry of evangelism, the exhortation to be wise suggests two concerns. First, the wise community exploits *every opportunity* it is given for evangelism. *Watchful* prayer makes one keenly sensitive to people and setting. In fact, O'Brien suggests that the middle voice of the verb *make the most* signifies "the personal interest" or involvement of believers in their environment (1982:241). But the reason for our activism is pointed and clear: this is a call not so much to be a "good Samaritan" as to share with Paul in the work of evangelism. Second, the wise community, eager to proclaim the gospel, engages the lost in *conversation [that is] full of grace, seasoned with salt.* This last phrase, so graphic and memorable, captures the wisdom of ancient rhetoric: ideological substance without personal style fails to convince people. If a believer, who has a wonderful story of conversion to tell, cannot tell it in a "salty," interesting way, the story will not be heard. Of course,

27). Paul preaches that God has chosen Gentiles out of their darkness for salvation in Christ (3:11). Against this backdrop, then, Paul's mission is made "necessary" by God's "commission" (1:25), since he has become an agent of God's redemptive plan for the Gentiles. Yet Paul's imprisonment makes it impossible to do what is "necessary": his work of evangelism.

lively stories, like "fine-sounding arguments," are sometimes used in the service of lifeless substance. In this case, however, the communication of the "word of truth" is undermined by uninteresting or incoherent words.

Paul may have mentioned *grace* to link human graciousness, a characteristic of effective communication, with divine grace. In this sense, the gospel of God's saving grace will find its audience through a gospel ministry characterized by a generous civility (see 3:12). The spiritual triumphalism that some evangelists exemplify today not only fails to edify the church but fails to attract an unsaved audience as well. Yet their rhetoric is often "salty," full of vibrant images and pungency, hardly dull and never boring. Evangelists know that an audience will never be attracted to new life by lifeless words, old clichés and tired slogans! Paul's wise exhortation is to bring humane graciousness together with carefully chosen words in our preaching ministry.

The meaning of the final phrase, *so that you may know how to answer everyone,* depends on whether it expresses the result of "gracious and salty" proclamation or describes its occasion. Probably the latter option fits this context best: the evangelist who makes the most of every opportunity finds a "gracious and salty" answer for every sincere query or malicious challenge facing the church.

Paul's Apostolic Concern for Insiders (4:7-17) Paul includes various instructions (4:7-9, 16-17) and personal greetings (4:10-15) in the letter's benediction to guide the church's response toward his coworkers. In one sense, these concluding words show the practical authority of Paul's apostleship: virtually everyone he mentions is given identity within the congregation by relationship to him. This is clearest in the instructions he gives for receiving Tychicus (see below, commentary on 4:7-9). Paul defines the congregation's vocation by his own. Therefore, while some continue to inspect this passage for clues to help reconstruct the chronology of Paul's life, its principal value remains theological: Paul's primary interest is to gird up his apostolic authority to strengthen the prospect for a successful evangelistic campaign, in keeping, then, with his preceding exhortation.

It is a prospect that seems imperiled. Paul refers to his imprisonment three times in this benediction (4:3, 10, 18) and says that he is sending Tychicus in order to tell the Colossians about *our circumstances* (4:8), presumably difficult. His cryptic aside about Mark (4:10) may suggest some internal strife within the mission's leadership (compare Acts 15:36-41); even Archippus's instructions (4:17) seem odd unless it is necessary for Paul to exhort him to *complete the work*. Further, Paul's strong and extraordinary endorsement of Epaphras (4:13) is unnecessary, given his previous association with this congregation (1:7-8), unless there is some trouble in his relationship with the Colossian believers (see introduction, and also my comments on 1:7-8). Lastly, Paul's admission that only a few Jews participated with him in the Gentile mission (4:11) may reflect the growing rift between the church and synagogue as well as between Gentiles and Jews within the church (Acts 15:1-4; 21:17-26; Gal 2:1—3:5).

Against this backdrop, then, Paul uses this letter's benediction to bolster support for his mission within a troubled community so that their prayers (4:2-6) and his (1:8-9) will not be in vain.

The Ministry of Tychicus (4:7-9) Paul often uses benedictions for personal commendations, often to solicit support for a colleague. The apostle's introduction of Tychicus to the Colossians carries considerable weight. He is more than a courier of personal regard—someone sent by Paul to field questions about his imprisonment so that the believers can pray more effectively for him (Wright 1987:155). The titles Paul gives Tychicus, *dear brother, a faithful minister and fellow servant,* suggest a role more important than that of a messenger. He was, in O'Brien's words, "a particularly valued colleague" (1982:247). In fact, the title *faithful minister* (*diakonos,* literally "servant," from which we derive "deacon") is used earlier to describe the ministry of both Epaphras (1:7) and Paul himself (1:23). Moreover, the title *fellow servant (syndoulos)* is used earlier (1:7) to describe Epaphras as one who participates equally with Paul in the Gentile mission. In effect, Tychicus is Paul's own designate to continue the ministry, at least at Colosse, during his imprisonment. Epaphras would have been the natural person for this ministry, since he first brought the gospel to Colosse; however, apparently his relationship with the Colossians is troubled and requires Paul's intervention (4:12-13).

Because of the various interruptions during his ministry (including imprisonment), Paul was unable to visit many Gentile congregations in person even though this was his desire. In Romans, for example, Paul repeats his desire to visit the Christian congregations in the world's most important city in order to "impart to you some spiritual gift to make you strong" (Rom 1:11; compare 15:23-4). Like the Colossian believers, those in Rome had never profited from the apostle's personal visit, a time when Paul could minister to them directly and they could benefit from his apostolic persona and gifts.

Paul's constant references in his letters to past and future visits are expressions of his apostolic authority. The gifts that Christ had given him (see Rom 1:5) have transformed him into a conduit of eschatological power, capable of empowering others to resist evil and grow in holiness, thereby preparing for the Lord's return. When he was unable to visit congregations in person, Paul sent substitutes (both people and letters) through which his apostolic ministry could continue to have its powerful effect (Funk 1967:249-68). Tychicus is one such substitute, Timothy is another (Phil 2:19; 1 Thess 3:6), and this very letter is a third. In this case, the apostle is "in chains" and unable to convey the gift of his apostleship to the Colossian believers in person. Because their faith is threatened by false teaching, he sends Tychicus as *minister* and *servant* to *encourage [their] hearts*—the very purpose Paul has assigned to himself (2:2).

This point is highlighted by the chiastic pattern of the text itself. Recall that a chiasmus is a literary device that arranges words and ideas into two parallel and inverted passages, with an odd member placed at the vertex, where the two passages intersect (ABCDC′B′A′). The odd phrase found at the vertex (D) helps the reader locate the passage's principal idea. Consider verses 7-9 in this light:

A Tychicus will tell you all the news about me (v. 7a).

  B He is a dear brother, a faithful minister and fellow servant in the Lord (v. 7b).

    C I am sending him to you for the express purpose that you may know about our circumstances (v. 8a)

      D and that he may encourage your hearts (v. 8b).

    C′ He is coming with Onesimus (v. 9a),

B′ our faithful and dear brother, who is one of you (v. 9b).
A′ They will tell you everything that is happening here (9c).

The chiastic shape helps us to identify the most important ingredient in the instructions Paul sends to the Colossians: *that [Tychicus] may encourage your hearts.* Paul's chief interest is that his ministry continue through Tychicus during his imprisonment (see Lohse 1971:171). The chiasmus also subordinates Onesimus to Tychicus, for it is the latter who is central to Paul's plans and additionally is called *faithful minister.* The credential added to Onesimus, *who is one of you* (4:9), suggests that his task is to help Tychicus gain entry into this Colossian community.

Greetings from Jewish Coworkers (4:10-11) The next three colleagues mentioned by Paul—Aristarchus, Mark and Jesus, who is called Justus—are Jewish believers and are said by Paul to be *the only Jews among my fellow workers for the kingdom of God.* Actually, the Greek text is more vague about their ethnicity than the NIV. The phrase translated "Jews" is literally "from the circumcised" *(ek peritomēs)* and may in fact refer to a specific group of Jewish Christian missionaries called "the circumcision party" (see Acts 10:45; 11:2; 15:1-5; Gal 2:12), whose membership included these three (Ellis 1978:116-28). Of course, we know that earliest Christianity sent different missions to various constituencies. In Galatians 2:1-10 Paul himself identifies two distinct missions, each with its own version of the gospel (Gal 2:7; compare Acts 15:19-21). What is less clear, especially in light of Paul's negative verdict against "the circumcision party" of Galatians 2:12, is the meaning of his positive reference to three of its members in this letter (although his high regard for Mark is less certain; see below).

In my view, we should not assume that Paul's words in Galatians describe a static sentiment; Galatians is a highly emotional book in any case, full of angry rhetoric that contrasts with the more cooperative language we find in Paul's other letters. While he has been called by Christ to evangelize primarily Gentiles (but also Jews; see Acts 9:15), there are others who are called to evangelize the Jews. The apostle understands this and celebrates them (see Gal. 2:7-10), so long as they do not substitute a more Jewish version of the gospel (Gal 2:11-16) for the one that has been given him by Christ for Gentile conversion (Gal 1:11-17).

Also, Paul may have identified these three Jewish evangelists as "being of the circumcision" in connection with the earlier reference to circumcision in his polemic against false teaching (2:10-12). If this is the case, the phrase bears subtle testimony against the Jewish content of the false teaching at Colosse: there are at least three Jewish-Christian teachers who support Paul and even share his imprisonment. In this sense, the *comfort* they have provided Paul is the knowledge that there is still support within the Jewish church for the Gentile mission and its gospel.

The parenthetical comment about Mark may be innocent enough: the Colossians are to *welcome him,* and Paul's *instructions* perhaps include a special task for him. However, Mark's relationship with Paul was troubled from the beginning (see Acts 15:36-41), and the *welcome* Paul encourages is conditioned on whether Mark actually arrives in Colosse. Still, I am inclined to take the tone of Paul's instructions as cautiously positive, since the conditional *if he comes to you* implies that he probably *will* come.

Greetings from and to Gentile Coworkers (4:12-15) Next comes Paul's greeting from Epaphras, who first preached the gospel to the Colossians (1:5-8). Because he is *one of [them],* Epaphras no doubt understands well the problems facing this congregation; in fact, I have argued that he may very well be the founding father of the Colossian congregation and therefore the more specific object of ridicule by the opponents of the Gentile mission in Colosse (see introduction, under "The Crisis at Colosse," as well as my comments on 1:7-8). Paul's commentary on Epaphras's personal commitment to the congregation indicates more than confidence that prayer is a critical ingredient in the work of the Gentile mission. Certainly the nurture of this congregation depends on Epaphras's *wrestling in prayer for you.* However, Epaphras's prayer that the Colossian believers *stand firm in all the will of God* (compare 1:9) indicates his commitment to them.

4:10 *If he comes to you* is a third-class conditional statement. The Greek *ean* (if) is followed by the aorist subjunctive form of the verb *come* and expresses an action that almost certainly will be completed. The phrase could be translated "when he comes to you." It alerts the congregation to prepare for Mark's visit and their ministry to him.

4:15 If Luke is the author of the Third Gospel and Mark (4:10) is the author of the Second, then Paul had close contact with two of the four writing Evangelists. Paul's appropriation

Further, Paul's phrase *mature and fully assured* extends his commentary on the importance of Epaphras's prayer for the Colossians. This phrase captures two themes in Paul's letter and therefore functions here to connect his concern for Epaphras with the content of what he has just written. According to O'Brien, the word *mature (teleios)* "touches on one of the key issues at Colosse in which members of the congregation were encouraged by false teachers to seek maturity or perfection through their philosophy (2:8) with its ascetic practices, visionary experiences and special revelations, rather than through Christ" (1982:253). Paul also uses this word to summarize his and God's purpose for mission: "so that we may present everyone perfect *[teleios]* in Christ" (1:28). The second term, *fully assured (plērophoreō),* belongs to the *plēroō* word-family, which Paul has used in confessing the core convictions of Colossian Christianity (1:9, 19; see also 4:17), in introducing his own mission (1:25; 2:2) and in arguing against the false teaching in Colosse (2:9-10). Paul's use of these two catchwords in describing the aim of Epaphras's prayer for the Colossians ties Epaphras with Paul in both the Colossian crisis and its resolution (see Lohse 1972:173-74).

This also may explain why Paul adds his extraordinary testimony of Epaphras's tireless campaign in the Lycus valley: *I vouch for him that he is working hard for you and for those at Laodicea and Hierapolis.* If we understand this comment in the light of the preceding one, Paul's reference to Epaphras's *working hard* may well combine with his *wrestling in prayer for you* to create a more favorable impression of him (so Schweizer 1972:240-41; Harris 1991:210-11). I am more inclined, however, to see it as a digression (as does O'Brien 1982:254), which allows Paul to *vouch* for Epaphras's commitment to the Colossian believers.

But why should Paul think his support for Epaphras is necessary now? Again, my speculation is that Epaphras, who is the principal architect of Colossian Christianity, has been discredited at home for some unknown

---

of Gospel traditions, however, is rather minimal; he seems interested in Jesus' death and resurrection more than his teaching and life, which are the substance of the Gospel narratives. Some modern scholars have even questioned whether Paul knew much about the Jesus of the Gospels. At least this point may be challenged by these references to the Evangelists, especially since Colossians was probably written after Mark wrote his Gospel.

reason, and that this has imperiled the work of the Gentile mission there. The coupling of *vouch* (from the word for "martyr," *martyreō)* with *working hard* (*ponos,* which emphasizes the painful outcome of hard labor) recalls the book of Revelation, where the faithful testimony (*martyria,* Rev 6:9) of the true disciple results in "pain" at the hands of evil powers and in the coming of Christ to bring this suffering to an end (*ponos,* Rev 21:4). Perhaps here too Paul uses these words to indicate that Epaphras is an exemplar of faithfulness, against the opinion of certain opponents.

Luke and Demas are joined together as they are in 2 Timothy 4:10-11; in the letter to Timothy, however, Demas has sadly deserted Paul "because he loved this world" (2 Tim 4:10), and Paul is left with only Luke. Whether Nympha is male (Nymphas) or female continues to be debated, since both forms are found in extant manuscripts of Colossians (O'Brien 1982:256). The question carries greater significance if a house church was generally led by the person who owned the home. If the homeowner here is a woman, as the NIV translation assumes, then a case could be made that female leadership was a part of the landscape of earliest Christianity. (Note also Paul's references to Priscilla in Rom 16:5 and 1 Cor 16:19, and Luke's narrative about Lydia in Acts 16, especially vv. 15, 40).

Final Instructions (4:16-17) The historical importance of Paul's final instructions is well known. On the basis of this single verse, a case has been made (first by Marcion around A.D. 150) that the letter of Ephesians is really this *letter from Laodicea*—a letter first written by Paul for Laodicean Christians and received from them by the Colossians, who passed it on to the Ephesians. This ancient opinion has received its modern draft by the eminent British scholar J. B. Lightfoot in the late 1800s and has since been widely accepted by others (see Wright 1987:160-61). On the other hand, Schweizer speculates that the Laodicean letter, rather than an edited book of Ephesians, might actually be the New Testament book of Philemon (1972:242), which I think is closer to the truth.

The case for the thesis that the *letter from Laodicea* is the New Testament Ephesians is cumulative, and it fails on two key points. First is the nature of the relationship between Colossians and Ephesians. Those who argue that the *letter from Laodicea* is Ephesians point out that the content of the two books is similar—a similarity that is obvious from even a cursory reading. On this basis, some contend that in 4:16 Paul's instruction is to read the two letters together, *the letter from Laodicea* with Colossians, presumably for a more nuanced understanding of the issues discussed in both letters. Historians argue, however, that a later composition will typically embellish upon and expand an earlier work. In this verse Paul writes that the Laodicean letter has already been written and sent, and that it has been read by the believers there; accordingly, it would be the earlier of the two letters. Yet clearly Ephesians is the fuller, more mature exposition of common themes; in the words of A. B. Hunter, it is the "quintessence of Pauline thought." More likely, Ephesians was written after Colossians and perhaps even depended on Colossians for its composition.

Second is the relationship between Ephesians and its first readers. This verse assumes that *the letter from Laodicea* had a specific address: the intended audience is the Christians at Laodicea. And if it had a specific address, we assume it also had a particular occasion: Paul wrote to the Christians at Laodicea to deal with a spiritual crisis there. But nowhere does Ephesians suggest that it was occasioned by a specific crisis in the life of a particular congregation. Probably it was written instead as an encyclical letter to circulate among several congregations for the purpose of instruction.

The more interesting historical aspect of this passage, in my mind, is its proposal to preserve and circulate Paul's writings—the earliest such proposal in the New Testament. Many speculate that the Pauline collection found in the New Testament had its origin in these instructions. More important, they illustrate why the church formed the New Testament: because a book written for a specific congregation was picked up by another and read for their spiritual benefit. The concerns of one related to the concerns of another. The writings subsequently gathered to form our biblical rule of faith were first picked up and read by congregation after congregation, from generation to generation, with spiritual profit. The *letter from Laodicea* was not preserved, even though it was written by the apostle, because it was not inspired by God to profit the wider Christian community (see 2 Tim 3:16). On the other hand,

Paul's letter to the Colossians was preserved and finally included in the New Testament because it was picked up and read again and again; the marks of God's inspiring activity were readily recognized by subsequent generations of believers, and we continue to this day to use Colossians for "teaching, rebuking, correcting and training in righteousness."

Archippus is mentioned in Philemon 2 as Paul's "fellow soldier." Here, Paul instructs him to *complete the work you have received in the Lord.* What that *work* is we do not know, although in Paul's writings the word for "work" *(diakonia)* generally refers to the work of ministry. The importance of Archippus's ministry is underscored by the expression *received in the Lord,* which may refer to a special commission not unlike Paul's own (compare 1:25). Houlden suggests that this ministry may be his leadership within the "headquarters household," mentioned in Philemon 2, and that Paul is reminding him of his strategic role for fear that he has fallen under the influence of the Colossian philosophy (1970:222). Indeed, the verbs *complete* (*pleroō;* compare 2:9-10) and *receive* (*paralambanō;* compare 2:6) recall Paul's contention that the "human tradition and basic principles of this world" (2:8), used by his opponents to promote an errant version of Christianity in Colosse, neglect Christ and so challenge the core convictions of his gospel (compare 1:25). In this light, perhaps Paul's instructions simply admonish Archippus to maintain the gospel of the Gentile mission in his house church.

Final Farewell (4:18) Paul prefaces his farewell with the assurance that this entire letter is from him and the request that the Colossians *remember [his] chains.* The exhortation to remember his imprisonment probably means to pray for his release (so O'Brien 1982:260; compare 4:2-4). In the wider context of Paul's writings, however, it may include an implicit request to pray for "the total work of the apostle . . . his preaching and his suffering on behalf of the entire church" (Lohse 1972:177). In the narrower frame of this benediction, it also serves as a reminder that the Colossians must now more than ever assume the hard work of Paul's missionary endeavor, since he is in *chains* (so Schweizer 1982:243).

Paul's letter closes as it began, in celebration of God's *grace.* Schweizer says this is as it should be, since "it is grace that represents the sole source of all effective power and help for both parties, the one who sends the letter and those who receive it" (1982:243). Paul finally asserts that God's empowering grace is *with you,* in the certain confidence that those who have participated in God's salvation with Christ will be sustained to the end.

Introduction to Philemon

The lasting importance of Philemon is not readily evident on first reading. It is an intimate letter, written to a slave owner, Philemon, to request that he forgive and even manumit his slave, Onesimus, and to reestablish a right relationship with him as a Christian "brother" and "partner." I contend, though, that the continuing importance of Paul's letter to Philemon for Christian nurture is precisely the same as for its first readers, even though currently it addresses different circumstances. Paul's point in writing to Philemon is this: *Spiritual conversion changes social relationships, making all equal in Christ.*

In Colossians, Paul wrote that faith in the Lord Jesus Christ necessarily results in the transformation of human relationships, including those between slave and owner (Col 3:5-17; 3:22—4:1). The apostolic preaching of the gospel yields this fruit because it is the trustworthy medium of God's salvation-creating grace (Col 1:3-12). God's grace abolishes evil, so there remains no social hierarchy of human value within the congregation that belongs to Christ. No social or economic class of believers is more important to God and to God's people than any other (Col 3:11). No believer should exercise power over another for selfish reasons. As disciples of Christ, himself a servant of God, we are servants of all, placing the interests of the other over our own (Mk 10:42-45; Phil 2:1-11).

The spiritual hierarchy within the faith community is based on its confession that Jesus Christ alone is Lord over all things (Col 1:15-20);

no other hierarchy is tolerated. The fruit of the gospel brings to an end our human tendency to arrange ourselves into classes, with certain people having power over other people. Simply put, Philemon illustrates the great theological truth that all believers have equal worth before God and all have equal access to God's grace; our relationships with others should embody this truth.

☐ Slavery in the First Century

To understand Philemon as an illustration of Paul's central moral claim that faith in Christ abolishes enmity between people (Eph 2:11-22), we must first of all understand something of Paul's social world.[1] Letters are not written in a vacuum but are shaped by the conventions and circumstances of the writer's world. Paul's letter to Philemon is certainly no exception to this rule of interpretation.

The Roman world of Paul's day was a complex society of classes. The empire's success and stability depended on maintaining proper relations between these social classes within many rural and urban cultures. The great majority of people belonged to the working class and lived a hand-to-mouth existence. Political and economic power belonged to the few who owned the farms and ruled the civil bureaucracies and the military. Life was hard and short for those who belonged to the working class. Without a network of influence, most workers were powerless to determine their destiny; upward social mobility was an impossibility for many.

One of the most important groups of workers was the slaves, especially within the urban culture. In the cities ruled by Rome nearly one-third of the population was owned, and a second third consisted of former slaves (freedpersons). Everywhere one looked, there were slaves living relatively normal lives. The slave class consisted of a variety of ordinary persons who were conscripted to work a variety of ordinary jobs. Some of these tasks were considered important in maintaining the cultural order, and considerable education and skill were required. Unlike the slaves and slave owners of pre-Civil War America, slave and master in the Roman Empire were often indistinguishable in race or religion, educa-

Notes: **Introduction** [1]Bartchy 1992b is the best available general introduction to the institution of Roman slavery. From a more detailed and scholarly perspective, the best of

tion or work. And even though it was against the law for a slave to own property, the historical record clearly shows that the opposite was more often true: slaves did own property and had money. So free people sometimes took the risk of selling themselves into slavery in order to find important and meaningful work—perhaps as often as impoverished parents sold their children into slavery so that they would survive.

Clearly, the treatment and status of slaves varied. The essential negative consequence of belonging to the slave class was that slaves had no legal right to the basic human freedoms granted to every Roman citizen, freeborn and freed. As a result, slaves were more easily exploited and abused. Whatever hope a slave had for a successful future was solely determined by the success of another—the master. A powerful owner determined the destiny of the powerless slave. Even if slave and master were equal educationally and financially, they were never political and social equals. Slaves were typically viewed as economic investments, and the owner had legal right to spend his dividend as he wished.

Some philosophers, especially among the Stoics, had taken up the cause of slaves in the Roman world, and by Paul's day certain reforms had been instituted to protect slaves from inhumane treatment. But no abolition movement existed, not even within the first-century church. The slaves formed a stable class of powerless people who generally served the interests of the powerful.

Another element of Paul's hierarchical and authoritarian world that may be especially important for our reading of Philemon was the patronage system. Similar to the slave-owner relationship, the interdependence of patron and client was useful in binding together higher and lower social classes of the social order. By supplying a letter of recommendation or even money in exchange for the client's loyalty and public expressions of honor, the patron would provide those on the lower end the opportunity to move up (Martin 1990:22-30). It may well be that the relationship between Onesimus and Paul was rooted in this social convention. Paul's letter to Philemon could be viewed as a patron's favor for his new client, Onesimus, helping to gain him a restored status within

several recent books on ancient slavery—both as a feature of the New Testament's social world and as a theological motif in Paul's writings—is Martin 1990.

Philemon's household and even in the Christian congregation that met in Philemon's home.

The earliest church was a part of this class-oriented world, and to a significant degree grew up in conflict with it. The memories of Jesus' ministry to society's least and last, coupled with Paul's insistence that in partnership with Christ all social barriers that prevent loving relationships between believers are dismantled, helped to form an alternative community within which slaves no longer were "investments" but rather sisters and brothers, even equal partners in the Christian enterprise.

Not surprisingly, the abolitionist movement in both North America and England had Christian roots. Most liberation movements within modern society have roots in biblical Christianity, because it teaches that every person—whether slave or free, black or white, male or female, rich or poor, influential or powerless—has an equal need for and access to God's saving grace and accepting love. God's salvation is offered to every person through Christ without prejudice. This spiritual truth is now embodied in the church's sociology: believers live together in common love and faith without prejudice in witness to God, whose love is poured out on every person equally. Philemon is today's reminder that relationships that accord with the values of God's reign represent an alternative to class structures and the enmity they naturally produce between people.

☐ The Occasion and Purpose of Philemon

In every letter of the New Testament is hidden a story about relationships—between author and first readers, between those readers and outsiders, between readers and God.[2] Many letters were written to repair broken relationships or fortify fragile ones. For instance, I think Paul's writing of Philemon was occasioned by two interrelated events that affected the relationship between two people. The first event destroyed the relationship between a slave, Onesimus, and his Christian owner,

---

[2]In contemporary scholarship, the most influential telling of Philemon's story is Peterson 1985. According to Peterson, Paul's letter to Philemon implies a story that begins with Philemon's conversion under Paul's ministry and the resulting spiritual debt (v. 19b), and continues with Paul's imprisonment (vv. 1, 9-10, 13, 23) about the same time that trouble between Philemon and his slave, Onesimus, developed (vv. 18-19a). This led Onesimus to seek out an imprisoned Paul for help in restoring his place in Philemon's household. Onesimus was converted by Paul and served him in prison (10-13). This creates a triangular

Philemon. According to verses 15 and 18, Onesimus had wronged Philemon in some significant way and had left his employment with some haste. Beyond this general scenario, we know few details: what were the circumstances that caused Onesimus to leave Philemon's household, and what possible peril has his wrongful departure produced for him?

Most scholars continue to suspect that Onesimus was a fugitive slave and left Philemon's service without permission because of some wrongdoing. Yet the evidence for this conjecture is quite meager. We know that Roman law gave Philemon permission to exact severe punishment for Onesimus's wrongdoing. However, we do not know whether Philemon was inclined to do so, or whether he was a Roman citizen and obligated to follow Roman law in any case. Even Paul's offer to repay Onesimus's "debt" in verse 19 may well be rhetorical and may not refer to an actual monetary debt (for the services of a slave). His expression of willingness to repay Philemon may therefore be ironical, underscoring that any relationship based on debts owed is wrongly conceived: there will always be someone else to whom a greater amount is owed.

In my view, many commentators exaggerate the peril of Onesimus's situation and the prerogatives of Philemon's social status. On this mistaken basis, some offer ingenious and highly influential reconstructions of the circumstances that occasioned the writing of this letter. For example, Knox, followed recently by Winter, argues that Archippus, a leader in the Colossian church (see Philem 2; Col 4:17), was the actual owner of Onesimus and thus the real recipient of the letter. Paul was asking Philemon, a Christian leader in Laodicea, to support his request that Archippus take Onesimus back without penalty. And Onesimus was the imprisoned Paul's messenger, carrying both Philemon—the "letter from Laodicea" mentioned in Colossians 4:16—and Colossians to Archippus at Colosse. As entertaining as Knox's story is, the lack of evidence from the text itself does not make it very convincing (see Winter 1987:1-15).

---

relationship in which Paul serves both slave and owner as spiritual patron. Paul acknowledges Philemon's good reputation and the work of his congregation (vv. 1-7) as the basis of making a request that wayward slave might return to compassionate owner to be reconciled (vv. 15-16) and restored (v. 17). With Onesimus, Paul sends this letter to Philemon with its offer to repay any necessary debt (vv. 18-19), with the prospect of Philemon's positive reply (vv. 20-21) and Paul's subsequent visit for confirmation (v. 22).

The second event, referred to in verses 10-11, was Onesimus's journey to Paul, who converted him to Christianity. Subsequently, Onesimus served Paul while in prison. From the letter we know nothing about the circumstances of their meeting or the legal nature of their relationship. Clearly, however, Paul's spiritual and personal relationship with Onesimus developed in the prison setting, and the apostle now feels compelled to intercede on this man's behalf. It should be said, against the opinion of a few modern scholars, that Paul does not seem at all interested in getting Philemon to grant Onesimus's services for himself (see Houlden 1970:225-26). Wright has correctly argued (1986:166-70) that the letter's wording suggests that Paul's single interest is for Philemon and Onesimus to be reconciled; he expresses no expectation of any personal benefit that might result. In fact, verse 15 seems to anticipate that Onesimus will stay on in Philemon's house rather than return to Paul's prison cell. Paul's tacit appeal to both his apostolic authority (v. 8) and future visit (v. 22) as well as the spiritual debt Philemon owes him (vv. 19-20) defines his role in the happy prospect of Onesimus's reconciliation with Philemon and manumission.

Paul may also wish to use his superior position to transform this troubled relationship, and perhaps to help Onesimus's standing within the congregation that meets in Philemon's home. While the latter element of Paul's purpose is rarely mentioned by commentators, the ecclesiastical metaphors Paul uses to contend for Philemon and Onesimus's reconciliation ("brother" and "partner") suggest that his real interest lies beyond Philemon's immediate household (which we know to include Apphia, his wife, as well as Onesimus), extending to the Christian church that meets in his home (Philem 3). Paul realizes that Onesimus's spiritual nurture is a corporate responsibility; since the Spirit is the resource of the faith community, nurture is carried out within the "household of faith" more than within Philemon's particular household.

The scenario recently suggested by Scott Bartchy is the most convincing to me. Building on his impressive knowledge of the legal aspects of Paul's social world—so critical to any discussion of slavery, whose var-

---

[3]Paul's interest in the entire congregation (rather than in just Philemon's spiritual well-being) is the point Derrett has recently made (1988:63-91). According to Derrett, Paul's real

ious aspects were carefully regulated by Roman law—Bartchy contends that Onesimus is not a fugitive at all (Bartchy 1992b). Rather, he is a slave who has done something that has turned out badly for Philemon—perhaps Onesimus is responsible for some loss of business or reputation (v. 18)—and turns to Paul to intervene on his behalf. Evidently Onesimus has heard enough about Paul from Philemon and from the congregation that meets in his home to know him as Philemon's much-respected friend and spiritual patron. Paul's evangelistic ministry had taken him into Asia Minor, where Philemon had heard the great apostle and come to faith under his ministry. No doubt Onesimus also is aware that, as Paul points out in the letter, Philemon owes Paul his very life (v. 19). Rapske even suspects that Onesimus, as a powerless slave, identified with Paul, a powerless prisoner, and appealed to him on that basis to bring pressure on Philemon to free him (Rapske 1991:187-203).

In short, Paul is Philemon's spiritual patron, and Onesimus goes to Paul to exploit this spiritual authority to his advantage. Finding him in prison, Onesimus himself becomes a believer under Paul's ministry. Paul becomes his spiritual patron and Christian brother too!

Bartchy correctly insists that Paul's ministry of reconciliation must be understood in the context of such a religious and legal "triangular scenario." That is, his appeal to Philemon, so carefully crafted in this letter, operates on a number of different levels. His purpose is to redefine Philemon's relationship to Onesimus: he wants to bring the two together into a new union with both spiritual and social consequences. His concern is for Philemon's spiritual nurture as much as for Onesimus's safety and status. In fact, it seems quite logical that with increased spiritual maturity, Philemon would recognize that if he is to treat Onesimus as a "partner" in Christ, he must stop treating him as his slave (v. 16) and manumit him.

Moreover, Paul's interest is for the entire fellowship.[3] In calling the congregation a "fellowship" (*koinōnia,* v. 6) and in naming himself and by implication Onesimus a "fellow" (*koinōnos,* v. 17), Paul links their common destiny, congregation and slave, to the decision Philemon is

---

concern is the implications of Onesimus's conversion for understanding the relationship of slaves to a congregation and to an owner who belongs to that congregation, especially in

asked to make. The emphasis on compassion *(splanchna)* in this letter confirms Paul's concern that the entire congregation first of all recognize Philemon as their spiritual exemplar, a status that is enhanced by his compassionate decision toward Onesimus. Second, Paul is concerned about Onesimus's future ministry and desires the church to include him in its gospel ministry as a spiritual equal, and now as the imprisoned apostle's personal agent in their midst. Until Paul is released from prison and can journey to Philemon's congregation for an apostolic visit (v. 22), he hopes that Onesimus will be an effective substitute and even a conduit for his apostolic gifts.

□ Paul's Imprisonment and Philemon's Onesimus

When we consider Paul's New Testament letters in the sequence they were written, we find that his understanding of God's relationship to those in Christ is constantly developing. While Paul's conviction that Jesus' death is messianic and redemptive remains unchanged, his understanding of the *implications* of Jesus' death grow and develop over time. Each personal experience and every new crisis encountered by his readers uncover new meanings for his firm and stable beliefs.

Prison changed Paul in two profound ways (see also the discussion of Paul's developing theology in my introduction to Colossians). In the letters he wrote from prison we find a diminished interest in Christ's Second Coming. In his early letters he seemed quite confident that Jesus would return in his lifetime (see 1 Thess 4:17), but that confidence seems to have shifted later, producing certain thematic shifts as well. In his prison writings, his emphasis is the present demonstration rather than the future disclosure of God's salvation, and therefore he focuses on the transforming results of Jesus' death and resurrection rather than the results of his return. Of course, Paul still hopes for Christ's return and believes in an end-time salvation; but this hope is no longer stated in

---

light of Deuteronomy 23:15; another key issue is the Christian nurture of a slave in comparison to other converts. These are points also raised by Barclay 1992:161-86. According to Barclay, the elements of the slave-owner relationship in the Roman world did not mesh with Paul's teaching about Christian relations. For Paul to have a "business-as-usual" attitude toward the conflict between Philemon and Onesimus could well have undermined the influence of his teaching at Colosse.

sharp apocalyptic tones. The cosmic transformation of all things is already under way in Christ (see Col 1:20).

Further, Paul emphasizes reconciliation within the church as a requisite for ministry. Paul's special vocabulary for the church in the prison letters envisions solidarity and equality: the church is "the body of Christ" (especially in Colossians and Ephesians), and the church is *koinōnia* (especially in Philippians and Philemon). This emphasis on an inclusive community in which all believers are equal partners is an important theological focus for interpreting Philemon.

Paul's own experience of powerlessness as a prisoner of Rome helps him identify with Onesimus's experience of powerlessness as Philemon's slave. Paul understands Onesimus's situation well. The rhetorical importance of his opening identification as "a prisoner for Christ Jesus" should not be glossed over, especially since he draws attention to his prisoner status repeatedly in this little letter. Typically, commentators are overly concerned with the historical why or where of Paul's imprisonment. Much more important is *how* his prison experience shaped Paul's understanding of the gospel: his sense of social alienation sharpened his understanding both of God's reconciling love and of the church's vocation to bear witness to that love in the world.

Perhaps the narratives of Paul's arrests found in Acts (e.g., 16:16-40; 21:27-36) help us understand the conflict provoked by Paul's ministry. Clearly, his preaching of the gospel challenged the convictions and values of the surrounding society; it signaled a whole new orientation toward life. Whether Paul's opponents were pagan merchants, as in Philippi, or Jewish religious leaders, as in Jerusalem, his preaching of the gospel called forth a community at odds with the prevailing economic and religious values. The gospel involves social as well as spiritual reform, and in Acts Paul's prison experience symbolizes the conflict between God's reign and the religious and political powers of this age.

Both of these scholars represent a shift in thinking about the purpose of Paul's letter, away from a simply personal intention (a concern for his friends and spiritual clients, Philemon and Onesimus) and toward a concern for the integrity of his mission and the well-being of this particular congregation. Significantly, these are concerns that Philemon shares with the other writings of the biblical canon.

Paul's prison writings, including Philemon, reflect this tension. These letters continue to serve the church as a pastoral exhortation that we are a people whose faith and life should challenge the social order (see Rom 12:2). When we continue to position ourselves to gain power over others rather than to empower them as agents of God's grace, our congregations and families will simply fail to bear witness to God in our world. As a result of this failure, the world's distance from God grows; society's various hierarchies—rich over poor, male over female, management over worker, government over citizenry, First World over Third World—become more repressive and dehumanizing; and God's grace is less able to penetrate a people hardened by the consequences of sin. Philemon promises, however, that God's grace is sufficient to transform power relationships within the church; and a transformed church will empower the social order for the good.

□ Philemon and the New Testament

Why did the early church include Philemon in the New Testament? What role in nurturing faith did the church imagine for Philemon? Some early Christian leaders, including the great Jerome, thought this Pauline writing should not be included in the biblical canon. In the second century, the ancient Syrian church dismissed Philemon because it supposedly deals with trivial things of life in this world (Lohse 1971:188). Many modern scholars agree, adding that unlike Paul's other epistles, Philemon is a private letter (verses 1 and 2, however, would seem to suggest otherwise; see my comments below). Philemon is so sparse in length and theological substance that many introductions to the New Testament do not include even a brief overview of it. Pastors, too, neglect Philemon, rarely finding it in the denominational lectionary or choosing to preach from it in any case: why bother, since its practical value for a modern readership seems to have diminished with the abolition of slavery?

In recent times a few scholars have even questioned whether Paul actually wrote Philemon; they say it lacks the magisterial tones of apostolicity. Most now do agree to Paul's authorship but contend that Philemon was added to the canon to give the more theologically substantial but deutero-Pauline book of Colossians a stamp of apostolic authority to justify its inclusion in the New Testament. John Knox, whose theory regarding the occasion of this letter I mentioned above, goes on to theorize that Philemon's Onesimus became Bishop Onesimus of the Ephesian church, and that it was he who later preserved and gathered together some of Paul's writings for circulation (Knox 1959). Knox hypothesizes that to give his Pauline collection greater authority, Onesimus included his own story within it.

Quite apart from these historical considerations, which are often too speculative to be of much use, the canonicity of Philemon is in fact a *theological* matter. Philemon continues to have authority in our lives because its content confirms and deepens our understanding of what it means to be God's people and to do as God's people ought. The ancient church recognized this book's divine inspiration through their use of Philemon in nurturing a Pauline (and therefore apostolic) understanding of Christian discipleship. Philemon was preserved by its first readers and eventually included in the New Testament because its readers have continually recognized the same thing: that Philemon is useful for forming a life and faith that is truly Christian.

Indeed, Philemon maintains certain theological convictions in common with other Pauline writings and shows how those convictions are applied to a particular relationship within a particular congregation of believers. The way Paul handles that situation continues to model how God's people should respond whenever social arrangements keep Christians from living out the truth that believers of all social backgrounds are equal in Christ. Thus, Onesimus represents all believers who are trapped in relationships and arrangements where they are powerless, while Philemon represents all believers who have power over others. Together, all the Philemons and Onesimuses of the world enter into Christ by faith, where everyone, whether slave or master, is reconciled with God and is one with all other believers. The difficult prospect we face, however, is to set aside our social differences and the values undergirding society's various hierarchies in order to build *koinōnia*—congregations of redeemed persons who have been given a new capacity to value and to love one another equally. Within Christ's church, God is an equal-opportunity God!

Brevard Childs has said that the church formed the New Testament canon in a way that would preserve a "dynamic" Paul whose theology, sense of mission and personal authority evolved over time and with controversy. Certainly, the New Testament always presents him as an authoritative preacher of God's gospel. But as indicated by his prison letters, the terms of his gospel were constantly adapted to the particular needs of particular audiences.

A growing, struggling, questioning church constantly needs a fresh word from God about how to respond to the Lord in faith and faithfulness. In my view, Philemon is such a word: in the midst of his new personal crisis, Paul addresses a new interpersonal crisis within a congregation of believers. The result is his letter to Philemon—a creative adaptation of the gospel to the life of God's people.

A final comment about the title of his composition is necessary. Titles to the writings in the New Testament canon, added long after they were written, reflect the intention of the church for Scripture rather than the intention of the authors themselves. In part, titles help us understand how scriptural writings should be read as a witness to God's gospel. Evidence within the document itself reveals that Paul did not write Philemon as a "private letter": he wrote it for Philemon as well as for all the other members of the congregation "that meets in your home" (v. 2). And yet the church's title for the canonical Philemon suggests that Paul wrote a private letter to a specific individual, that it addressed the crisis of a single believer (Philemon) and so that its ongoing purpose for Christian nurture is more personal than congregational. The discrepancy between the composition's title and its opening greeting forces us to ask: If the Bible's role is to form our Christian faith, and if each writing's title was chosen by the ancient church to guide the Bible's readers toward that end, how are we helped by viewing Philemon as resolving a personal crisis of faith?

My response to this important question is only provisional; I would point us to the biblical Wisdom tradition exemplified by Proverbs, the book of James and even by Jesus in the Sermon on the Mount (Mt 5—7). The Wisdom tradition keenly emphasizes the individual's obedient response to God's word and will. The whole is composed of parts, and the well-being of each part determines the well-being of the whole. There is, then, a corporate reason for the emphasis on personal action: the individual believer's response determines the destiny of the whole community. According to James, for example, the salvation of the entire community is imperiled by a single believer's abusive language (Jas 3:2-8). Perhaps a similar calculus interprets the title of Paul's letter: Philemon's response to Paul's request helps to determine the spiritual formation of the entire congregation that meets in his home. Further, those of us who adapt Paul's request of Philemon to the situations we face are reminded that our individual response of faith and obedience will have its positive effect in others.

This point is reinforced by the personal terms of Paul's request throughout the body of his letter. We are reminded by the letter's congregational address along with its private request that threats to a congregation's faith are sometimes focused in the struggles of an individual member. In such cases, sermons and exhortations, while delivered to the whole congregation, are actually intended for very specific ears, for we know that if the individual responds, the whole community will be restored and revived.

Outline of Philemon

1-3 ______ Paul's Greeting

4-7 ______ Paul's Prayer

8-22 ______ Paul's Request

- 8-9 ______ Paul's Relationship to Philemon
- 10-11 ______ Paul's Relationship to Onesimus
- 12-16 ______ Onesimus's Relationship to Philemon
- 17-22 ______ Paul's Relationship to Philemon

23-25 ______ Paul's Benediction

COMMENTARY

Philemon

□ Paul's Greetings (vv. 1-3)

The significance of epistolary greetings goes beyond identifying author and audience; it is more than saying hello. The author's salutation, however conventional and formal, specifies the nature of the relationship between author and audience and even draws lines around the conversation being carried on by the letter in hand. Meanings are more readily and rightly determined in terms of this "rhetorical relationship" formulated by the letter's opening words. Thus, Philemon and the others mentioned in verse 2 hear the following request for Onesimus's restoration in terms of Paul, whose importance (and therefore the legitimacy of his appeal) is made clear by his opening self-introduction: the author is *a prisoner of Christ Jesus.* It is a claim so important to Paul's purpose that he repeats it thrice in the body of this very short letter (vv. 9, 13, 23).

Paul's first audience is also made clear by his greeting. His address establishes an intimacy, even solidarity, with his readers—they are "dear brothers and sisters" and "coworkers and soldiers"—that can only increase the impact of his request and enhance the prospect of its compliance. And while it is true that Paul's salutation, found in verse 3, is rather conventional, it does present his essential understanding of what it means to belong to the church. He writes for the true Israel of God—an inclusive community called out of the world by the preaching of the gospel in order to bear witness to God's salvation within the world order (see commentary on Col 1:2). That is, the readers of Paul's letter must finally understand his subsequent request for Onesimus's restoration to reflect what it means to be the church and to do as the church ought.

The Author (v. 1) Paul's introduction of himself is both similar and dissimilar to his Colossians greeting (Col 1:1-2). As before, he refers to Timothy as his cowriter (in some sense) and calls him *brother* (see commentary on Col 1:1). Unlike Colossians, where Paul cites his apostolic credentials to give his subsequent polemic greater legitimacy, he refers to himself here as *a prisoner of Christ Jesus,* thus introducing immediately an important motif for the rest of his letter (see introduction). Certainly, Paul intends to convey more than his historical situation (contra O'Brien 1983:271); in fact, he is not first of all a prisoner of Rome but a prisoner of Christ Jesus. His appellation interprets his literal imprisonment as a worshipful act—an act of devotion to Christ, of obedience to his calling. Paul does not appeal to his apostolic office (see vv. 8-10), not because it might offend his readership, close friends all (contra Melick 1991:348), but because the personal costs exacted by his imprisonment "allow him to speak to the community with greater authority" (Lohse 1971:189).

The use of *prisoner* without the article is unusual and may suggest that Paul uses it as part of his proper name, which regularly is given without an article (Harris 1991:244). Since added names suggest the nature of a person's calling (Jesus is "Savior," Peter is "Rock"), Paul may well identify himself as Christ's prisoner to indicate the very substance of his missionary task and its costs. Further, he may be implying that the costliness of Christian ministry is the result of the revolutionary content of his message, thereby preparing Philemon for the revolutionary character of Paul's request of him. Paul's message bears witness to a new social

Notes: **1-3** Scholars often use Philemon as an example of the ancient literary genre of the religious letter. The four parts of a Pauline letter—greetings, thanksgiving, main body, benediction—serve as a helpful pattern for us to follow in studying Philemon. On the

order, and for that reason he finds himself in jail. This prepares us, then, for a radical word concerning the relations between a Roman slave and his owner.

While Paul's imprisonment represents his missionary identity, it is Jesus for whom Paul is imprisoned. The response Paul strongly desires from Philemon springs from his orientation toward discipleship: because of Christ Jesus, Philemon should respond favorably toward Onesimus, even though it may be costly and at odds with the surrounding social order.

The Audience (vv. 1-2) As the first person mentioned, Philemon is Paul's principal addressee. J. Knox contended that Paul's principal addressee is rather Archippus; his opinion, however, has not been accepted by scholars (see introduction; also see O'Brien 1983:266). Perhaps Philemon is named first because he is the patron of the household church that meets in his home and not because Paul's request will be directed primarily to him. Yet Paul's affectionate greeting of him as *dear friend and fellow worker* suggests a more significant intent. Actually, "dear friend" translates a single word, *agapētos,* "beloved one." Elsewhere in his writings Paul uses this as a term of affection for believers (Rom 1:7) and congregations (Phil 2:12). Paul further refers to Philemon as a *fellow worker,* which identifies him as one among others (see v. 24) who worked with Paul in the Gentile mission.

In his epistolary greetings, Paul's view of his addressees largely determines what is said to them and how they are treated. Paul views Philemon as a trusted and dear colleague and treats him as a peer and friend. Precisely this same attitude undergirds Paul's request that Philemon view the slave Onesimus as a brother and partner in faith.

Certainly, however, Philemon is not Paul's only addressee. Two other names are mentioned, Apphia *our sister* and Archippus, along with *the church that meets in [Philemon's] home.* The exact identities of Apphia and Archippus are unknown. Most scholars speculate that Apphia is Philemon's wife; her name is Phrygian, she is a Christian *sister,* known to Paul, and Paul places her name alongside Philemon's in the address

significance of epistolary greetings, see my commentary on Col 1:1-2.

1-2 For helpful introductions to household congregations within earliest Christianity, see Banks 1980 and Meeks 1983:74-110.

(Lightfoot 1876:306-8). Probably this Archippus is the one mentioned in Colossians 4:17, where Paul's cryptic exhortation suggests that he has fallen prey to the Colossian "philosophy" (see commentary on Col 4:17). The reference to him here as a *fellow soldier* tells a different story. According to O'Brien, the term Paul uses to address Archippus designates him as one who has "played an important part in assisting Paul in his missionary labors, and has faithfully stood at his side through persecution and trial—perhaps even imprisonment" (O'Brien 1983:273).

Paul's reference to the household church is important for two reasons. In the rhetorical pattern of this letter, Paul's opening address establishes an important contrast between a secular household, where slaves are an underclass and often exploited, and the Christian household or church, where slaves are loved and treated as equal partners in the faith. Also, Paul's reference to a household church reminds the contemporary reader that believers first met in private homes rather than in buildings in the public square. We should not suppose that living rooms are somehow better places to worship God than downtown sanctuaries. I am reminded of John's great vision of the New Jerusalem, in which he noted that he saw no temple during his tour of the city because "God and the Lamb are its temple" (Rev 21:22). Worship is not determined by places or buildings but by the spiritual vitality of the relationships between a people, God and the Lamb. In fact, Paul's reference to Philemon's house church may well indicate that Christianity was still an unofficial, underground religious movement in Colosse, or that it was such a new work that a social structure had not yet been fashioned. Nevertheless, Paul addresses his readers as the *church,* composed of people whom God has called out of the world for salvation.

The Greeting (v. 3) Paul's conventional greeting finally comes in verse 3, and as usual contains both the traditional Greek salutation, *grace (charis),* and the traditional Jewish salutation, *peace (eirēnē* = shalom). The theological point Paul's greeting makes is that for him the church of God includes every believer, whether Jew or Greek (see commentary on Col 1:2). In Philemon Paul adds the phrase *and the Lord Jesus Christ* (which many ancient manuscripts add to Colossians 1:2 as well) to indicate that the congregation receives its salvation-creating grace and its experience of "peace with God" from God through Christ (see Rom 5:1-11).

□ Paul's Prayer (vv. 4-7)

Some of the most significant explorations of the literary genre of Paul's letters have been in the second parts of his letters, where he gives thanks to God and then offers a prayer on behalf of his audience. Generally speaking, such expressions of thanksgiving and petition serve three purposes: (1) to establish good rapport between Paul and his first readers, so that they will respond positively to the advice that follows, (2) to set forth in the context of thanksgiving the religious ideals or moral virtues toward which the congregation should aspire, and (3) in the petitions offered, to introduce the spiritual crisis that threatens the readership's spiritual advance. Paul's epistolary thanksgiving functions, then, as a critical preface to what follows in the letter's main body (see also commentary on Col 1:3-12). Not only are specific goals established and a motive given for following the apostolic advice, but the crisis that might undermine these goals is sometimes suggested. We should take particular care to explore the meaning of the special vocabulary that Paul uses in this part of his letters, since it will often form the basis for the advice that follows in the main body.

In the case of Paul's letter to Philemon, the ecclesial ideals established in thanking God are *faith* and *love* (v. 5). The implied threats to these twin ideals are, first, whether the faith of Philemon (Paul's thanksgiving has a single person in mind) will be shared in a sufficiently active way (v. 6) and, second, whether his love, which Paul claims has given him *great joy and encouragement,* will continue to refresh *the hearts of the saints* (v. 7)—including Onesimus, as we will see.

Thanksgiving (vv. 4-5) Paul gives thanks to God for his friend Philemon. His language is emphatic—adding personal pronouns to emphasize that he is the subject of the sentence and Philemon is its object—and immediate, expressing the verbal ideas in the present tense. Not only is the content of Paul's thanksgiving formed by current reports of Philemon's faith and love, but Paul is ready to *always* thank God for Philemon's Christian witness. The iterative force of the present tense of Paul's thanksgiving impresses the reader with the security of their relationship: Paul continually gives God thanks for the continuing good reports he hears of Philemon's faith and love.

Paul often uses a triad of Christian virtues, such as faith, hope and love, to express his thanks to God for his readers; he highlights qualities that characterize mature Christian life (see commentary on Col 1:4-5). Although only two are mentioned in this letter, they constitute the Christian ideals he desires to find in Philemon's life. Certainly Paul reworks the triad to introduce his subsequent appeal: Philemon is characterized by the very virtues that will forge a restored relationship with Onesimus.

The Greek syntax of verse 5 is difficult and remains contested among commentators. Literally, the verse is a participial phrase that expresses the cause of Paul's thanksgiving: "hearing of your love and the faith that you have for *[pros]* the Lord Jesus and for *[eis]* all the saints." In untangling this verse's grammatical knot, Harris (1991:249-50) discusses its three possible meanings: (1) Philemon's *love* and *faith* may characterize his relationships with both the Lord Jesus and the saints (so NEB, JB, NASB); (2) Philemon's *faith* (but not his *love*) may characterize his relationships with both Jesus and the saints (so RSV); or (3) the verse may be an inverted parallelism (AB:B'A'), keyed by the two different prepositions for *for*. In this case, the "hearing of your love" is parallel to "for *[eis]* all the saints" and "the faith that you have" is parallel to "for *[pros]* the Lord Jesus." This third possibility is preferable (so Harris). Unfortunately, I think, the NIV obscures this parallelism by reversing its order. Paul actually mentions Philemon's *love* for the *saints* first and again last for emphasis, since his appeal to Philemon on behalf of Onesimus will require his love most of all.

Petition (vv. 6-7) After Paul thanks God for Philemon, he prays for him. The content of his petition actually reverses the terms of his thanksgiving: first he prays for Philemon's *faith* (v. 6) and then for his *love* (v. 7). O'Brien contends that Paul's intercessory prayer for Philemon is that he may acquire sufficient faith and love from God to respond favorably to the request to reconcile himself with Onesimus (1983:279). Most commentators, however, link the opening clause *that you may be active in sharing your faith* with *my prayers* (v. 4) rather than with *as I re-*

6 While *faith* is articular, "the faith," in verses 5 and 6, Paul is clearly speaking of Philemon's faith rather than a formal system of beliefs that Philemon might hold to. The use of the article renders Philemon's faith as a definite substance—something that is visible and demonstrable to others—rather than something inward and private, between Philemon and Christ only. More critical is the function of the genitive, "the sharing *of* your faith," in

member you (v. 4) as O'Brien would have it (see Harris 1991:250-51). Paul's prayer is not for Philemon's character, for which Paul has just given thanks, but for the *koinōnia* or *sharing* of Philemon's faith. In this case, Paul has in mind "the mutuality of Christian life which springs from a common participation in the body of Christ" (Wright 1986:175). He is mainly interested in the kind of fruit that God harvests in the relations between believers (see commentary on Col 1:5-12). Paul's implied prayer, then, is that Philemon welcome Onesimus gladly as an equal *koinōnos* (translated "partner" in v. 17) in the faith.

We should not underestimate the strategic importance of Paul's use of *koinōnia* to focus this petition for Philemon. Unfortunately, *koinōnia* is difficult to define with any precision (see Koch 1963:183-87; Wall 1992:1003-10; also Wright 1986:176; O'Brien 1983:279-81). In the ancient world, it defined a whole community of persons in which something is shared in common and as essential for life. In Paul's handling of this word, the community is a *koinōnia* in the sense of sharing a faith and missionary praxis. Wright adds that "Christians not only belong to one another but actually become mutually identified" (1986:176); that is, *koinōnia* takes place where believers recognize that other believers are essential for their well-being. Paul is therefore praying that Philemon's personal faith in Christ be worked out in appreciation of the important roles that other believers, including Onesimus, have in his spiritual formation in Christ.

Koinōnia, then, requires a particular understanding of the church's corporate life. God calls each believer into a congregation and provides each with certain gifts and opportunities to minister to other believers, so that all may be brought to maturity together in Christ Jesus (1 Cor 12; Eph 4:1-16). This sense of partnership marks out a congregation's *koinōnia* and is found where persons view one another as equals in worth and importance. It aims at partnership with Christ in God's salvation, so that with him we are able to find those resources necessary to enable

---

the context of Paul's petition. I agree with O'Brien and others (cf. Harris 1991:251) that the genitive is subjective and envisions the fruit that faith produces. That is, Paul assumes Philemon is a believer—a person who has faith; so he prays that Philemon's faith will produce the fruit of *koinōnia* that will extend to the likes of Onesimus.

us to minister, to love, to view one another as important and valuable. Christianity is about a transformation of the way we see and think about other people. When we begin to view others as those with whom life and faith are shared equally in Christ, arrogance and bigotry are finished.

Further, in referring to Philemon's *faith* Paul probably has in mind his public demonstration of Christian faith rather than his personal faith in Jesus Christ. While the immediate result of Philemon's faith is *koinōnia,* the ripple effect is extraordinary: out of the experience of *koinōnia* comes a *full understanding of every good thing we have in Christ.* Critically, the word translated "understanding" *(epignōsis)* refers not to theoretical knowledge but to knowledge acquired by experience. Paul is speaking about *every good thing* Philemon experiences while *in Christ,* where God's grace is found.

The NIV takes Paul's phrase *eis Christon* (literally "toward Christ") as meaning virtually the same as his important formula *in Christ* (see commentary on Col 1:2 and Col 1:15-17; also see O'Brien 1983:281). However, I think Paul's meaning here is telic (see Harris 1991:252-53) and envisions the christological aim or direction of spiritual formation. That is, our experience of divine grace moves us toward unity with Christ (Eph 4:13; see Wright 1986:177). In sum, Paul's first petition is that Philemon's faith produce *koinōnia,* which will enable the kind of understanding that matures him spiritually.

Paul's second petition is for Philemon's *love.* Unfortunately, the NIV omits a connecting "for" *(gar)* that links verses 6 and 7 together: ". . . we have in Christ. *For* your love has given me . . ." The impression left by the NIV is that verses 5 and 7 rather than verses 6 and 7 are bound together as complementary notes of Paul's thanksgiving for Philemon's spirituality. Paul's point, however, is to join verses 6 and 7 by a connecting "for" *(gar),* integrating them as a single petition (see Harris 1991:253). In this sense, verse 7 complements the central idea of verse 6, *koinōnia,* and reveals Paul's incentive for prayer: the essential characteristic of and incentive for *koinōnia* is love. Since Philemon's capacity to love is confirmed, Paul remains confident that his prayer will be answered by Philemon's positive response to his request. Yet in another more implicit sense verse 7 extends Paul's petition for Philemon's faith to include the prospect of a future demonstration of his previous love.

To further develop the connection of *love* and *koinōnia,* Paul introduces another catchword into the petition—*hearts (splanchna).* Like *koinōnia, splanchna* is a difficult word to translate. Literally it refers to human entrails. According to Greek psychology, however, one's *splanchna* or "guts" is where the visceral feelings of compassion are produced; compassion is a "gut feeling." The image created is that compassion is not a detached emotion; rather, it is an experience of lovers who are moved by and toward someone else. For example, Luke uses the verbal form of this same word in two of Jesus' most beloved parables to illustrate true discipleship: how the good Samaritan is disposed toward the rejected, hurt man (Lk 10:33) and how the father is disposed toward his prodigal son (Lk 15:20). Each had compassion on and was moved toward the needy other. Compassion is not to pity someone but to be drawn toward another in order to love and care for that person. One might draw intriguing parallels between Onesimus and the prodigal son and between Philemon and the son's father. The restoration of Philemon's relationship with Onesimus—receiving his troubled slave back into his home (see commentary on verse 17)—requires from him the very same compassion that was required from the father to welcome his prodigal son back home.

For Paul, compassion is both the capacity to love and the experience of being loved. His prayer for Philemon is for a greater capacity to love; but such compassion is also the experience of those *saints* he has *refreshed.* In this way, the compassionate heart is the mark of the *koinōnia* of shared faith. More important, Paul's prayer introduces in a positive way what the main body of his letter develops: that the compassion and so *koinōnia* of the congregation are now threatened by the problem between Onesimus and Philemon. Given Paul's twofold petition, then, the reader realizes that Philemon's response to Paul's appeal will largely determine whether the congregation's witness to the gospel in Colosse will survive.

□ **Paul's Request (vv. 8-22)**

The main body of any letter from Paul deals more specifically with the crisis at hand. In this case the crisis is neither doctrinal nor a confused morality; Paul does not write to correct Philemon or members of his congregation. Certainly, getting the ideas of Christian faith straight is always Paul's concern and therefore always at least implicit in his writings. In making his appeal to Philemon in this letter, however, Paul is mainly interested in getting relationships straight. For him, the essential fruit of the "word of truth" is transformed relationships—a point clearly and decisively developed in his letter to the Colossians.

To understand the full gospel is to be guided and empowered toward newness of life with and for other persons. Because such changes in our relationships demonstrate devotion to the transcendent Lord God, they are often at odds with the surrounding secular order. The social conflict that emerges from being the church in an anti-God world stems from the revising and reforming of relationships. It is on the border between these two conflicting worlds that Paul finds Philemon.

Paul's request is that Philemon provide more concrete evidence—adding to the faith and love already given (vv. 4-7)—that God has indeed "rescued him from the dominion of darkness and brought him into the kingdom of the Son God loves" (see commentary on Col 1:13-14). On the surface, the problem has to do with Onesimus's status as a slave and believer. However, on closer reading the real crisis proves to have more to do with Philemon's status before God than with Onesimus's status before Philemon. Philemon's exemplary status within the church is being tested by the decision he must make with respect to Onesimus. The real purpose of Paul's letter is to convince Philemon to make a radical choice of *splanchna* that will help to mark out his congregation as one where the *koinōnia* of faith is found. In this light, then, Paul's request intends two results: it intends a change in Onesimus's social status, presumably through his manumission, and it intends a change in Philemon's spiritual status, presumably through his reconciliation with Onesimus as a brother and partner in the faith.

Many recent scholars have called attention to Paul's rhetorical skill in crafting his appeal to Philemon. Literary analysis of Paul's letter reveals a conventional threefold pattern of "deliberative request," common in the ancient world, which seeks to persuade another to a different point

8-22 For the rhetorical patterns found in Philemon, see Church 1978:17-33; Peterson

of view while maintaining the integrity of both parties concerned.

The first part of such a writing, the "exordium," prepares the reader to hear a request by establishing a conducive atmosphere—of friendship, for instance, or worship (as in Heb 1:1-4). We may view Paul's epistolary prayers of thanksgiving and petition (vv. 4-7) as already functioning in this way. But if we want to study the main body of this letter as deliberative request, we need to understand that by setting aside his apostolic authority for the sake of his love for Philemon (vv. 8-9), Paul allows his audience to make a choice that is not coerced but will be issued with charity and integrity.

The second part of the request offers proof that the writer has the reader's (in this case Philemon's) best interests at heart. Thus Paul makes his appeal for Onesimus only after establishing that his relationship with Philemon is neither controlling nor coercive (v. 10). Paul's appeal is backed up by a series of reasons that a favorable decision for Onesimus would actually be to Philemon's advantage, enhancing his reputation as a Christian leader (vv. 11-16).

The final part of deliberative rhetoric is the "peroration," in which the author repeats his appeal but posits it on a more personal basis (vv. 17-22).

Paul's Relationship to Philemon (vv. 8-9) Paul's appeal to Philemon on Onesimus's behalf begins with irony: he sets aside his apostolic authority, along with the more assertive, demanding argument it would yield, for a more gentle form of persuasion. In defining his relationship to the church along lines of friendship, finally stressing his need for Philemon's love (v. 9), Paul establishes that his intent is not coercive but collaborative.

O'Brien says that the word translated "boldness" *(parrēsia)* refers to Paul's openness to speak intimately to Philemon, and he contends that to understand this word in terms of political authority is incorrect (1983:287-88). Yet by coupling it with *order,* which usually refers to an authoritative demand given by one in a superior position over another, Paul suggests that candor is justified by his right to rule. That is, the

1988; Schenk 1987; and Bartchy 1992a.

apostle could make demands if he wanted; he could force Philemon on religious grounds to do what he asks. This passage may even be a caveat, warning Philemon that his position within the church could be imperiled if he fails to comply with Paul's request.

However, the opening conjunction, *therefore,* already indicates that Paul's appeal will correspond to his prayer for Philemon, in which he thanks God for his friend's love. His use of *in Christ* roots his appeal in a place where God's salvation is shared and where any legal or fraternal obligation Philemon feels toward Paul can only be deepened and secured. This is why Paul's *appeal* to Philemon is tendered *on the basis of love.* As Wright points out, Paul seeks a free decision rather than a coerced obedience, since this is the more loving and Christian way (1986:180).

The word translated "appeal" *(parakaleō)* is part of Paul's special vocabulary. In Paul's use, it rarely implies a contrast to a command that might have been made instead. Rather, Paul usually "appeals" for prayer for some personal difficulty or for others' support (for instance, Rom 15:30-31). This deeper logic informs our understanding of the passage. First, it provides another, more implicit link between Paul's appeal and his earlier prayer for Philemon: his request is based on the confidence of answered prayer that Philemon will act compassionately *(splanchna)* toward Onesimus and so increase the sense of partnership *(koinōnia)* within their household congregation. Second, Paul's appeal naturally draws attention away from personal authority and to personal need: he is an *old man and now also a prisoner.* Paul's appeal is rooted, therefore, in his awareness of his own need for Philemon's generous support.

The meaning of *old man (presbytēs)* is contested. Harris, agreeing with O'Brien (1983:290), prefers to understand it as "ambassador" (1991:259-60). But this would require us to substitute another, albeit almost identical, word *(presbeutēs)* for the one Paul actually uses. Without textual support, even with Lightfoot's claim that the two are almost identical in meaning, I am reluctant to agree. Paul's appeal is not made as an "ambassador" of Christ but as an *old man* who has great emotional and physical need of Philemon's love. Against Wright, who argues for a symbolic meaning of age (1986:180), I think that Paul's advancing age and imprisonment have literally cost him dearly. The difficulty of his circumstances now obliges Philemon to come to his aid by granting his request. Paul's appeal is made within a culture where the request of an elderly person would be granted; not to do so would have been considered shameful (Bartchy 1992a).

Paul's Relationship to Onesimus (vv. 10-11) Paul now introduces Onesimus into his letter, yet not first of all as Philemon's slave but as Paul's *son.* Paul does not tell the story behind this letter; letters are not narratives, even though a letter may imply the story of its occasion (see introduction). So we do not know the details of how Onesimus found Paul in prison, under what circumstances or why; nor do we know how he became a believer.

Why Paul waits this long to mention Onesimus in his letter is yet another matter of speculation. To contend that Paul delays referring to Onesimus because he fears offending Philemon or feels Philemon must first be "buttered up" is unwarranted (see O'Brien 1983:290). Rather, this first mention of Onesimus is part of Paul's rhetorical strategy: repeating his appeal (first made in verse 9) in terms of Onesimus's conversion and transformed character (v. 11) will more effectively persuade Philemon to do what Paul requests. Moreover, Paul's appeal presumes that his relationship with Onesimus will prove decisive in moving Philemon toward a new perception of his slave.

Paul defines his relationship with Onesimus as that of a father and son. While *son* is often found in Jewish writings as a metaphor for the student of a rabbi, it probably is used here as a metaphor of conversion. Paul uses it with *became (gennaō),* as in the birth of a son. In this way "Paul views the process of bringing Onesimus to spiritual birth in a comprehensive glance" (Harris 1991:261). While considerable affection seems to be implicit in Paul's emphatic reference to Onesimus as *my son,* Paul's primary purpose is to declare Onesimus a true believer. Further, Onesimus's conversion obligates him to Paul in the very same way Philemon's does: both are Paul's spiritual sons. This will become important when Paul seeks to redefine the nature of Onesimus's relationship to Philemon: as Paul's sons, they are now brothers (see v. 16; so O'Brien 1982:291).

Onesimus's name derives from a root that means "beneficial" (compare v. 20), and his service to an imprisoned Paul is testimony to his name. Onesimus is introduced into the sentence last and in apposition to Paul's reference to his conversion. Thus, his name may well be his new Christian name, indicating his new birth in Christ.

This possibility seems plausible because of the additional statements of verse 11, which extend the importance of Onesimus's name. The idiom "then . . . but now" *(pote . . . nyni de)* is employed frequently by Paul to introduce the general results of Christ's death and the specific results of conversion. In the case of Onesimus, conversion in Paul's prison cell has resulted in his personal transformation: once he was *useless (achrēstos)* but now he is *useful (euchrēstos).* These two words are frequently contrasted in ancient moral literature and typically refer to a person's character more than to the quality of one's work (O'Brien 1982:291-92). According to Paul, the gospel yields the fruit of virtue; spiritual conversion results in a better person who enjoys transformed relationships with others (see commentary on Col 3:5-11).

This point is deepened by the recognition that the common root of these two words *(chrēstos)* sounds the same as the word for Christ *(Christos).* Wright argues that Paul uses a pun, as was common in ancient literature, to draw attention to the changes that have taken place in Onesimus now that he is in Christ (1986:182). This pun may have additional value in reminding Philemon and his congregation that Onesimus's personal transformation illustrates the sort of change that Christ's death initiates (see commentary on Col 1:21-23).

Yet Paul is emphatic that the results of Onesimus's transformation benefit not only himself but also Philemon: Onesimus *has become useful both to you and to me.* What an extraordinary claim! We can surely imagine how Onesimus has been a blessing to the imprisoned Paul in his old age; but it is surprising to learn that the departed Onesimus may be useful to Philemon as well. Paul mentions Philemon first, since he will no doubt want to see for himself the dramatic change that has taken place in Onesimus before he grants Paul's request (so Lohse 1971:201). In any case, the point is rhetorical: Paul's surprising assertion provides the focal point for the next part of his appeal. The practical reason Philemon should agree to Paul's request has now been introduced: because Onesimus is useful to you too.

Philemon's Relationship to Onesimus (vv. 12-16) Paul claims that Onesimus's conversion has resulted not only in his personal transformation but in his usefulness to Philemon. This new situation could not have been immediately clear to Philemon; after all, Onesimus's apparent uselessness has caused him to seek Paul's help, and he is still a slave who is the likely object of Philemon's displeasure (see introduction). In this light, the next section of Paul's letter answers Philemon's unspoken but rather practical question: *How* is the believer Onesimus now useful to me? Why should Paul send him back to me?

Several recent commentators have argued that Paul is probably not motivated to send Onesimus back to Philemon for legal or financial reasons. Onesimus was probably not a fugitive slave; Philemon was probably not a Roman citizen; and in either case Roman law is unclear on what Paul's responsibilities were in this triangular relationship (see introduction). Clearly, Paul steadfastly resists thinking of Philemon as Onesimus's legal owner. The story behind Paul's appeal is a profoundly religious one and has social implications: Philemon is to regard Onesimus as his Christian "brother" (v. 16) and "partner" in the faith (v. 17), which makes their owner-slave relationship no longer possible. So Paul is sending Onesimus back to Philemon for their reconciliation; they are both his spiritual sons, and he is the religious patron and responsible for the nurture of both. In my view, under these new and revolutionary circumstances Philemon's only real option is Onesimus's manumission.

Against this religious background, Paul describes Onesimus's twofold usefulness to Philemon: first, he has been Philemon's effective substitute in serving Paul's needs in prison (vv. 12-13), and second, he will be an effective stimulus to Philemon's spiritual growth as his brother in Christ and his partner in the life of the congregation (vv. 14-17). Both benefits are finally understood and appreciated in terms of Paul's paternal and patronal relationship with his two spiritual "sons" and clients; both benefits intend to redefine Philemon's relationship with Onesimus so that Philemon will see Paul's request for their rapprochement (and no doubt for Onesimus's manumission) as in his best interests. In fact, once this particular slave-owner relationship is skillfully redefined by Paul, Onesimus's newly perceived usefulness to Philemon may be rewarded with manumission on more common grounds: a slave's effective service to his master.

The biblical story of Philemon and Onesimus tells its current hearers that our common status in Christ is more than simply a spiritual or eschatological reality. When Paul writes that there is neither a slave nor a master class in Christ, since all are equal (see commentary on Col 3:11), he is articulating a principle that is sociological as well as christological (compare Gal 3:28; Eph 2:11-22). While the social dimension of the gospel should not replace the call to a saving relationship with the Lord, we must understand that God's grace rearranges the various conventions and hierarchies that order society's status quo (that is, "the present evil age"; see Rom 12:2; Gal 1:4). Biblical believers, then, are not surprised that the great majority of the social-transformative movements, such as the nineteenth-century women's suffrage and abolitionist movements and the twentieth-century human rights and prolife movements, are deeply rooted in Christian teaching and indebted to the work of faithful Christians (see Dayton 1990). In my view, the importance of Philemon within the New Testament collection of Pauline letters is that it provides a concrete illustration of this important element of Pauline teaching. So we need to preach and teach Philemon, to remind each other that Christian discipleship includes both a personal and a public praxis.

Onesimus as Philemon's Useful Substitute (vv. 12-13) In justifying his appeal that Philemon take Onesimus back into his home, Paul is well aware that Onesimus's solicitation of his support has created a delicate situation: a non-Christian slave has come to the apostle, in prison, to gain some advantage over his Christian master. He must make reconciliation possible by asking a trusted colleague for a radical act: the manumission of his slave (see introduction). The motives to which Paul appeals are deeply rooted in Philemon's spiritual obligations to him as spiritual father.

First, Paul is not *sending* Onesimus back to Philemon, who is probably not a Roman citizen, for legal reasons to secure his official consent (see above; here I differ from O'Brien, Wright and others), but rather because he is Paul's *very heart* (or *splanchna,* which means compassion; see commentary on verses 6-7). For this reason, Paul states his personal preference that Onesimus remain with him in prison.

While it is not clear why Paul should speak of Onesimus as his *very heart,* two possibilities seem best: (1) the imprisoned Paul may be designating Onesimus as his agent, so that by delivering this letter to Philemon, Onesimus can be the mediator of Paul's *heart* (or compassion) in his absence (O'Brien 1982:293); or (2) Onesimus himself may be a source of compassion for the imprisoned Paul. I am inclined toward the second meaning, since it best explains Paul's hesitancy in sending Onesimus home. He has been Paul's faithful servant (v. 13) and has been his only source of compassion while he is *in chains for the gospel.* Yet when Paul prayed for Philemon's compassion in verse 7, *heart* was coupled with *koinōnia* and indicated the requisite capacity of a nurturing congregation. Perhaps Paul implies the same here: Onesimus is useful to Philemon as one who has the capacity for compassion and therefore can help Philemon and his household church reach its ideal of *koinōnia* (see Phil 1:5).

A second and perhaps more critical reason is located in the purpose clause at the end of verse 13, where Paul says that Onesimus's ministrations are *so that he could take [Philemon's] place.* Paul's language is of substitution, suggesting he "assumes that Philemon would have wished to attend to Paul's needs personally if such had been possible" (Harris 1991:264). Such are the obligations of the spiritual son to his father and of the indebted client to his patron. Moreover, Paul has already expressed his confidence in Philemon's capacity and readiness to dispense compassion in order to build Christian partnership (v. 7). Rather than stressing Onesimus's usefulness as *his* substitute or proxy, Paul underscores Onesimus's usefulness as Philemon's substitute in the important work of heartfelt servanthood (see commentary on vv. 18-19). Ironically, Onesimus continues to function as Philemon's slave, but now as Paul's servant.

Finally, Paul's word choice for *helping (diakoneō)* is striking because it comes from a different word for "slave" from the one he then uses in verse 16 *(doulos).* According to O'Brien, Paul uses words from the *diakoneō* family when speaking of gospel ministry (as in Col 1:7, 23, 25; 4:7, 17) rather than of the degrading work associated with a prisoner's slave (1982:294). But it seems to me that Paul's intent is more ironical: Onesimus is no longer a slave (*doulos,* v. 16), even though his labor of love could well be seen as degrading work; rather, he is Paul's minister and therefore a useful substitute for Philemon. On this basis, then, Philemon's manumission of Onesimus can be rightfully granted.

Onesimus as Philemon's Useful Brother in Christ (vv. 14-16) A second purpose clause, *so that any favor you do will be spontaneous and not forced,* focuses the second part of Paul's explanation of Onesimus's usefulness to Philemon, and why his manumission (that is, the specific *favor* asked of Philemon) makes good sense. Why is Paul concerned that Philemon not be pressured into this decision? Surely Paul understands that Philemon may perceive him as exploiting their relationship to Onesimus's unfair advantage. Under such circumstances, his granting Paul's *favor* would be a hollow triumph and might even create bitterness between them. Sharply put, Paul here imagines a situation where his explicit appeal (manumission) is granted, but its implicit objective (reconciliation) is not accomplished. Paul's solution to this potential problem is to maintain Philemon's honor: the condition for the *favor* is that it be *spontaneous and not forced;* it must be an act of worship, freely offered to God (see O'Brien 1982:294-95).

In light of his concern for Philemon's honor, Paul's anticipation of the spiritual aftermath of Onesimus's manumission transforms the conventional perceptions of the relationship between a manumitted slave and his former master. Yet even before describing this new perception in verses 16 and 17, Paul mentions that Philemon's choice must be pressure-free and made in the awareness that his separation from Onesimus was short-term and not permanent (v. 15). While the meaning of the phrase *he was separated from you* remains contested among scholars, many now take it as a reference to the outworking of God's will rather than to Onesimus's fugitive status. The verbal voice is passive, implying that something or someone besides Onesimus is responsible for Onesimus's action. (O'Brien calls this a "divine passive" because it suggests the working out of God's will; 1982:295.) Further, Paul couples this phrase with the adverb *perhaps (tacha),* which is sometimes used in Jewish literature to introduce a theological exposition. For Paul, Onesimus's departure provides the setting for the work of God. Thus, Chrysostom's suggestive comparison of this text with the Old Testament Joseph story about divine providence (Gen 45:4-8; 50:15-21) seems quite right to me (see O'Brien 1982:295; Wright 1986:184-85): in both cases, God's redemptive purposes are achieved by the act of freeing a slave.

Given the importance of allusions to Old Testament types and texts in Paul's writings (see Hays 1988), Paul may have the Joseph story in mind as he writes his appeal to Philemon. That is, Paul recognizes Onesimus to be a type of the biblical Joseph. The relationship between the two may well suggest Paul's principal theological conviction in this case: God's good intentions for people are often worked out in the redemptive consequences of choices that free brothers make about slave brothers. Of course, in Joseph's story a bad choice (brothers' selling another brother into slavery) results in a good end because of divine intervention. In this case, Philemon's good choice (a "brother" manumitting another "brother" from slavery) would result in a similar end. From God's perspective, then, Philemon's favorable decision, which has been shown to make sense in light of Onesimus's past usefulness to him, would make even more sense when he considers the prospect of a redemptive result.

The intriguing comparison between *for a little while* and *for good* (*aiōnion,* literally "for an eternity") refers less to a changed social status (although see Harris 1991:266) than to the eternal destiny of both brothers, Philemon and Onesimus, who will share together the salvation of God (so O'Brien 1982:296). Paul's point is not that our decisions about social conventions bear witness to our convictions about God; rather, our convictions about God ought to prompt our decisions about the social order. Because Philemon trusts that God purposes good ends for God's people, Paul trusts that he will make a natural, free decision about Onesimus that will result in good.

Curiously, Wright does nothing with his interesting suggestion that Paul's use of *aiōnion* is an allusion to the teaching on Hebrew slaves found in Exodus 21 (1982:185, n. 1; see also Moule 1968:156). According to the legal code in Torah, the slave who rejected his sabbath manumission in order to stay with his master (see Ex 21:1-5) was first "brought" by the master *to God* as the condition for "lifelong" (literally "eternal") service (see Ex 21:6). In the Old Testament, God and eternity together frame a central tenet: whatever God's people consecrate to their eternal God in worship must then be embodied in their ongoing life together. I would argue that this is Paul's point here: Philemon is expected to make decisions toward his slave that embody his worship of God.

The results of Philemon's act of worship in manumitting Onesimus are twofold: (1) Onesimus is no longer a slave but a *brother* (v. 16), and (2) Onesimus is no longer a slave but a "partner" (v. 17). In both senses of their new relationship as brothers and partners in Christ, Onesimus acquires new responsibilities of spiritual usefulness to Philemon.

Some scholars do not think Paul envisions Onesimus's manumission from slavery, since *no longer as a slave* refers to his spiritual but not social status. While I agree that Paul chooses his words carefully, I do not agree that he makes a formal distinction between the social and spiritual realms so that the two cannot be fully integrated in Christ (see commentary on Col 1:15-20 and 3:22—4:1). The phrase makes a rhetorical point: Paul does not presume Onesimus's emancipation because such a decision is Philemon's to make freely, so the presumption would contradict Paul's earlier statement (v. 14).

Further, to contend that Philemon can make perceptual but not substantial changes in his relationship with Onesimus fails to integrate "seeing" with "doing" in the new creation. If Philemon decides to "see" Onesimus *as a dear brother* (compare this with Paul's greeting of Philemon in verse 1, "dear friend"), then his decision must be to emancipate him. Paul's additional phrase *he is very dear to me but even dearer to you* recalls his earlier expression of love for Onesimus as his "son" (v. 10). If both Philemon and Onesimus are Paul's spiritual sons, then they are indeed brothers in the Lord.

The fundamental shift of Onesimus's social status from "slave" to "dear brother" is repeated in the phrase *both as a man and as a brother in the Lord.* Again, Paul does not suppose that the social (*as a man,* literally "in the flesh") and the spiritual *(as a brother)* can be kept as two disjointed spheres of human existence. While God's creation includes both the visible and the invisible, they are integrated and held together by the one Lord. Thus, the spiritual well-being of the congregation will always be demonstrated publicly by the well-being of its

16 The intriguing interplay between the superlative ("very much dear") and comparative ("even more dear") forms of *mala,* which are tied together by "how much more" *(posos),* reflects the rabbinical rhetorical device called *Qal Wehomer,* which makes something great-social relationships (see commentary on Col 1:3-12; 3:1-11; 3:12-17). Harris's interpretation, so common among evangelicals, that Paul is speaking of a change of attitude rather than a change of social relationship—so that Onesimus will resume his position as a household slave, as before his conversion (Harris 1991:268)—fails to observe the calculus of Paul's gospel. In fact, Paul's letter to Philemon clarifies and extends the ethical implications of the gospel set forth in the household code of his letter to the Colossians (3:22—4:1). The book of Philemon's moral vision is that social hierarchies, such as the one between a powerful owner and his powerless slave, are dismantled in Christ. The presence of *koinōnia* within a society of classes, hitherto divided between those who have power and value and those who do not, gives public testimony to the empowering grace of God.

Paul's Relationship to Philemon (17-22) In conclusion, Paul returns to his relationship with Philemon (see 1:8-9) in order to restate his request for Onesimus's manumission in terms of four demands, which are predicated on his (vv. 10-11) and Philemon's (vv. 12-16) relationship to the slave. Critically, Paul makes each demand of Philemon with the exchange of Paul's payment for Onesimus's debt in mind (see Peterson 1985:290-91). While Paul addresses Philemon in an emphatically personal way, each demand, tied to the idea of an exchange, illustrates Paul's Christology: Christ became what we are so that we might become what he is (see especially the commentary on Col 1:18-20).

The logic of Paul's words is inescapable: If Philemon and Onesimus are indeed brothers in Christ and spiritual children of Paul, then they are also partnered with Christ to participate together in God's salvation. Christ's exchange for their common salvation obligates Philemon (and Paul too!) to exchange his right to Onesimus for his salvation (or manumission). Each demand Paul makes aids Philemon in understanding that Christ's exchange for him must be concretely demonstrated by welcoming his slave home as an equal *partner (koinōnos)* in the *koinōnia* of the congregation's life (v. 17); or by paying another's debt (vv. 18-19);

er than a good thing that much greater. Restating this phrase in terms of a *Qal Wehomer*, then, Paul's implied argument is that "if Onesimus is dear to me, how much more greatly should he be dear to you, Philemon."

or by showing compassion (for a third time, *splanchna* is used) toward another (vv. 20-21); or by providing a room in his home to a guest (v. 22). Such are the requirements of being a new creature in Christ.

Paul surely recognizes that Onesimus constitutes a testing of Philemon's faith in Christ, even as he knows that Philemon's willingness to exchange personal rights for a generous response will not only produce greater *koinōnia* in his household but also demonstrate publicly that he has been transformed by God's salvation-creating grace. Paul is the patron of both men; thus, while he asks for Onesimus's emancipation, he seeks to secure Philemon's honor and standing within his church.

Welcome Onesimus as Me! (v. 17) The first exchange of the imprisoned Paul for the returning Onesimus has to do with their common status as *partners (koinōnoi)* within the faith community (*koinōnia;* see commentary on v. 6) to which Philemon also belongs. As a theological abstraction and spiritual reality, this substitution is perhaps not terribly difficult to swallow. Onesimus's recent conversion to Christianity did result in a new parity with both Paul and Philemon. They are all believers; they all share the very same promises and convictions; they are partners, some more senior than others, in the same religious "firm."

Yet Paul demands that Philemon *welcome* Onesimus as though *he* were Philemon's apostle and patron. The verb translated "welcome" *(proslambanō)* suggests the personal reception of one into another's home—a hospitable "homecoming" (Harris 1991:272). There is nothing abstract about this substitution, since it presumes an actual encounter between two persons. Onesimus is a crisis that Philemon cannot avoid; his conversion cannot be acknowledged from afar. Philemon must deal with Onesimus in person, first recognizing and honoring him as Paul's substitute, but then welcoming him as though he were a spiritual partner like Paul within the very household he once served as a slave.

Paul's challenging request serves a practical end. He realizes that religious conversions, such as those experienced by both Philemon and Onesimus, have very public results; they are not events that just happen to one and are then privatized and compartmentalized so they do not intrude on one's other activities. Conversion joins the believer with Christ in the cosmic salvation of God, whose grace transforms every aspect of human life. Philemon and Onesimus both must realize, as we all must, that in the crisis of a difficult reunion, we are sometimes forced to admit that how we relate to one another has changed with the changes that have taken place in us. For example, the changes that have taken place in our son, who is away from home at college, and in us, who experience a home without him, have changed forever the way we talk to and think about each other.

The previous arrangement between Onesimus and Philemon as slave and owner has been changed by their experience of grace. They are now *partners (koinōnoi)* in a *koinōnia,* where they share a new capacity to love one another as never before. The result of granting Paul's request is envisaged by the coupling of the words *partner* and *welcome* in characterizing the homecoming of Onesimus: he will be included as a member of the congregation, the equal of everyone in the house he once served as slave. Philemon is no longer his lord but a brother; they are partnered together with the Lord Jesus for their mutual salvation.

Charge Onesimus's Debt to Me! (vv. 18-19) The second demand Paul makes of Philemon is ironical. On the one hand, the reader supposes that Paul is offering to make good whatever financial or business loss Philemon has suffered as a result of Onesimus's failure (whatever that might be). While Paul owes Philemon nothing, even as Christ owes us nothing, he involves himself in Onesimus's affairs in order to pay his debt, whether financial or interpersonal, even as Christ (who knew no sin) took upon himself the sins of us all (so Rom 5:6-11). Paul's involvement has a firm christological basis.

Yet behind Paul's offer is the common awareness that he is Philemon's spiritual patron—that Philemon is obliged to Paul even as Onesimus is. At day's end, then, Paul's offer to pay Onesimus's costs—*if he has done you any wrong or owes you anything*—is canceled by Philemon's own debt—*you owe me your very self.* The force of Paul's words is neither coercive or paternalistic but firmly persuasive. Even the rhetorician's trick of mentioning the unmentionable (*not to mention that you owe me;* compare v. 8) does not seem heavy-handed (see Wright 1986:188). It rather calls attention to what is true about Paul's relationship with both Philemon and Onesimus and perhaps explains, therefore, why he requests a change in Onesimus's status but then offers to pay all his debts: the spiritual reality (what Philemon owes Paul) naturally yields a social result (what Paul requests of and offers to Philemon).

Harris says that the final reference to Philemon's debt to Paul in verse 19 qualifies Paul's offer to pay off any monetary debts; however, there are no legal debts in view (see introduction). Paul's concern is reconciliation, not the settling of debts (Harris 1991:274); and reconciliation will have its result in Onesimus's freedom.

Further implicit in Paul's offer is that Onesimus himself has satisfied Philemon's obligation to Paul (and therefore paid his debt in full) by taking care of Paul's needs while in prison (see commentary on v. 13). Behind the prospect of Paul's exchange, then, is the satisfaction of Onesimus's. What Paul offers to do as an agent of God's reconciling grace has already been done by Onesimus! There is a sense, then, that Onesimus has already proved himself as Philemon's *brother* and *partner;* it is left then to Philemon to acknowledge his debt to Onesimus by treating him as his *brother* and *partner* as well.

Show Me Compassion! (20-21) The NIV fails to translate Paul's opening "yes" *(nai),* which introduces his subsequent wish as a more emphatic repetition of his request that Philemon welcome Onesimus as a *partner* (Harris 1991:275). While Paul recognizes that such a radical departure from social convention would derive from Philemon's status *in the Lord,* he also recognizes in the parallel phrase that Philemon has a proven capacity for "refreshing hearts" (see commentary on vv. 6-7). Now, having made his request, the apostle translates his earlier thanksgiving into an emphatic, personal demand: Philemon, *refresh my heart in Christ.*

Again we find that in concluding his request, Paul emphasizes Philemon's spiritual capacity to *refresh my heart* (*splanchna,* v. 20). The believer's participation *in the Lord / in Christ* transforms his capacity to act in "refreshing" ways that build *koinōnia* (see commentary on vv. 6-7). Paul's confidence that Philemon will treat both him and Onesimus, for whom he is substitute, in the same way he has treated the other saints is based on what takes place *in Christ.*

Prepare My Room! (v. 22) The final demand seems to be made as an afterthought: *And one thing more: Prepare a guest room for me.* Yet Robert Funk has called attention to the theological importance of these offhand references to Paul's itinerary that are found in most of his writings (Funk 1967; also Jervis 1991; Wall and Lemcio 1992:142-60). Funk suggests that Paul's declared interest in visiting a congregation (such as in Rom 1:10; 15:22-24; 1 Thess 2:17-18; 3:11) or a person (in the case of Philemon) is a metaphor of his apostolic authority and power: until Christ's parousia, Paul stands in for Christ as his substitute for God's redemptive power (see commentary on Col 4:7-9). When he comes to visit (the "apostolic parousia"), the power and truth of God's reign are present in him. Paul visits people, then, to test and empower them for ministry. In this sense, the stated reason for Paul's visit and the congregation's prayers implies the hope of dispensing the gift of his apostleship. In fact, *restored* (*charizomai,* literally "to give a gift") may very well have a double meaning: on the one hand it refers to Paul's release from prison (a gift in answer to the congregation's prayers), and on the other hand it refers to Paul's opportunity to now give this congregation the "gift of his apostleship" (compare Rom 1:5, 10-11).

Another more pointed way of saying this is that without the benefit of Paul's apostolic gift, Philemon will not be well grounded in the truth and praxis of Christian faith. Indeed, Paul's request for Onesimus's emancipation would be imperiled by spiritual immaturity. True, he wrote letters and sent others in his place when circumstances prevented him from coming in person; but these were inferior substitutes for his own apostolic persona, which conveyed the full powers of the apostolic charisma God had given him. For this reason, the letter he now writes to Philemon and even Onesimus's role as his substitute are second best: Paul wants to visit Philemon and the others in person to fortify their resolve with regard to Onesimus.

This interpretation is at odds with many commentators who think Paul's remark carries no implied threat or warning. However, if we recognize this verse as another use of Paul's "apostolic parousia" motif, we must also suppose that the intent of his anticipated visit is not friendly and casual but apostolic and official (although certainly neither unfriendly nor unwelcome). More than anything else that might come from such an official visit, the apostle wants to make certain that his request is acted on by Philemon and that the results in the congregation's life are positive. If not, then Paul's ministry in person would no doubt enable Philemon to mature to the point of granting Paul's request. R. P. Martin is surely correct is saying, then, that Paul's mention of his travel plans is "no courtesy gesture" but a convention of his writing used to "drive home a point" (1991:145).

□ Paul's Benediction (vv. 23-25)

Greetings (vv. 23-24) Paul's closing words greet his readers on behalf of certain colleagues who are also mentioned in his later Colossian letter and who are no doubt known and perhaps important to the Gentile mission there. Especially important in this regard is Epaphras (v. 23), whose relations with the Colossian church he found to be strained (see commentary on Col 4:12-13) and who is the implied subject of Paul's later Colossians letter (see commentary on Col 1:7).

The reference to him here as *my fellow prisoner for Christ Jesus* singles him out among the others (v. 24), who are simply *fellow workers* (see commentary on Col 4:11 and Philem 1). If naming Epaphras a *prisoner* symbolizes his spiritual valor and vitality, which is likely because *for Christ Jesus* is added, then Paul's reference to Epaphras may be more than a reference to his physical circumstances. Further, if indeed it is Epaphras, the founder of the Colossian church (see commentary on Col 1:7-8), who greets Philemon, its current leader, then Paul may well be sending a tacit message: be like Epaphras, who is imprisoned for Christ's sake.

Closing Prayer (v. 25) Typically, Paul's last word to his readers reminds them of the availability of *the grace of the Lord Jesus Christ:* living within Christ's lordship will enable his disciples, especially Philemon, to respond to the apostle's advice (see commentary on Col 4:23). Martin adds that this prayer is a "liturgical grace that situates the letter in the house congregation at worship" (1991:145), reminding current readers that all Paul's writings are for nurturing the worshiping community.

Paul often adds the phrase *with your spirit* to his benediction (compare Gal 6:18; Phil 4:23; also 2 Tim 4:22). Not just a fuller but equivalent expression of "with you," this concluding phrase suggests the collaboration of Christ's Spirit, who mediates his grace, with Philemon's human spirit, which receives it and applies it to life (Wall 1979:128-44). Such an image lies at the very core of Paul's participatory Christology: God's salvation-creating grace transforms the believer who actively collaborates with Christ in the ongoing work of God.

Bibliography

Abbott, T. K.

1897 *The Epistles to the Ephesians and to the Colossians.* International Critical Commentary. Edinburgh: T & T Clark.

Agnew, F. H.

1986 "The Origin of the NT Apostle-Concept." *Journal of Biblical Literature* 105:75-96.

Aune, David

1987 *The New Testament in Its Literary Environment.* Library of Early Christianity. Philadelphia: Westminster Press.

Aus, Roger

1979 "Paul's Travel Plans to Spain and the 'Full Number of Gentiles' of Romans 11:25." *Novum Testamentum* 21:232-62.

Balch, David

1981 *Let Wives Be Submissive: The Domestic Code in 1 Peter.* Missoula, Mont.: Scholars Press.

Bandstra, A. J.

1964 *The Law and the Elements of the World.* Kampen: KOK.

Banks, Robert

1980 *Paul's Idea of Community: The Early House Churches in Their Historical Setting.* Grand Rapids, Mich.: Eerdmans.

Barclay, John

1991 "Paul, Philemon and the Dilemma of Christian Slave-Ownership." *New Testament Studies* 37:161-86.

Bartchy, S. Scott

1973 *Mallon Chresai: First Century Slavery and the Interpretation of 1 Corinthians 7:21.* Missoula, Mont.: Scholars Press.

1992a "Philemon, Epistle to." In *Anchor Bible Dictionary.* 6 vols. New York: Doubleday, 5:305-10.

1992b "Slavery, New Testament." In *Anchor Bible Dictionary.* 6 vols. New York: Doubleday, 6:65-73.

Beker, J. Christiaan
1980 *Paul the Apostle: The Triumph of God in Life and Thought.* Philadelphia: Fortress.

Bornkamm, Günther
1975 "The Heresy of Colossians." In *Conflict at Colossae.* Ed. F. O. Francis and W. A. Weeks. Sources for Bible Study. Missoula, Mont.: Scholars Press, pp. 123-45.

Bruce, F. F., and E. K. Simpson
1984 *The Epistles to the Colossians, to Philemon and to the Ephesians.* The New International Commentary on the New Testament. Grand Rapids, Mich.: Eerdmans.

Brueggemann, Walter
1990 "The Preacher, the Text and the People." *Theology Today* 47:237-47.

Caird, G. B.
1976 *Paul's Letters from Prison.* Oxford: Oxford University Press.

Cannon, George
1983 *The Use of Traditional Materials in Colossians.* Macon, Ga.: Mercer University Press.

Church, F. F.
1978 "Rhetorical Structure and Design in Paul's Letter to Philemon." *Harvard Theological Review* 71:17-33.

Crouch, J. E.
1972 *The Origin and Intention of the Colossian Haustafel.* Forschungen zur Religion und Literatur des Alten und Neuen Testaments 109. Göttingen, Germany: Vandenhoeck & Ruprecht.

Dayton, Donald
1990 *Discovering an Evangelical Heritage.* Peabody, Mass.: Hendrickson.

Derrett, J. D. M.
1988 "The Functions of the Epistle to Philemon." *Zeitschrift für die neutestamentliche Wissenschaft* 79:63-91.

Dibelius, Martin
1953 *An die Kolosser, Epheser an Philemon.* Handbuch zum Neuen Testament. 3rd ed. Rev. by H. Greeven. Tübingen, Germany: J. C. B. Mohr.

Doty, William

1973 *Letters in Primitive Christianity.* Guides to Biblical Scholarship. Philadelphia: Fortress.

Dunn, James D. G.

1977 *Unity and Diversity in the New Testament.* Philadelphia: Westminster Press.

1980 *Christology in the Making: A New Testament Inquiry into the Origins of the Doctrine of the Incarnation.* Philadelphia: Westminster Press.

1983 "The New Perspective on Paul." *The Bulletin of the John Rylands Library of the University of Manchester* 65:94-122.

1990 *Jesus, Paul and the Law.* Louisville, Ky.: Westminster/John Knox Press.

Ellis, E. Earle

1971 "Paul and His Co-workers." *New Testament Studies* 17:437-52.

1978 "Prophecy and Interpretation in Early Christianity." *Wissenschaftliche Untersuchungen zum Neuen Testament* 18. Tübingen, Germany: J. C. B. Mohr, pp. 116-28.

Fishbane, Michael

1986 "Inner Biblical Exegesis: Types and Strategies of Interpretation in Ancient Israel." In *Midrash and Literature.* Ed. G. H. Hartman and S. Budick. New Haven, Conn.: Yale University Press, pp. 19-37.

Francis, Fred

1975 "Humility and Angelic Worship in Col 2:18." In *Conflict at Colossae.* Ed. F. W. Francis and W. A. Meeks. Sources for Bible Study. Missoula, Mont.: Scholars Press, pp. 163-207.

Funk, Robert

1967 "The Apostolic *Parousia:* Form and Significance." In *Christian History and Interpretation: Studies Presented to John Knox.* Ed. W. Farmer. Cambridge: Cambridge University Press, pp. 249-68.

Harris, Murray

1991 *Colossians and Philemon.* Grand Rapids, Mich.: Eerdmans.

Harrison, P. N.

1950 "Onesimus and Philemon." *Anglican Theological Review* 32:268-94.

Hays, Richard

1988 *Echoes of Scripture in Paul.* New Haven, Conn.: Yale University Press.

Hooker, Morna
1973 "Were There False Teachers in Colossae?" In *Christ and Spirit in the New Testament: Studies in Honour of C. F. D. Moule.* Ed. B. Lindars and S. S. Smalley. Cambridge: Cambridge University Press, pp. 315-31.

Horsley, Richard
1977 "Wisdom of Word and Words of Wisdom in Corinth." *Catholic Biblical Quarterly* 39:224-37.

Houlden, J. L.
1970 *Paul's Letters from Prison.* Pelican Commentaries. Philadelphia: Westminster Press.

Hummel, Charles E.
1991 *The Prosperity Gospel.* Downers Grove, Ill.: InterVarsity Press.

Jervis, Ann
1991 "The Apostolic 'Parousia' of Romans Reconsidered: Form, Function and Significance." Paper presented to the Society of Biblical Literature, Kansas City, Mo.

Käsemann, Ernst
1964 *Essays on New Testament Themes.* Naperville, Ill.: Allenson.

Knox, John
1959 *Philemon Among the Letters of Paul.* 2nd ed. Nashville: Abingdon.

Koch, E. W.
1963 "A Cameo of Koinonia: The Letter to Philemon." *Interpretation* 17:183-87.

Kümmel, Werner
1975 *Introduction to the New Testament.* Nashville: Abingdon.

Lampe, Paul
1985 "Keine 'Sklavenflücht' des Onesimus." *Zeitschrift für die neutestamentliche Wissenschaft* 76:132-37.

Lightfoot, J. B.
1890 *Saint Paul's Epistles to the Colossians and to Philemon.* 9th ed. London: Macmillan.

Lincoln, Andrew
1981 *Paradise Now and Not Yet: Studies in the Role of the Heavenly Dimension in Paul's Thought with Special Reference to Eschatology.* Society for New Testament Studies Monograph Series 41. Cambridge: Cambridge University Press.
1990 *Ephesians.* Word Biblical Commentary. Waco, Tex.: Word Books.

Lohse, Eduard

1971 *Colossians and Philemon.* Trans. W. Poehlmann and R. Karris. Hermeneia. Philadelphia: Fortress.

1976 *The New Testament Environment.* Nashville: Abingdon.

Martin, Dale

1990 *Slavery as Salvation.* New Haven, Conn.: Yale University Press.

Martin, Ralph

1991 *Ephesians, Colossians and Philemon.* Interpretation. Atlanta: John Knox Press.

Meade, David

1989 *Pseudonymity and Canon: An Investigation into the Relationship of Authorship and Authority in Jewish and Christian Tradition.* Grand Rapids, Mich.: Eerdmans.

Meeks, Wayne

1983 *The First Urban Christians.* New Haven, Conn.: Yale University Press.

Melick, R. R.

1991 *Philippians, Colossians, Philemon.* The New American Commentary. Nashville: Broadman.

Moule, C. F. D.

1962 *The Epistles of Paul the Apostle to the Colossians and to Philemon.* Cambridge Greek Testament. Cambridge: Cambridge University Press.

Munck, Johannes

1959 *Paul and the Salvation of Mankind.* London: SCM Press.

O'Brien, Peter

1982 *Colossians and Philemon.* Word Biblical Commentary. Waco, Tex.: Word Books.

Olasky, Marvin

1992 "The Return of Spiritism." *Christianity Today* 36 (December 14): 20-24.

Percy, Ernst

1946 *Die Probleme der Kolosser- und Epheserbriefe.* Acta Societas Humananorum Litterarum Lundensis 39. Lund, Germany: Gleerup.

Peterson, Norman

1985 *Rediscovering Paul: Philemon and the Sociology of Paul's Narrative World.* Philadelphia: Fortress.

1988 "Philemon." In *Harper's Bible Commentary.* Ed. J. L. Mays. San Francisco: Harper & Row, pp. 1245-48.

Rapske, B.
1991 "The Prisoner Paul in the Eyes of Onesimus." *New Testament Studies* 37:187-203.

Reicke, Bo
1951 "The Law and This World According to Paul." *Journal of Biblical Literature* 70:259-76.

Rowland, Christopher
1983 "Apocalyptic Visions and the Exaltation of Christ in the Letter to the Colossians." *Journal for the Study of the New Testament* 19:73-83.

Schenk, W.
1987 "Der Brief des Paulus an Philemon in der neueren Forschung." *Aufstieg und Niedergang der römischen Welt* 25:3134-55.

Schweizer, Eduard
1982 *The Letter to the Colossians: A Commentary.* Trans. A. Chester. Minneapolis: Augsburg.
1988 "Slaves of the Elements and Worshipers of Angels: Galatians 4:3, 9 and Colossians 2:8, 18, 20." *Journal of Biblical Literature* 107:455-68.

Scott, E. F.
1930 *The Epistles of Paul to the Colossians, Philemon, Ephesians.* Moffatt New Testament Commentary. London: Hodder & Stoughton.

Shogren, G. S.
1988 "Presently Entering the Kingdom of Christ: The Background and Purpose of Colossians 1:12-14." *Journal of the Evangelical Theological Society* 31:173-80.

Stendahl, Krister
1977 *Paul Among Jews and Gentiles.* Philadelphia: Fortress.

Stuhlmacher, Peter
1975 *Der Brief an Philemon.* Evangelisch-katholischer Kommentar zum Neuen Testament. Zurich: Benziger.

Vawter, Bruce
1971 "The Colossians Hymn and the Principle of Redaction." *Catholic Biblical Quarterly* 33:62-81.

Wall, Robert
1979 *The Nature of Obedience in the Ethics of Paul.* Th.D. diss., Dallas Theological Seminary.

1988 "Wifely Submission in the Context of Ephesians." *Christian Scholars' Review* 17:272-85.

1990 "The New Testament Use of the Old Testament." In *Mercer Dictionary of the Bible.* Ed. W. Mills. Macon, Ga.: Mercer University Press, pp. 614-16.

1991 *Revelation.* The New International Biblical Commentary. Peabody, Mass.: Hendrickson.

Wall, Robert, and Eugene Lemcio

1992 *The New Testament as Canon: A Reader in Canonical Criticism.* Journal for the Study of the New Testament, Supplement Series 76. Sheffield, U.K.: Sheffield Academic Press, pp. 161-207.

Wink, Walter

1984 *Naming the Powers: The Language of Power in the New Testament.* Philadelphia: Fortress.

Wright, N. T.

1986 *Colossians and Philemon.* Tyndale New Testament Commentaries. Grand Rapids, Mich.: Eerdmans.

1990 "Poetry and Theology in Colossians 1:15-20." *New Testament Studies* 36:444-68.

Winter, Sara

1987 "Paul's Letter to Philemon." *New Testament Studies* 33:1-15.